THE BOOK OF
ABSINTHE

A CULTURAL HISTORY

PHIL BAKER

GROVE PRESS
New York

First published in the UK in 2001 by Dedalus Ltd.

Printed in the United States of America
Published simultaneously in Canada

PUBLISHER'S NOTE: As of this printing, Absinthe is currently illegal for consumption in the United States. The Publisher and the Author do not advocate or endorse usage of any substances described herein. Any information regarding the usage of Absinthe is meant purely for reference purposes.

FIRST AMERICAN EDITION

Library of Congress Cataloging-in-Publication Data

Baker, Phil, 1961–
    [Dedalus book of absinthe]
    The book of absinthe : a cultural history / Phil Baker.
        p. cm.
    Originally published: The Dedalus book of absinthe. Sawtry, U.K. : Dedalus, 2001.
    Includes bibliographical references and index.
    ISBN 0-8021-3993-0
    1. Absinthe—Social aspects. 2. Absinthe—History. 3. Absinthe in art. 4. Drinking customs—France—History—19th century. I. Title.

GT2898.B35 2003
394.1'2—dc21   2003044823

Grove Press
841 Broadway
New York, NY 10003

03 04 05 06 07   10 9 8 7 6 5 4 3 2 1

CONTENTS

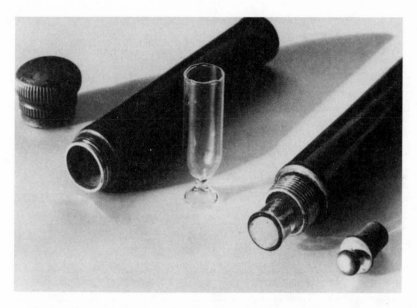

Toulouse-Lautrec's absinthe cane. Photo Musée
Toulouse-Lautrec, Albi.

Prologue
Three Coffins in the Morning

News of a particularly ugly tragedy swept across the European headlines in the month of August 1905. A thirty one year old man named Jean Lanfray, a Swiss peasant of French stock, had drunk two glasses of absinthe, taken his old army rifle out of the cupboard, and shot his pregnant wife in the head. When his four year old daughter Rose appeared in the doorway to see what was happening, he shot her too. He then went into the room next door, where his two year old daughter Blanche was lying in her cot, and blasted her as well. At this point he tried to shoot himself but botched it, and staggered across the yard to fall asleep holding Blanche's dead body.

Next morning, now in police custody, Lanfray was taken to see the corpses of his wife and children. They were laid out dead – and here creeps in the kind of horribly picturesque touch that might have pleased Dickens – in three differently sized coffins. It must have been a sobering sight.

The public reaction to the Lanfray case was extraordinary, and it focused on just one detail. Never mind the fact that Lanfray was a thoroughgoing alcoholic, and that in the day preceding the murder he had consumed not only the two absinthes before work – hours, in fact, before the tragedy – but a crème de menthe, a cognac, six glasses of wine to help his lunch down, another glass of wine before leaving work, a cup of coffee with brandy in it, a litre of wine on getting home, and then another coffee with *marc* in it. Never mind all that, or the fact that he was known to drink up to five litres of wine a day. People were in no doubt. *It must have been the absinthe that did it.* Within weeks, a petition had been signed by local people. 82,450 of them. They wanted absinthe banned in Switzerland, and in the following year it was. No drink, not even gin in Hogarth's London, has ever had such a bad reputation.

Chapter One
What Does Absinthe Mean?

L'Absinthe by Benasset. Copyright Musée Carnavalet.

"You tell me you have become an *absintheur* – do
you know what that means?"

Marie Corelli, *Wormwood*

What does absinthe mean? It is one of the strongest alcoholic
drinks ever made, with an additional psychotropic potential
from the wormwood it contains, but the *idea* of absinthe has
developed a mythology all of its own. Even the word has a
strange ring to it. It barely sounds like an alcoholic drink at all,
although it does sound like a substance of some kind, recalling
amaranth – a never-fading flower symbolising immortality –
and nepenthe, a sorrow-lulling drink or drug, and also a
carnivorous plant.

As we shall see, wickedness is often to the fore when people
talk about absinthe, particularly in the English-speaking
world. But it isn't quite *sin* that we're dealing with here,
although it's somewhere in the same spectrum. Absinthe
doesn't necessarily have the creeping luxuriousness of sin. It's
too powerful, for one thing. Absinthe – particularly in France
– has often meant something a bit more brutal and degraded:
it isn't so much about sin as *vice*.

Having begun as a tonic in Switzerland at the close of the
eighteenth century, absinthe became associated with the
French colonial army in Algeria by the middle of the nineteenth. Taking a glass of absinthe became respectable and
almost universal bourgeois habit under the gilded Second
Empire, but by the Empire's end it was already developing
two rather more particular and dangerous meanings. It
was associated on the one hand with poets, painters, and
Bohemianism in general, and on the other with working class
alcoholism (particularly after the horrors of 1870–71, when
the Franco-Prussian War was followed by the uprising and

annihilation of the revolutionary Paris Commune). The absinthe problem grew worse in the 1880s, when failing grape crops resulted in absinthe becoming cheaper than wine. Eventually these meanings came together at the junction where Bohemia meets Skid Row, spelling out a generalized ruin for artists and workers alike. Absinthe − no longer "the green fairy" but "the green witch" and the "queen of poisons" − became the demonized object of a moral panic. It was by now strongly associated with insanity, and it became popularly known as "the Charenton omnibus", after the lunatic asylum at Charenton. "If absinthe isn't banned," a French prohibition campaigner wrote, "our country will rapidly become an immense padded cell where half the French will be occupied putting straitjackets on the other half."

The French did ban absinthe in 1915, scapegoating it for the national alcohol problem, and for the French army's unreadiness for the First World War. But it lived on in Spain and Eastern Europe, and now, in the aftermath of a new *fin-de-siècle*, absinthe is back, bringing all its connotations with it. For three recent writers on the subject, absinthe has a spread of meanings: for Regina Nadelson it suggests "sweet decadence" and "a history rich in carnal and narcotic connotation", while as a social problem, it was "the cocaine of the nineteenth century". For Barnaby Conrad its history is one of "murder, madness and despair", and it "symbolized anarchy, a deliberate denial of normal life and its obligations". And for Doris Lanier, absinthe was "associated with inspiration and freedom and became a symbol of French decadence" − so much so that for her the word "absinthe" evokes "thoughts of narcotic intrigue, euphoria, eroticism, and decadent sensuality".

And in addition to all that, absinthe will always be associated with the old *fin-de-siècle*: the 1890s of Oscar Wilde and Ernest Dowson at the Café Royal, and the French symbolists who preceded the English Decadence, such as Verlaine and Rimbaud. In London, before the current revival, attitudes to absinthe were always bound up with impressions of Paris, and with what Aleister Crowley says somewhere is "the average

Cockney's idea of Paris as a very wicked place". It is an attitude to France and all things French that lasted well into the second half of the twentieth century. Take Lou Reed's line "like a dirty French novel – ooohhh" on the Velvet Underground track 'Some Kinda Love', or Patti Smith on the cover of the Smith fanzine *White Stuff*, posing with a lurid pulp edition of Montmartre writer Francis Carco's novel *Depravity*.†

Depravity is certainly the keynote of Marie Corelli's 1890 anti-absinthe novel *Wormwood*, a book so sublimely over the top it makes *The Phantom of the Opera* look like *Pride and Prejudice*. It tells the story of Gaston Beauvais, a once decent and intelligent man who becomes a complete moral leper through his fatal encounter with absinthe, and brings total ruin upon himself and all around him. "Let me be mad", cries Beauvais:

> . . . mad with the madness of *Absinthe*, the wildest, most luxurious madness in the world! *Vive la folie! Vive l'amour! Vive l'animalisme! Vive le Diable!*

Corelli soon makes it clear that aside from the absinthe, Gaston has another filthy personal problem. He is French.

> The morbidness of the modern French mind is well known and universally admitted, even by the French themselves; the open atheism, heartlessness, flippancy, and flagrant immorality of the whole modern French school of thought is unquestioned. If a crime of more than usual cold-blooded atrocity is committed, it generally dates from Paris, or near it; – if a book or a picture is produced that is confessedly obscene, the author or artist is, in nine cases out of ten, discovered to be a Frenchman.

† Carco ("the author", says the jacket, "of ONLY A WOMAN and PER-VERSITY") was an eminent French novelist before the 'Berkley 35 cents Library' got its hands on him, a winner of the Grand Prix du Roman of The Académie Française and a member of the Académie Goncourt.

[. . .] There are, no doubt, many causes for the wretchedly low standard of moral responsibility and fine feeling displayed by the Parisians of today – but I do not hesitate to say that one of those causes is undoubtedly the reckless Absinthe-mania, which pervades all classes, rich and poor alike. Everyone knows that in Paris the men have certain hours set apart for the indulgence of this fatal craze as religiously as Mussulmans have their hours for prayer. . . The effects of its rapid working on the human brain are beyond all imagination horrible and incurable, and no romanticist can exaggerate the terrific reality of the evil.

It must also be remembered that in the many French cafés and restaurants which have recently sprung up in London, Absinthe is always to be obtained at its customary low price, – French habits, French fashions, French books, French pictures, are particularly favoured by the English, and who can predict that French drug-drinking shall not also become *à la mode* in Britain?

Having been introduced to "the Fairy with the Green Eyes" by his friend Gessonex, a mad artist, Beauvais embraces destruction by way of a melodramatically horrible descent that takes him to the Paris morgue and the cemetery at Père Lachaise *en route*. "You tell me you have become an *absintheur*," says Gaston's father "do you know what that means?"

"I believe I do," I replied indifferently. "It means, in the end, death."
"Oh, if it meant only death!" he exclaimed passionately. . . . "But it means more than this – it means crime of the most revolting character – it means brutality, cruelty, apathy, sensuality, and mania! Have you realised the doom you create for yourself. . .?"

Gaston ends up a veritable Mr Hyde, "a slinking, shuffling beast, half monkey, half man, whose aspect is so vile, whose body is so shaken with delirium, whose eyes are so murderous, that if you met me by chance in the day-time, you would probably shriek for sheer alarm."

But you will not see me thus – daylight and I are not friends. I have become like a bat or an owl in my hatred of the sun!. . . At night I live; at night I creep out with the other obscene things of Paris, and by my very presence, add fresh pollution to the moral poisons in the air!"

———

It is easy to laugh at Marie Corelli, but perhaps she deserves our grudging respect. And she makes absinthe sound like something the Addams Family might crack open at Christmas: this is absinthe as bottled doom.

The history of absinthe has some sobering themes: addiction, ruin, and mortality. Bitter rather than sweet, the aesthetic charge it carries is not so much beautiful as awesome, or sublime in the old sense of the word (the sense in which Edmund Burke used it in his proto-Gothic essay 'A Philosophical Enquiry into Our Ideas of the Sublime and Beautiful'). The sublime involves awe, and feelings not unlike terror. A writer on the Internet mentions the Old Absinthe House at New Orleans and notes that the marble bartop is "allegedly pitted from ancient absinthe spillage. One wonders, though, what absinthe does to the human body *if it can eat through solid rock*" [my emphasis]. It is probably the water dripping and not the absinthe at all, but the frisson is palpable; people *want* absinthe to be fearful stuff, with the distinctive form of pleasure that fearful things bring.

Richard Klein has argued that cigarettes are sublime. They have, he says, "a beauty that has never been considered as unequivocally positive; they have always been associated with distaste, transgression and death." Co-opting Kant into his argument, he defines the sublime as an aesthetic category that includes a negative experience, a shock, a menace, an intimation of mortality, the contemplation of an abyss. If cigarettes were good for you, says Klein, they would not be sublime: but,

> Being sublime, cigarettes resist all arguments directed at them from the perspective of health and utility. Warning smokers or neophytes of the dangers entices them more powerfully to the edge of the abyss, where, like travellers in a Swiss landscape, they can be thrilled by the subtle grandeur of the perspectives on mortality opened by the little terrors in every puff. Cigarettes are bad. That is why they are good – not good, not beautiful, but sublime.

If we follow Klein's argument, then absinthe is even more sublime.

So, to contemplate the history of absinthe is a pleasure with a shudder in it. It is not unlike the feeling invoked by Thomas de Quincey in his discussion of what he calls the "dark sublime". He argues that it is not only great things that are sublime (mountains, or storms), but that small things can be sublime as well, by virtue of their associations: the razor, for example, with which a murder has been committed, or a phial of poison. . .

But enough of all this ruin and darkness. It is time to call the first witness for the defence.

———

Aleister Crowley (1875–1947) commandeered the legacy of the late nineteenth-century occult revival so effectively that in the twentieth century his name was virtually synonymous with magick. He liked to be known as The Great Beast, after the monster in the Book of Revelations, and when he was vilified by the Beaverbrook newspapers in the 1930s he achieved widespread notoriety as "the wickedest man in the world". Somerset Maugham knew him in Paris – the character of Oliver Haddo in Maugham's novel *The Magician* is based on him – and of the many verdicts on Crowley, Maugham's is the most succinct: "a fake, but not entirely a fake."

In Paris, Crowley hung out in the upstairs drinking room at a restaurant called Le Chat Blanc in the Rue d'Odessa (where Maugham met him). This was back in the days when Pernod was a major brand of absinthe, and not the pastis it was later forced to become. Crowley was an inveterate practical joker, and when his long suffering friend Victor Neuburg came to join him in Paris, The Great Beast couldn't resist giving him some advice:

> He had been warned against drinking absinthe and we told him that was quite right, but (we added) many other drinks in Paris are terribly dangerous, especially to a nice young man like you; there is only one really safe, mild, harmless beverage and you can drink as much of that as you like, without running the slightest risk, and what you say when you want it is "Garcon! Un Pernod!"

This advice led to various misadventures. Crowley's own absinthe drinking took place not in Paris but in New Orleans, where he wrote his absinthe essay 'The Green Goddess':

> What is there in absinthe that makes it a separate cult? The effects of its abuse are totally distinct from those of other stimulants. Even in ruin and in degradation it remains a thing apart: its victims wear a ghastly aureole all their own, and in their peculiar hell yet gloat with a sinister perversion of pride that they are not as other men.
>
> But we are not to reckon up the uses of a thing by contemplating the wreckage of its abuse. We do not curse the sea because of occasional disasters to our marines, or refuse axes to our woodsmen because we sympathise

with Charles the First or Louis the Sixteenth. So therefore as special vices and dangers pertain to absinthe, so also do graces and virtues that adorn no other liquor.

For instance:

It is as if the first diviner of absinthe had been indeed a magician intent upon a combination of sacred drugs which should cleanse, fortify and perfume the human soul.

And it is no doubt that in the due employment of this liquor such effects are easy to obtain. A single glass seems to render the breathing freer, the spirit lighter, the heart more ardent, soul and mind alike more capable of executing the great task of doing that particular work in the world which the Father may have sent them to perform. Food itself loses its gross qualities in the presence of absinthe and becomes even as manna, operating the sacrament of nutrition without bodily disturbance.

There is another other section of particular interest, where Crowley considers absinthe and artistic detachment. There is beauty in everything, he says, if it is perceived with the right degree of detachment. The trick is to separate out the part of you that really "is", the part that perceives, from the other part of you that acts and suffers in the external world. "And the art of doing this", he adds, "is really the art of being an artist." Absinthe, he claims, can bring this about.

At one point Crowley raises the already rather Masonic tone of his essay even higher by quoting a poem in French. "Do you know that French sonnet 'La légende de l'Absinthe?'", he asks the reader. It would be surprising if very many readers did, because he had written it himself. He published it separately in the pro-German propaganda paper *The International* (New York, October 1917) under the pseudonym "Jeanne La Goulue": a famous Moulin Rouge star painted by Toulouse-Lautrec.

Apollo, mourning the demise of Hyacinth,
Would not cede victory to death.
His soul, adept of transformation,
Had to find a holy alchemy for beauty.
So from his celestial hand he exhausts and crushes
The subtlest gifts from divine Flora.
Their broken bodies sigh a golden exhalation
From which he harvested our first drop of – Absinthe!

In crouching cellars, in sparkling palaces,
Alone or together, drink that potion of loving!
For it is a sorcery, a conjuration,
This pale opal wine aborts misery,
Opens the intimate sanctuary of beauty
– Bewitches my heart, exalts my soul in ecstasy.

                                        Aleister Crowley

Absinthe used to be found wherever there was French culture; not only in Paris and New Orleans but in the French
colonies, notably French Cochin-China (Vietnam). In his
Confessions, Crowley recounts an incident in Haiphong
that he found "deliciously colonial". A large building on
the corner of a main street was to be demolished, but the
Frenchman in charge of the work could not be found. Finally
the overseer of the construction workers ran him to ground in
a combined drinking house and brothel, where he was solidly
under the influence of absinthe. But he was still able to talk,
and perfectly happy to calculate the explosive charge required
using a stub of pencil on the marble slab of his table. He
slipped up with his decimal point, however, and a charge of
dynamite a hundred times too big took down not just the
building on the corner but the entire block. No doubt
the absinthe was to blame: as Crowley helpfully reminds us,
it is "not really a wholesome drink in that climate".

———

Aleister Crowley would be in favour of absinthe. He had to be: he was the wickedest man in the world. For a more impartial judge, we can turn to George Saintsbury. Saintsbury (1845–1933) was once the grand old man of English letters. Unashamedly pleasure-oriented in his approach to literature, he was a master of the connoisseurial 'wine-tasting' mode of literary criticism, with its almost mystical overtones. What has been called, "the social mission of English criticism", had no appeal for Saintsbury. Social conscience was never his strong point, and his idea of heaven would probably have been reading Baudelaire while sending little children up chimneys. George Orwell mentions Saintsbury in *The Road to Wigan Pier*, with a kind of back-handed admiration for his politics. "It takes a lot of guts," says Orwell, "to be *openly* such a skunk as that."

A bearded, bespectacled, appropriately Mandarin-looking old man, Saintsbury was famed for his extreme erudition, his odd but often brilliant judgements (Proust reminded him of Thomas De Quincey, for example), and his phenomenally rambling syntax. A fragment has been preserved for posterity: "But while none, save these, of men living, had done, or could have done, such things, there was much here which – whether either could have done it or not – neither had done."

Saintsbury's extreme connoisseurship of wine and other drinks led to a Saintsbury Society being formed in his honour, back in the hedonistic 1920s, which still exists. Before he died he was particularly adamant that there must never, ever be a biography written of him. What did he have to hide? We don't know. But here he is on absinthe, from the liqueur chapter of his famous *Cellar Book*:

> . . . I will not close this short chapter without saying something of the supposed wickedest of all the tribe – the 'Green Muse' – the water of the Star Wormwood, whereof many men have died – the *absinthia taetra*, which are deemed to deserve the adjective in a worse sense than that which the greatest of Roman poets

meant.† I suppose (though I cannot say that it ever did me any) that absinthe has done a good deal of harm. Its principle is too potent, not to say too poisonous, to be let loose indiscriminately and intensively on the human frame. It was, I think, as a rule made fearfully strong, and nobody but the kind of lunatic whom it was supposed to produce, and who may be thought to have been destined for lunacy, would drink it 'neat' [. . .]

A person who drinks absinthe neat deserves his fate whatever it may be. The flavour is concentrated to repulsiveness; the spirit burns 'like a torch light procession'; you must have a preternaturally strong or fatally accustomed head that does not ache after it.

There is another reason for not drinking it neat, which is that this would lose the ritualistic, drug-like fascination of preparing it according to a method: "you lose all the ceremonial and etiquette which make the proper fashion of drinking it delightful to a man of taste." More about the various methods later, but Saintsbury's is one of the most lovingly described.

When you have stood the glass of liqueur in a tumbler as flat-bottomed as you can get, you should pour, or have poured for you, water gently into the absinthe itself, so that the mixture overflows from one vessel into the other. The way in which the deep emerald of the pure spirit clouds first into what would be the colour of a star-smaragd [an old name for an emerald], if the Almighty had been pleased to complete the quartette of star-gems. . .

And here we have to interrupt Saintsbury for a moment, strange old buffer that he is. He is about to say that watching the pure spirit turn cloudy is *a very agreeable experience*, but before he gets there he is going to sidle, by way of a footnote,

† Lucretius, *De Rerum Natura*, Book IV Prologue. Lucretius meant it was bitter.

into a digression about his love of jewels, and the rarity of star gemstones. The star gems, he says in his lipsmacking little note, are

> As yet only a triad – sapphire (which is pretty common), ruby (rarer), and topaz, which I have never seen, and which the late Signor Giuliano, who used to be good enough to give me much good talk in return for very modest purchases, told me had seen only once or twice. But an ordinary emerald in cabochon form, represents one of the stages of the diluted absinthe very fairly.

So. He likes the way that absinthe turns first into emerald. . .

> and then into opal; the thinning out of the opal itself as the operation goes on; and when the liqueur glass contains nothing but pure water and the drink is ready, the extraordinary combination of refreshingness and comforting character in odour and flavour – all these complete a very agreeable experience. Like other agreeable experiences it may no doubt be repeated too often. I never myself drank more than one absinthe in a day. . .

Saintsbury's curious little testimony brings out a number of salient points, all of which we shall meet again later: the strength of absinthe, its bad reputation, the element of ritual involved in drinking it, and its persistent affinity with aestheticism.

———

Corelli is against absinthe, Crowley is for it, and Saintsbury is nicely (even *exquisitely*. . .) balanced. But for each of them, living through the heyday of absinthe, we can see that it was already a mythic substance.

Writing about the idea of an "ideal drink", Roland Barthes suggests it should be "rich in metonymies of all kinds"; it should, in other words, be rich in all those part-for-the-whole, tip-of-the-iceberg associations and symbolic workings of why we want what we want. People who like the idea of Scotland can drink Scotch; people who believe in transubstantiation can drink the blood of Christ; and people who drink wine can be happy in the knowledge that it's about grapes and sunshine and good soil and vineyards and what-have-you. When Keats wants wine, in 'Ode to a Nightingale', he wants it "Tasting of Flora and the country-green, / Dance, and Provencal song, and sunburnt mirth! / O for a beaker full of the warm South!" It is not unlike the methods of advertising.

Whatever absinthe means, it is not a beaker full of the warm south. It is an industrial product, as synthetic as Dr Jekyll's potion, and whatever metonymies are in play are not from the rural landscape but from urban culture. Aestheticism, decadence, and Bohemianism are well to the fore, along with the idea of nineteenth-century Paris and 1890s London. As an advert for Hill's brand of absinthe has it, with no apologies to The Artist Formerly Known As Prince: "TONIGHT WE'RE GONNA PARTY LIKE IT'S 1899!"

Chapter Two
The Nineties

Aubrey Beardsley's cover for Vincent O'Sullivan's *Houses of Sin*, published by Leonard Smithers in 1897. Wilde told Beardsley his drawings were like absinthe.

Absinthe will forever be associated with the *fin-de-siècle* decadence of the 1890s, the absinthe decade. Max Beerbohm's incomparable comic creation Enoch Soames – the author of two slim collections of verse entitled *Negations* and *Fungoids* – could hardly have drunk anything else. We first meet Soames at the old Café Royal, "in that exuberant vista of gilding and crimson velvet set amidst all those opposing mirrors and upholding caryatids, with fumes of tobacco ever rising to the pagan and painted ceiling". Beerbohm and the painter William Rothenstein invite him to sit down and have a drink:

And he ordered an absinthe. *'Je me tiens toujours fidèle'*, he told Rothenstein, *'à la sorcière glauque.'* [I am forever faithful to the glaucous witch]
'It is bad for you', said Rothenstein drily.
'Nothing is bad for one,' answered Soames. *'Dans ce monde il n'y a ni de bien ni de mal.'* [In this world there is neither good nor bad]
'Nothing good and nothing bad? How do you mean?'
'I explained it in the preface to *Negations*.'
'*Negations*?'
'Yes; I gave you a copy of it.'
'Oh yes, of course. But did you explain – for instance – that there was no such thing as good or bad grammar?'
'N-no,' said Soames. 'Of course in Art there is the good and the evil. But in Life – no.' He was rolling a cigarette. He had weak white hands, not well washed, and with finger tips much stained by nicotine. 'In Life there are illusions of good and evil, but' – his voice trailed away to a murmur in which the words 'vieux jeu' and 'rococo' were faintly audible.

Soames is not just a bad poet but a Diabolist; a devil worshipper, or thereabouts:

> "It's not exactly worship", he qualified, sipping his absinthe. "It's more a matter of trusting and encouraging."

Talentless, posturing, and desperate, Soames sells his soul to the Devil in return for the promise of posthumous fame. But he was on the highway to hell in any case. He was an absinthe drinker.

———

The 1890s were a bizarre decade, often seen as the end of the old Victorian certainties and decencies, and the birth of the Modern. It was a time of "fantastic attenuations of weariness, fantastic anticipations of a new vitality". Wilde and Beardsley reigned, but amid the extreme preciousness, Grub Street poverty was endemic among writers in a way that it had not been for the Romantics and the earlier high Victorians.

There was a new attention to urban subjects and urban squalor, which was partly a response to grim London conditions and partly the influence of French writers such as Baudelaire. Homosexuality was coming to the fore as a coded tendency within aestheticism, only to be driven underground again after the Oscar Wilde trial in 1895. People felt they were living in a time of crisis and decline, exacerbated by the tendency to think in centuries: the *fin-de-siècle* is often a strange time, whether it is the 1590s, with the dark and morbid spirit of its proto-Jacobean drama, or the 1790s, with the French revolution and the guillotine. Writers with a grounding in classics and Latin felt that they were living through something akin to the decline and fall of the Roman Empire, and the decadence of Petronius. Occultism and High Catholicism were gaining converts. Pessimism and despair reigned, notably in the work of the quintessential Nineties poet Ernest Dowson, not to mention the verse of Enoch Soames. Peter Ackroyd provides an elegant role call;

> ". . .those doomed poets and writers who make up the generation of the Nineties and who arrive in our midst with the intoxicating perfume of hot house flowers from that strange conservatory known as the *fin-de-siècle*; Richard Le Gallienne is here, together with Swinburne and Dowson and Symons, forming a strange litany of fluted lust and hopelessness."

One night in 1890, the essayist and minor poet Richard Le Gallienne was offered some absinthe by the poet Lionel Johnson. Le Gallienne remembers that they were walking back from a public house after closing time, and Johnson invited him up to his rooms in Grays Inn, Holborn, for a final drink. Looking back in 1925, Le Gallienne says that Johnson's warning on the stairs still makes him smile as he writes, "for it was so very 1890": "I hope you drink absinthe, Le Gallienne," said Johnson, "for I have nothing else to offer you."

> I had just heard of it, as a drink mysteriously sophisticated and even Satanic. To me it had the sound of hellebore or mandragora. I had never tasted it then, nor has it ever been a favourite drink of mine. But in the '90s it was spoken of with a self-conscious sense of one's being desperately wicked, suggesting diabolism and nameless iniquity.

Immediately those all-important associations and connotations came into play: "Did not Paul Verlaine drink it all the time in Paris! and Oscar Wilde and his cronies, it was darkly hinted, drank it nightly at the Café Royal."

> So it was with a pleasant shudder that I watched it cloud in our glasses, as I drank it for the first time, there alone

with Lionel Johnson, in the small hours, in a room paradoxically monkish in its scholarly austerity, with a beautiful monstrance on the mantelpiece and a silver crucifix on the wall.

(A monstrance is a luxuriantly ornamental piece of High Church ornament, not unlike a reliquary, in which the consecrated Host is exposed for adoration). Johnson was a founder member of the Rhymers Club, a group of poets who met at the Cheshire Cheese in Fleet Street, including Le Gallienne, Dowson, Arthur Symons, and W.B.Yeats, who was a great admirer of Johnson's poetry. Johnson was a *fin-de-siècle* figure but he was some distance from being a true Decadent himself, as his sharp essay on the Decadents shows.

First of all – says Johnson in his 1891 essay 'The Cultured Faun', published in *The Anti-Jacobin* – the true Decadent should be soberly dressed (just as much as William Burroughs in his "banker drag", or T.S.Eliot, Aubrey Beardsley was noted for dressing like a man who worked in insurance, which he once did; he was said to look like "the man from the Prudential"). Then, says Johnson, the Decadent should be nervous, attracted to High Church ritual, cynical, and above all a worshipper of beauty; even if life also contains harsh and terrible realities, such as absinthe addiction.

Externally, our hero should cultivate a reassuring sobriety of habit, with just a dash of the dandy. None of the wandering looks, the elaborate disorder, the sublime lunacy of his predecessor, the 'apostle of culture'. Externally, then, a precise appearance; internally, a catholic sympathy with all that exists, and 'therefore' suffers, for art's sake. Now art, at present, is not a question of the senses so much as of the nerves. . . Baudelaire is very nervous. . . Verlaine is pathetically sensitive. That is the point: exquisite appreciation of pain, exquisite thrills of anguish, exquisite adoration of suffering. Here comes in the tender patronage of Catholicism: white tapers upon the high altar, an ascetic and beautiful young priest, the great gilt monstrance, the subtle-scented and mystical incense. . .

To play the part properly a flavour of cynicism is recommended: a scientific profession of materialist dogmas, coupled – for you should forswear consistency – with gloomy chatter about 'The Will to Live'. . . finally conclude that life is loathsome yet that beauty is beatific. And beauty – ah, beauty is everything beautiful! Isn't that a trifle obvious, you say? That is the charm of it, it shows your perfect simplicity, your chaste and catholic innocence. Innocence of course: beauty is always innocent, ultimately. No doubt there are 'monstrous' things, terrible pains, the haggard eyes of an *absintheur*, the pallid faces of 'neurotic' sinners; but all that is the portion of our Parisian friends, such and such a 'group of artists' who meet at the Café So-and-So.

Johnson was received into the Catholic Church in the same year that this essay was written, and he had a distinctly austere streak in his character. He once said to Yeats that he wished people who denied the eternal and permanent nature of damnation would realise how unspeakably *vulgar* they were.

Johnson's agonised religious and monarchistic (in fact neo-Jacobite) sensibility can be seen from two of his most famous poems, 'The Dark Angel' and 'By the Statue of King Charles at Charing Cross'. He slid into alcoholism after a doctor – with what now seems like criminal negligence – advised him to take up drinking for his insomnia. Yeats chronicles his decline in his *Autobiographies*. Le Gallienne could already see trouble in store on that night in Grays Inn, feeling that absinthe was "too fierce a potion" for a man as delicate as Johnson. But Johnson was devoted to alcohol, "because, particularly in the form of his favourite absinthe, it has for a time so quickening and clarifying an effect on the intellectual and imaginative faculties." Later he developed a tendency to persecution mania, and believed that detectives were following him. A good friend of Ernest Dowson,

Johnson haunted the pubs of Fleet Street and died in 1902, after falling off a bar stool.

—

Johnson's fellow Rhymer Arthur Symons played a key role in shaping the 1890s. He edited the influential periodical *The Savoy*, and he wrote studies of Baudelaire, Walter Pater and Oscar Wilde, as well as his major work *The Symbolist Movement in Literature* (1899), which made modern French poetry better known in England and was regarded as something of a manifesto. He had already written an essay on 'The Decadent Movement'. Symons's own poetry is quintessentially Nineties in its impressionistic handling of sleazy urban subjects – theatres and cafés, equivocal actresses or prostitutes, and the life of lodgings and digs – complete with what were then 'unpoetic' details such as cigarettes and gas. At the same time he is capable of a heavy flowery aestheticism, and more fantastic touches such as the gaslit streets in his poem 'London':

. . . and in the evil glimpses of the light,
Men as trees walking loom through lanes of night
Hung from the globes of some unnatural fruit.

His 1892 collection *Silhouettes* contains his poem 'The Absinthe Drinker':

The Absinthe-Drinker

Gently I wave the visible world away.
Far off, I hear a roar, afar yet near,
Far off and strange, a voice is in my ear,
And is the voice my own? The words I say
Fall strangely, like a dream, across the day:
And the dim sunshine is a dream. How clear,
New as the world to lover's eyes, appear
The men and women passing on their way!

The world is very fair. The hours are all
Linked in a dance of mere forgetfulness.
I am at peace with God and man. O glide,
Sands of the hour-glass that I count not, fall
Serenely: scarce I feel your soft caress,
Rocked on this dreamy and indifferent tide.

It is a companion piece to his earlier and more vicious poem 'The Opium-Smoker', which begins well ("I am engulfed, and drown deliciously") but ends badly, revealing a rat-infested garret.

Symons was associated by reputation with drink and hashish, but he had only a slight experience of them. Havelock Ellis believes Symons to have drunk absinthe only once, with Ellis himself outside a Paris café. This is probably an underestimate, but Symons was certainly no addict. Perhaps mindful of his reputation, Symons wrote in *London: A Book of Aspects*

I have always been curious of sensations, and above all of those which seemed to lead one into 'artificial paradises' not within everybody's reach. It took me some time to find out that every 'artificial paradise' is within one's soul, somewhere among one's own dreams. . . The mystery of all the intoxicants fascinated me, and drink, which had no personal appeal to me, which indeed brought me no pleasures, found me endlessly observant of its powers, effects, and variations.

He would have had plenty of opportunity to observe it with friends such as Dowson and Johnson. Symons's absinthe-free lifestyle did not protect him from a catastrophic nervous breakdown in 1907, but it may have contributed to his longevity, compared to his absinthe-drinking comrades. He survived Dowson, Johnson and Wilde by almost half a century, living on into the distant future of 1945.

—

The fortunes of aestheticism, decadence, and 'Art for Art's sake' rose and fell with Oscar Wilde's own, ascending from around 1880 and crashing disastrously in 1895. Wilde was a disciple of Walter Pater, whose book *The Renaissance* contained a manifesto of nihilistic aestheticism in its 'Conclusion'. "It is my golden book", Wilde said, "I never travel anywhere without it; but it is the very flower of decadence; the last trumpet should have sounded the moment it was written." Wilde himself wrote the other great English decadent work, his novel *The Picture of Dorian Gray*. Smouldering resentment against Wilde flamed into the open in 1895, when he was found guilty of homosexual offences and sent to prison, moving to France after his release in 1897.

The French *litterateur* Marcel Schwob was an acquaintance of Wilde, and he has left a wickedly exaggerated picture of the aesthete as he knew him in 1891. Wilde was, "a big man, with a large pasty face, red cheeks, an ironic eye, bad and protrusive teeth, a vicious childlike mouth with lips soft with milk ready to suck some more. While he ate – and he ate little – he never stopped smoking opium-tainted Egyptian cigarettes." To complete this unappetising picture, Schwob adds that he was also, "A terrible absinthe-drinker, through which he got his visions and desires."

In reality Wilde was not such a terrible absinthe drinker at that period, and his attitude to it seems to have varied with time; his drinking in general grew heavier as his life grew more unhappy, and eventually he came to like it. He once told the art critic Bernard Berenson "It has no message for me", and he confessed to Arthur Machen – partial to a glass himself † – that "I could never quite accustom myself to

---

† The second edition of Machen's book *Hieroglyphics*, "has for frontispiece a photograph of myself. It seems to express great gloom, righteousness and austerity. What it really expresses are my sentiments during the process of 'sitting.'

'Oh Lord!' I was saying to myself, 'why should I waste my time being photographed at Baron's Court this blessed Sunday, when I might be drinking my absinthe. . .?'"

absinthe, but it suits my style so well." He did accustom himself to it in the end, and in Dieppe, after his downfall, he said, "Absinthe has a wonderful colour, green. A glass of absinthe is as poetical as anything in the world. What difference is there between a glass of absinthe and a sunset?"

Wilde developed what his biographer Richard Ellmann calls "romantic ideas" about absinthe, and he described its effects to Ada 'The Sphinx' Leverson:

> "After the first glass, you see things as you wish they were. After the second, you see things as they are not. Finally you see things as they really are, and that is the most horrible thing in the world."
> "How do you mean?" asked Leverson.
> "I mean disassociated. Take a top-hat! You think you see it as it really is. But you don't, because you associate it with other things and ideas. If you had never heard of one before, and suddenly saw it alone, you'd be frightened, or laugh. That is the effect absinthe has, and that is why it drives men mad."

This awful de-familiarisation has all the hallmarks of a real drug experience. Then Wilde went on, perhaps less convincingly:

> "Three nights I sat up all night drinking absinthe, and thinking that I was singularly clearheaded and sane. The waiter came in and began watering the sawdust. The most wonderful flowers, tulips, lilies, and roses sprang up and made a garden of the café. 'Don't you see them?' I said to him. '*Mais non, monsieur, il n'y a rien.*'"

The other thing that Wilde said made you see things as they really are was prison, which is a sobering thought.

Wilde always liked to raise the tone of his conversation by quoting himself, and he gave a slightly variant account of the effects of absinthe to John Fothergill, who went on to become something of a sensation as a 'gentleman pub-keeper' in the

1930s. When he was younger, Fothergill had known Wilde, and Wilde told him – "all in his great heavy drawl" – of the three stages of absinthe drinking. This time:

> The first stage is like ordinary drinking, the second when you begin to see monstrous and cruel things, but if you can persevere you will enter in upon the third stage where you see things that you *want* to see, wonderful curious things. One night I was left sitting, drinking alone, and very late in the Café Royal, and I had just got into this third stage when a waiter came in with a green apron and began to pile the chairs on the tables. 'Time to go, Sir,' he called out to me. Then he brought in a watering can and began to water the floor. 'Time's up, sir. I'm afraid you must go now, sir.'
> – 'Waiter, are you watering the flowers?' I asked, but he didn't answer.
> 'What are your favourite flowers, waiter?' I asked again. 'Now, sir, I must really ask you to go now, time's up,' he said firmly. 'I'm sure that tulips are your favourite flowers,' I said, and as I got up and passed out into the street I felt – the – heavy – tulip – heads – brushing against my shins."

Wilde's last days were grim. An ear infection, believed to be a result of syphilis, grew worse and worse; an operation failed to clear it up, and Wilde seems to have died from meningitis. He was understandably preoccupied with death during his final period, and he wrote to Frank Harris, "The Morgue yawns for me. I go and look at my zinc bed there." Ellmann notes that Wilde really did visit the Paris morgue.

Some weeks after his ear operation, he got up and went with some difficulty to a café, where he drank absinthe before walking slowly back, and rallied enough to produce his famous statement (for a woman named Claire de Pratz) that, "My wallpaper and I are fighting a duel to the death. One or the other of us has to go." His friend Robbie Ross said, "You'll kill yourself, Oscar. You know the doctor said absinthe was poison for you." "And what have I to live for?" said Wilde. It was a wretched time, but Wilde didn't have the monopoly of good lines. "I dreamt I was supping with the dead", he said to Reggie Turner. "My dear Oscar," said Reggie "you were probably the life and soul of the party."

In his epilogue to Wilde's life, Ellmann notes of his later days that "a constant sense of ill-being" was checked, but not eliminated, by brandy and absinthe. Drinking itself is the subject of one of Wilde's less well-known quips, set against the nineteenth-century fashion for declaring that all kinds of things, from rare beefsteak to seaside air, could somehow cause intoxication. "I have discovered", said Wilde, "that alcohol taken in sufficient quantity produces all the effects of drunkenness."

———

The vultures had been gathering over Wilde for some time before his trial; there was strong anti-decadent feeling in the last two decades of the nineteenth century. It is noticeable that when absinthe is mentioned in English poetry of the time, it is – with the honourable exception of Dowson and Symons – usually a sign of either Frenchness or wickedness, or both. To understand more of absinthe's public image at this period, we need to plumb the depths of bad verse.

The French connection is natural enough, and it figures in W.S.Gilbert's song 'Boulogne' (which includes the immortal rhyme "You can sit in a café with gents rather raffy"). More than that:

> If you're French in your taste, you can pull in your waist,
> and imbibe, till all consciousness ceases
> Absinthe and vermouth, with the Boulonnais youth,
> and play billiards like mad for franc pieces –

Which all seems like fair comment. Robert Williams Buchanan, on the other hand, has more of an axe to grind.

Buchanan is – as they say – 'not much read these days'. And deservedly so. But in his own day he was a prolific versifier, and a great man for the moral high ground. If he is remembered at all now, it is for his rooting out of decadence and depravity, notably in his attacks on Swinburne ("unclean", "morbid", "sensual") and the Pre-Raphaelites, whom he attacked in his 1871 essay 'The Fleshly School of Poetry'. There were a lot of people Buchanan disapproved of, and in one of his poems, 'The Stormy Ones', he puts them all on a ship. The "stormy ones" are the writers Buchanan hates – Byron, Alfred de Musset, Heinrich Heine, and others, all of them "Lords of misrule and melancholy" – aboard their ship of fools:

> For up at the peak their flag is flying –
> A white Death's head, with grinning teeth, –
> 'Eat, drink, and love, for the day is dying'
> Written in cypher underneath.
>
> 'Vanity! Vanity! Love and Revel!'
> 'Take a sip of absinthe, my dear!'
> 'Religion's a bore, but I like the Devil!'
> These are some of the words you hear. . .

Heinrich Heine was a German Romantic poet who lived and died in Paris, and who was disapproved of in Victorian England. When Charles 'Water Babies' Kingsley was asked by his children who Heine was, all he felt the need to say was, "A bad man, my dears, a very bad man", a reply which seemed to George Saintsbury to be one of the touchstones of bone-headed Victorian moralism. Buchanan wrote another poem about Heine in his own right, in which he figures as a morally dodgy gnome:

> In the City of absinthe and unbelief,
> The Encyclopaedia's sceptic home,
> Fairies and trolls, with a gentle grief,
> Surrounded the sickly gnome.

The gnome ends up dead and buried in Montmartre cemetery, which Buchanan no doubt felt was the best place for him. And there (where he's "laid asleep") "in the moonlight and the gloom, / The spirits of Elfland creep!"

Buchanan puts up a far less fey performance when he gets his teeth into wicked French novels, breeding like pullulating reptiles and promoting world-weary *ennui*:

> . . . what d'ye call the dreary
> Heavy-hearted thing and weary,
> In old weeds of joy bedizen'd?
> By the shallow French 'tis christen'd
> *Ennui*! Ay, the snake that grovels
> In a host of scrofulous novels,
> Leper even of the leprous
> Race of serpents vain and viprous,
> Bred of slimy eggs of evil,
> Sat on by the printer's devil,
> Last, to gladden absinthe-lovers,
> Born by broods in paper covers!

There are more scrofulous novels to come with "F. Harald Williams" (otherwise F. W. D. Ward, 1843–1922) in his 1894 *Confessions of a Poet*. He is another prolific churner-out of moral doggerel and it is not easy to say whose verse is worse, Buchanan's or Williams'. In Williams' poem 'The Triumph of Evil' we meet a devil, Goniobombukes. Goniobombukes is congratulating himself on the success he is having with those writers who are really his puppets, writing "with devilled pens". He knows that the times as a whole are going his way:

> And the sty of *absinthe* and French novels
> In their nude and naughty stage undress,
> Is the temple in which fashion grovels
> Still more low the louder to confess.

———

It is a pleasure to turn from Buchanan, Williams, and Goniobombukes to Robert Hichens, author of the brilliant anti-decadent satire *The Green Carnation*, published anonymously in 1894. Wilde had instructed some of his friends to wear green carnations in their buttonholes for the 1892 premiere of *Lady Windermere's Fan*. Since one of the characters on stage was also wearing one, without any further explanation, this gave the public the deliberately mystifying impression of an obscure and cryptic secret fraternity of some kind. These dyed carnations could be obtained from a shop in London's Royal Arcade, and since they never occur in nature they fitted in with the decadent cult of artificiality, and became the emblem of aestheticism.

If *The Green Carnation* has a fault it is that it is too subtle, and comes perilously close to the attitudes it is supposed to be parodying. It is only occasionally that its inventions are unequivocally comic, like the practise of *secret Bovril drinking* ("It makes one feel so wicked!").

Hichens was a member of the Wilde circle, and his novel features a "Mr.Amarinth" (Wilde) and his friend "Reggie" (Bosie, Lord Alfred Douglas). Ellmann comments that its fictional veneer was so thin that it reads more like a documentary than a parody.

> "And who started the fashion of the green carnation?"
> "That was Mr.Amarinth's idea. He calls it the arsenic flower of an exquisite life. He wore it, in the first instance, because it blended so well with the colour of absinthe."

The green-yellow colour of absinthe did chime perfectly with the 1890s, where green and yellow were 'aesthetic' colours. In the anti-aesthetic comic opera *Patience* (1881), W.S.Gilbert had already lampooned the "greenery-yallery, Grosvenor Gallery" sort of young man, and green and yellow are the colours in Wilde's ostentatiously, provokingly aestheticized 1889 vision of London, 'Symphony in Yellow', where the buses are like yellow butterflies and the pale green Thames is like a rod of jade.

Even in its heyday – in England, though not in France – the aura of faintly ludicrous aestheticism and damnation surrounding absinthe was ripe for parody. It is mentioned earlier in Hichens's novel when Reggie vaunts his own divided nature, split between the very good and the very bad, with an explanation that skips elegantly from absinthe to psychogeography:

> When I am good, it is my mood to be good; when I am what is called wicked, it is my mood to be evil. I never know what I shall be like at a particular moment. Sometimes I like to sit at home after dinner and read *The Dream of Gerontius*. I love lentils and cold water. At other times, I must drink absinthe, and hang the night hours with scarlet embroideries. I must have music, and the sins that march to music. There are moments when I desire squalor, sinister, mean surroundings. . . The mind has its West End and its Whitechapel.

The Green Carnation spelt the end of friendship between Wilde and Hichens, and Wilde was particularly mortified by rumours that he had written it himself. Hichens may have done Wilde more damage than he intended with the book's depiction of the relationship between Amarinth and Reggie. The Marquis of Queensberry – Bosie's father, and Wilde's nemesis – was not amused when he read it.

—

Wilde's disgrace took *The Yellow Book* down with it. This notorious periodical had been published by John Lane at The Bodley Head in Vigo Street, but after Wilde's arrest in 1895 the public mood turned against aestheticism and decadence. A mob attacked The Bodley Head – or "The Sodley Bed", as Aubrey Beardsley called it – and smashed its windows. John

Lane lost his nerve and sacked Beardsley; Wilde was arrested on April 5th and Beardsley was fired from the art editorship on April 11th. The *Yellow Book's* successor was *The Savoy*, edited by Arthur Symons: Beardsley's original cover featured a cherub urinating on a copy of *The Yellow Book*.

In 1895 Symons, Beardsley, and Dowson all went to Dieppe, and in August the artist Charles Conder wrote to William Rothenstein that Arthur Symons had arrived in town, taken a room in the same hotel, and had "just written a poem as to the Dieppe sea being like absinthe – original, n'est-ce pas?"

The oppressive atmosphere in London was one of the main reasons why the decadents and aesthetes gathered in Dieppe, although even there Beardsley didn't feel entirely safe. "There isn't a gendarme in France", he complained, "who hasn't got a photograph of me or a model of my penis about his person."

One of the leading lights of the Anglo-*absintheurs* at Dieppe was the publisher Leonard Smithers, a pivotal figure in the literary world of the 1890s, remembered by Rothenstein as "a bizarre and improbable figure" and described by Symons as "My cynical publisher Smithers, with his diabolical monocle." Smithers' life story has been exaggerated and largely told by his enemies, so he is remembered as a shady pornographer with evil proclivities. There was more to him than that.

Smithers prided himself on publishing "what all the others are afraid to touch". He rallied to support the Decadents after the Wilde affair, and set up *The Savoy* with Symons and Beardsley at the helm. It was named after the hotel, which was then a mere six years old. The Savoy Hotel promised electric lighting and "artistic furniture throughout", and it also happened to be the location where Wilde's offences were alleged to have taken place. *The Savoy* was Smithers's flagship, but his other achievements are impressive. He published Wilde's *Ballad of Reading Gaol* (originally published anonymously as the work of prisoner C.3.3.) and *The Importance of Being Earnest*. He also published books by Max Beerbohm, Beardsley,

Symons and Dowson, along with more curious and scrofulous items such as Aleister Crowley's *White Stains: The Literary Remains of George Archibald Bishop, a Neuropath of the Second Empire*, and the simply unclassifiable, such as the memoirs of Marie-Antoinette's hairdresser Leonard, or *Alone: An Introspective Work*, described as the internal ramblings of a female lunatic of lesbian and religious tendencies.

As for Smithers's murkier side and his reputation for depravity – which caused many people, such as Yeats, to shun him – his business was firmly grounded in the clandestine, *sub rosa* world of Victorian pornography. This was a gigantic subterranean industry in which almost anything was available, from explicit daguerreotypes to books bound in human skin (something which Smithers occasionally used to sell in his antiquarian catalogues, although there is no suggestion that he had any bound himself). At the height of his career Smithers had his premises at 4 and 5 Royal Arcade, off Old Bond Street, from where he sold "continental literature" and material of the kind that booksellers used to catalogue as "curiosa" and "facetiae". Wilde described Smithers as a publisher of very limited editions, "accustomed to bringing out books limited to an edition of three copies, one for the author, one for [himself], and one for the Police".

Wilde seems to have liked Smithers, describing him as "a delightful companion and a dear fellow." He described him to Reggie Turner: "His face, clean-shaven as befits a priest who serves at the altar whose God is Literature, is wasted and pale – not with poetry, but with poets, who, he says, have wrecked his life by insisting on publishing with him. He loves first editions, especially of women: little girls are his passion. He is the most learned erotomaniac in Europe." Can this really be as sinister as it sounds to our modern ears? We just don't know. But whatever it means, it doesn't seem to have bothered Wilde. In a rather inscrutable 1898 letter to Robbie Ross, Wilde writes that Smithers had been to visit him in Paris: "He was quite wonderful, and depraved, went with monsters to the sound of music, but we had a good time, and he was very nice."

Smithers seems to have been one of those people for whom drinking absinthe was a sacrament and a mark of caste; like a member of a special club he wrote to Wilde from London

> Since I last wrote to you I have neglected absinthe, and have drunk whisky and water, but I have distinctly seen the error of my ways, and have gone back to absinthe.

"Dowson sends his love", Smithers added at the bottom of the letter, "and he is gushing over the poem at the present moment." This was Wilde's *Ballad of Reading Gaol*, which Smithers was in the process of publishing.

In due course Wilde would write from France and ask Smithers to lay flowers on Dowson's grave for him. Smithers too came to a bad end. He lived hard: Rothenstein, among others, thought that absinthiated late nights with Smithers were ruining the health of Dowson and Beardsley. Smithers not only went bankrupt – confirming the old Victorian adage that if you really care for art you end up poor – but he graduated from absinthe to chlorodyne (a mixture containing chloroform, morphine, ether, and ethanol). He was probably driven to this by the pain from a stomach complaint, itself aggravated by alcohol and lack of food, and he finally died from gastric trouble and cirrhosis of the liver. One of his former authors, Ranger Gull, recognised him in the gutter of Oxford Street, starving, and gave him some money. Six months later he was dead, in what have been called, "circumstances of extreme horror", and described as being like, "something out of a Russian novel".

In 1907 Smithers' wife and son were called to a house near Parson's Green, Fulham, on what would have been Smithers' forty-sixth birthday. The house had been stripped completely bare; this alone must have been a strange sight for the people who found it, considering the cluttered domestic interiors that the Victorians and Edwardians were accustomed to. Except for a couple of wicker baskets and fifty empty bottles of chlorodyne, there was nothing in the house except Smithers' dead body. This had also been stripped completely; even the diabolical monocle was gone.

Chapter Three
The Life and Death of Ernest Dowson

William Rothenstein's picture of Ernest Dowson. According to Max Beerbohm, Rothenstein was a rare witness to the existence of Enoch Soames. Photo copyright National Portrait Gallery.

The definitive member of the "tragic generation" of 1890s decadents was Ernest Dowson, who wrote some of the most quintessentially Nineties poetry. Dowson's melancholy and self-destructive absinthe-drinking life has been extensively mythologised and romanticised, beginning with Arthur Symons' 1896 piece on him in *The Savoy*. There was "something curious in the contrast of a manner exquisitely refined, with an appearance generally somewhat dilapidated", says Symons, and "without a certain sordidness in his surroundings he was never quite comfortable, never quite himself"; in fact he had "that curious love of the sordid, so common an affectation of the modern decadent, and with him so genuine." One of Dowson's friends said that after his death an autopsy would find 'Art for Art's sake' engraved on his heart, and his biographer Jad Adams has written that "his dedication to art was nothing short of religious; his life was a human sacrifice."

Dowson's melancholy view of the world circles around themes of wistful yearning for an impossible ideal, and a sense that decay is inevitable – or that it has happened already – and everything is lost. His poetry is centred on erotic devotion, unrequited love, lost love, and parting by death. Influenced by the French Symbolists and by Latin literature, Dowson's work might be relentless but it is never laboured, and he brings it off with a musical lightness of touch. A contemporary reviewer noted his, "almost morbid grace and delicacy, which can only be conveyed by Rossetti's word gracile, and a decadent melancholy". Some of his phrases have an almost Biblical simplicity and resonance, and have since become film and novel titles: "gone with the wind"; "stranger in a strange land"; "days of wine and roses". And if the latter sounds cheerful, the context is "they are not long, the days of wine and roses".

Dowson was liked by almost everyone who knew him, Aubrey Beardsley being one of the very few exceptions. Beardsley was commissioned by Leonard Smithers to decorate the cover of Dowson's *Verses*, which he did with a Y-shaped arabesque. He liked to say that it meant "*Why* was this book ever written?" Beardsley was a waspish character, and he disliked both Wilde and Dowson. If Frank Harris can be trusted, Oscar Wilde once likened Beardsley's drawings to absinthe:

"It is stronger than any other spirit and brings out the subconscious self in man. It is like your drawings, Aubrey, it gets on one's nerves and is cruel."

Despite Beardsley's own reputation, he disliked the Decadent movement and resented his public identification with it. It may be that Beardsley – who was dying young through no fault of his own, slowly fighting a losing battle with tuberculosis – particularly despised Dowson for his suicidal lifestyle.

Dowson was never quite the same, said a friend, after both his parents committed suicide. This was perhaps an exaggeration: his father may have died of natural causes, although there was a widespread belief among Dowson's friends and possibly family that he had killed himself. Six months later Dowson's mother, who had always been unstable, unquestionably did kill herself.

Dowson's father owned a failing dock in East London – Bridge Dock, later called Dowson's Dock – and it ruined the Dowsons' lives with financial worry and eventual bankruptcy. But even this wasn't the worst thing in Dowson's existence. He fell desperately in love with a twelve year old girl named Adelaide, or 'Missie', the daughter of a restaurant owner in Sherwood Street, Soho. Dowson's motives were honourable, and he waited faithfully ("in my fashion", as we shall see) for this vision of purity to grow old enough to marry him. When she finally came of age she married a waiter, and Dowson never really recovered.

Dowson's adoration of little girls was not a purely personal kink. An outgrowth of the Romantic cult of the child, it was one of the more absurd nineteenth-century fashions, and seems to have been something of an Oxford thing, Lewis Carroll being another famous case. It is worth disentangling Dowson's passion for girls from paedophilia in the modern sense: for Dowson, the whole point of adoring little girls seems to have been precisely that there was nothing sexual about it. Dowson was deeply shocked by newspaper reports about a man who ran off with a schoolgirl and lived with her in Hastings, eventually receiving six months in prison. "The worst of it", he wrote to a friend in September 1891, "was that it read like a sort of foul and abominable travesty of – pah, what is the good of hunting for phrases. You must know what I mean. . . This beastly thing has left a sort of slimy trail over my holy places." This cult of the little girl was a widespread decadent phenomenon, and *Punch*, wielding its commonsensical humour like a truncheon, gave the whole business a sharp tap on the head with its spoof poem published in September 1894, 'To Dorothy, My Four-Year-Old Sweetheart.'

Dowson's friends found his love for children to be charming evidence of his purity of heart. Dowson himself wrote about the 'cult of the child' and related it to the pessimism and disillusionment of the age. His own temperament was deeply pessimistic: he described the world as " a bankrupt concern" – shades of Dowson's Dock – and life itself as "a play that ought to have been damned on the first night." When a friend reminded him that there were still books, dogs and seven-year-old girls, Dowson replied that in the end the books make you yawn, the dogs die, and the little girls grow up. A not untypical Dowson poem, 'Dregs', includes the lines

> The fire is out, and spent the warmth thereof,
> (This is the end of every song man sings!)
> The golden wine is drunk, the dregs remain,
> Bitter as wormwood and as salt as pain;
> And health and hope have gone the way of love
> Into the drear oblivion of lost things.

Jad Adams quotes an Oxford contemporary of Dowson, who remembered his philosophical pessimism as being largely based on his reading of the German philosopher Schopenhauer: "He never changed the opinion, then formed, that nature and humanity are, in the mass, abhorrent, and that only those writers need be considered who proclaim this truth, whether subtly or defiantly." Certainly nobody ever regarded Ernest Dowson as a healthy mind in a healthy body. He wrote from the failing dock to a friend, "I feel like a protoplasm in the embryo of a troglodyte. If you see a second hand, roomy coffin, fairly cheap will you please purchase same and have it sent down here."

One of the few things not to pall on Dowson was drink, especially absinthe. "Whisky and beer for fools; absinthe for poets", he would say; "absinthe has the power of the magicians; it can wipe out or renew the past, annul or foretell the future." Writing to Arthur Moore in October 1890, he asks:

How is your health? The absinthe I consumed between nine and seven of the morning on Friday seems to have conquered my neuralgia, but at some cost to my general health yesterday! The curious bewilderment of the mind after much absinthe! One's ineffectual endeavours to compass a busy crossing! The unreality of London to me! How wonderful it is!

Seven in the morning? It is a horrendous regime. Not only the bewilderment but the curious unreality are very vivid, like Wilde's de-familiarisation of the top hat.

On another occasion Dowson and Lionel Johnson shouted, late at night, up at their friend Victor Plarr's window in Great Russell Street. Plarr's light promptly went out. Dowson wrote to Plarr to apologise for having "violated the midnight silence of Great Russell Street"; "Forgive me if it was real and not an absinthe dream," he says, "as many things seem nowadays." Something of the dreamlike quality of a night out with

Dowson is captured in R. Thurston Hopkins' memoir 'A London Phantom'.†

Dowson's Aunt Ethel preferred his more sensible brother, Rowland, and remembered Ernest as a Jekyll and Hyde character, writing beautifully (she was thinking of his translation work, from which he scratched a living) "and then taking awful drugs, absinthe and other things. . . He was a queer mixture, clever but a fearfully weak character and like a madman when he got drink or drugs."

Dowson was a small, lightly built individual of great urbanity and politeness, but after he had been on the absinthe he would pick fights with Guardsmen. He was taken in for being drunk and disorderly so often that a magistrate greeted him with, "What, you here again Mr Dowson?" Arthur Symons remembers:

Sober, he was the most gentle, in manner the most gentlemanly of men; unselfish to a fault, to the extent of weakness; a delightful companion, charm itself. Under the influence of drink he became almost literally insane, certainly quite irresponsible. He fell into furious and unreasoning passions; a vocabulary unknown to him at other times sprang up like a whirlwind; he seemed always about to commit some act of absurd violence.

Frank Harris gives a grim picture of a night out with Dowson in the East End: "a nightmare; I can still hear a girl droning out an interminable song meant to be lively and gay; still see a woman clog-dancing just to show glimpses of old, thin legs, smiling grotesquely the while with toothless mouth; still remember Dowson hopelessly drunk at the end screaming with rage and vomiting insults."

Dowson's Jekyll-and-Hyde personality extended into his love life. W.B.Yeats writes of Dowson's devotion to the restaurant-keeper's daughter, with whom he played a chaste game of cards once a week: "that weekly game of cards," says

† Which can be found whole at the back of this book.

Yeats, "that filled so great a share of Dowson's emotional life."
He adds that "Sober, he would look at no other woman, it was
said, but, drunk, desired whatever woman chance brought,
clean or dirty." This situation is the basis of Dowson's famous
poem 'Cynara', the first verse of which runs:

> Last night, ah, yesternight, betwixt her lips and mine
> There fell thy shadow, Cynara! Thy breath was shed
> Upon my soul between the kisses and the wine;
> And I was desolate and sick of an old passion,
> Yea, I was desolate and bowed my head:
> I have been faithful to thee, Cynara! In my fashion.

He is always haunted by his previous love, and he is unable to
lay it to rest with prostitutes or riotous living:

> I cried for madder music and for stronger wine,
> But when the feast is finished and the lamps expire,
> There falls thy shadow, Cynara! The night is thine . . .

Yeats writes that one of the Rhymers Club members (possibly
Symons) had seen Dowson drunk in a Dieppe café with what
Yeats rather haughtily calls, "a particularly common harlot" –
evidently a bit of a shocker, even by Dowson's standards – and
Dowson had caught him by the sleeve to whisper excitedly
that they had something in common. "She writes poetry!" he
said, "It is like Browning and Mrs Browning!"

Dowson's letters are filled with references to his absinthe
drinking, giving a picture of an 1890s night life that would
give anyone the shakes. On a typical evening, Dowson and his
friends would meet at a public house on Shaftesbury Avenue,
the Cock, and those arriving after about six would generally
find Dowson there already, with his glass of absinthe before
him, scribbling verses on a scrap of paper or an envelope.
Around seven they would move on, either to the theatre,
which Dowson wasn't particularly fond of, or to Sherwood
Street for dinner at the restaurant where he fell in love with
Adelaide. Sometimes the nights were heavier, like the one

described below from July 1894, when Dowson went drinking with an actor called Charles Goodhart. The background is that Dowson and his friends have been looking after a sick girl called Marie, probably an actress, who had taken a drug overdose and developed a 'brain fever' as a consequence; everyone has been under great stress.

Goodie and I met in the evening. He had a charming man with him, a twenty-ton opium eater, who had run away with his cousin and is now to marry her. We met at 7 and consumed four absinthes apiece in the Cock till 9. We then went and ate some kidneys – after which two absinthes apiece at the Crown [a public house on the Charing Cross Road]. After which, one absinthe apiece at Goodie's club. Total 7 absinthes. These had seriously affected us – but made little impression on the opium-eater. He took us back to the Temple in a cab. This morning Goodhart and I were twitching visibly. I feel rather indisposed; and in fact we decided that our grief is now sufficiently drowned, and we must spend a few days on nothing stronger than lemonade and strychnine. But the previous strain on our nerves had been terrible. I wish you had seen more of Marie. Her charm was really remarkable – it was not only men but women that it struck. She made an immediate conquest of Missie and her mother who didn't at all take to Hoole's or Marmie's irreproachable fiancées – in fact of everyone who came across her.

But I must say I'm deucedly glad she's gone.

Write and give me your nouvelles – and forgive any incoherences in this scrawl. My hand has a palsy of the first quality, and my head is full of noises.

Some of these mornings were enough to give even Dowson second thoughts about the green stuff. Writing to Arthur Moore in February 1899, he heads his letter "Whisky v Absinthe"; "In the High Court of Justice Intoxicating Liquors Division":

On the whole it is a mistake to get binged on the verdant fluid. As a steady drink it is inferior to the homely Scotch. . . awoke this morning with jingling nerves and pestilential mouth. . . I understand that absinthe makes the tart grow fonder. It is also extremely detrimental to the complexion. . . I never presented a more deboshed [sic] appearance than I do this morning.

Dowson usually referred to absinthe in more positive terms. He and his friends drank regularly at the Café Royal, near Piccadilly, an opulent establishment modelled on the great French cafés of the Second Empire, where he always looked forward to a glass. "Would the gods I had some absinthe on board. Good old Café Royal", he wrote to Arthur Moore, and later, "We will walk to the Royal and absinthe; that may restore me. . .". This was a matter of months before his death. Closer still, he wrote "I will one day stay my tremulous course outside No.7 [Lincoln's Inn Fields, where Arthur Moore lived] – and we will absinthe – be it never so deleterious."

Dowson's absinthe prose-poem, 'Absintha Taetra' (Terrible Absinthe), is remarkable for the anxiety that it conveys (with the "tiger eyes" of the future), and its sense of a man hunted down and beset by both future and past. With absinthe, an artificial paradise is revealed, at least for a little while, and the piece attempts to render a druggish experience that goes beyond ordinary drunkenness. But like Arthur Symons's 'The Opium Smoker', the point is that nothing is really altered.

'Absintha Taetra'

Green changed to white, emerald to an opal: nothing
    was changed.
The man let the water trickle gently into his glass, and as
    the green clouded, a mist fell from his mind.
Then he drank opaline.
Memories and terrors beset him. The past tore after him
    like a panther and through the blackness of the
    present he saw the luminous tiger eyes of things to be.

But he drank opaline.

And that obscure night of the soul, and the valley of
humiliation, through which he stumbled were
forgotten. He saw blue vistas of undiscovered
countries, high prospects and a quiet, caressing sea.
The past shed its perfume over him, to-day held his
hand as it were a little child, and to-morrow shone
like a white star: nothing was changed.

He drank opaline.

The man had known the obscure night of the soul, and
lay even now in the valley of humiliation; and the
tiger menace of the things to be was red in the skies.
But for a little while he had forgotten.

Green changed to white, emerald to an opal: nothing
was changed.

Dowson's regime had a disastrous effect on him. Another
member of the Smithers circle, Vincent O'Sullivan, author of
Houses of Sin, remembered Dowson:

Dowson's neglect of his personal appearance went to
lengths which I have never seen in anybody else still on
the surface, and hardly in bums and beats. . . The thing
about Dowson was that he did not want to remedy it. . .
to spend money on baths and clothes and remedies
seemed to him to be putting money to the wrong
account.

This description (which is also a remarkably early use of the
word 'beat') gives some indication why the fastidious
Beardsley despised him. Arthur Symons described Dowson as
looking like Keats, but his life took its toll on his appearance.
When Smithers published Knut Hamsun's *Hunger*, it had a
grim cover picture by William Horton, and Oscar Wilde
claimed this picture was "a horrible caricature of Ernest". He
wrote to Smithers, "The picture on *Hunger* grows more like
Ernest daily. I now hide it." Shades of *Dorian Gray*. . .
Dowson was a loyal friend to Wilde after his downfall, and

William Horton's cover for Knut Hamsun's *Hunger*, published
by Leonard Smithers in 1899. Wilde claimed the picture was
"a horrible caricature of Ernest", and that likeness
increased daily until he had to hide it.

spent time with him in France. These were bad days for
Dowson, who was in the depths of his miseries over Adelaide,
but they had their peaceful moments: writing to Reggie
Turner from Berneval-sur-Mer, Wilde adds "Ernest had an
absinthe under the apple trees!" He had written to Alfred
Douglas the day before, teasing him about the dating of his
letters. "Do you ever really know the day of the month?" he
asks, and adds, "I rarely do myself, and Ernest Dowson, who is
here, never." Wilde always defended Dowson's drinking.
When somebody said, "It's a pity he drinks so much
absinthe," Wilde shrugged his shoulders and said: "If he
didn't drink, he would be somebody else. *Il faut accepter la
personnalité comme elle est. Il ne faut jamais regretter qu'un poète est
saoul, il faut regretter que les saouls ne soient pas toujours poètes.*†

---

† "You have to accept personality for what it is. You shouldn't regret that
a poet is a drunk, instead you should regret that drunks are not always
poets"

Some of Dowson's habits seem to have rubbed off on Wilde. Dowson persuaded him to go to a heterosexual brothel to acquire what he called "a more wholesome taste", but Wilde didn't altogether enjoy it. "It was like cold mutton", he said quietly to Dowson when he emerged again, and then (loudly, so that the cheering crowd who had followed them could hear), "But tell it in England, for it will entirely restore my character." Wilde also seems to have followed Dowson in his drinking. Writing to Dowson and asking "Why are you so persistently and perversely wonderful?", Wilde adds:

I decided this morning to take a Pernod. The result was marvellous. At 8.30 I was dead. Now I am alive, and all is perfect, except your absence.

A few days later he wrote Dowson a note to entice him over: "My dear Ernest, Do come here at once: Monsieur Meyer is presiding over a morning meal of absinthe, and we want you."

Dowson was an ardent Francophile, and he spent a long time in Paris ("the only city", as he called it), where he almost starved. Writing from 214 rue Saint-Jacques, he tells Arthur Moore that he and Connell O'Riordan are finding things hard: "Connell smokes and drinks nothing in order to have his two square meals and I tighten my belt in order to allow myself a sufficiency of cigarettes and absinthe. As for women. . . we dare not even look at them." Writing to O'Riordan, then safely back in London, Dowson details a few days of his life. The night before he has managed to get a free dinner at the house of the Vicomte de Lautrec (not the painter, although Dowson also knew him), where they also smoked hashish and played ouija. "We got a message from Satan", Dowson reports, "but he appeared to have nothing of the slightest importance to say."

Now, after an absinthe at the D'Harcourt café, and spending his last money on tobacco and cigarette papers, Dowson is back home *"chez moi"* for a bread roll, a piece of Brie and half a bottle of wine; he puts a sketch of his table top in the letter, numbering the items along with his "various literary effects".

Next day he has to buy a bread roll instead of a stamp, and on the third day he continues the unposted letter: "this morning lo there was a letter and £1 and I went out with tears of gratitude in my eyes and had an absinthe and afterwards a breakfast."

Dowson had been received into the Catholic Church at Brompton Oratory in September 1891, and in London he was in the habit of dipping his crucifix into his absinthe before he drank. In Paris he attended the beautiful church of Notre Dame des Victoires, which previously "I only knew from Huysman's marvellous novel"†; "I was immensely impressed by the sort of wave of devotion which thrills through the whole crowded congregation." Jad Adams recounts that when he was in Dieppe, Dowson would spend hours in a side chapel of the church at Arques, kneeling in adoration before a painting of St. Wilgefortis, known in France as Livrada. Wilgefortis was the daughter of a pagan king, but she became a Christian and took a vow of virginity. When her father wanted to marry her off to the King of Sicily, Wilgefortis prayed for God's help to avoid the marriage, and this arrived when she grew a beard. When the King of Sicily decided not to marry her after all, her father had her crucified instead. It was to this bearded female martyr that Dowson addressed his devotion, evidently moved by her story. As Adams comments, "You could always count on Dowson to be out of the ordinary."

Aside from simple alcoholism, we can see those metonymic, part-for-the-whole associations at play in Dowson's drinking; when he drank absinthe in London he was drinking Paris, and when he dipped his crucifix in it, he was drinking his religion.

Inevitably his physical and mental health began to break under the life that he was leading. In 1899 he was staying at the Hotel Saint Malo in the Rue d'Odessa and drinking heavily, chiefly in the Latin Quarter and the all night market workers' bars around Les Halles. Along with the artist Charles

† I.e. Huysmans' *En Route* (1895).

Conder he went to La Roche Guyon to take a break from the punishing Paris routine, but by now he was showing pronounced symptoms of absinthism. Conder wrote to William Rothenstein that Dowson, "had a fit in the morning which left his mind in a most confused state and with a most extraordinary series of hallucinations. I left him there as he refused to come to Paris."

Dowson did return to Paris later, and it was there that his friend Robert Sherrard found him, "slumped over a table sticky with absinthe". Dowson's nerves were now completely shot, and he told Sherrard he was afraid to go back to his hotel room. He had become terrified of a statue on the mantelpiece. "I lie awake and watch it," he said; "I know that one night it means to come down off its shelf and strangle me."

Sherrard was another drinker, and a duellist. Dowson described him as, "charming but the most morose and spleenful person I have yet encountered. His conversation is undiluted vitriol." Sherrard was capable of shouting anti-Semitic slogans and firing his revolver into the ceiling. Nevertheless, it was Sherrard and his wife who took Dowson in and looked after him at the end of his life, in their house – sometimes rather genteelly described as a cottage, but in fact an ordinary terraced house in the shabby suburb of Catford, South-East London, with another family downstairs – where Dowson died.

Dowson liked to reminisce about Paris, and he told Sherrard that he felt literary life hadn't worked out for him. "In future", he said, he would devote his energies to something else. Dowson was coughing badly, and Sherrard fetched him some ipecuanha wine from a chemist. The coughing continued, and Sherrard sent for a doctor. While he was gone, Dowson told Sherrard's wife, "You are like an angel from heaven, God bless you." Sherrard returned, and as he lifted Dowson into a sitting position to ease his breathing and mop his forehead, Dowson's head slumped. He was thirty-two.

Wilde wrote from Paris to Leonard Smithers – who was himself bankrupt by now – and asked him to put some flowers on Dowson's grave. Wilde's letter contains his famous epitaph on Dowson: "Poor wounded wonderful fellow that he was, a tragic reproduction of all tragic poetry, like a symbol, or a scene. I hope bay-leaves will be laid on his tomb, and rue, and myrtle too, for he knew what love is." On the centenary of Dowson's death the Eighteen Nineties Society laid a wreath of rue, rosemary and myrtle on Dowson's headstone, after which members of The Lost Club poured absinthe over his grave.

Homeless, toothless, intermittently insane, Dowson had lasted until 1900. He could hardly have died in a more fitting year. W.B. Yeats recalled the Nineties coming to an abrupt end:

> Then in 1900 everybody got down off his stilts; henceforth nobody drank absinthe with his black coffee; nobody went mad; nobody committed suicide; nobody joined the Catholic church; or if they did I have forgotten.

He was wrong about the absinthe.

Chapter Four
Meanwhile In France

Paul Verlaine in the Café Procope, inkwell and absinthe in front of him. Photo copyright Bibliothèque Nationale.

Gaston Beauvais, the doomed absintheur of Marie Corelli's *Wormwood*, is a man with literary aspirations: he has even written a short study of Alfred de Musset. Musset was among the first of the major French poets to fall victim to absinthe, although it comes to look like an occupational hazard as the nineteenth century goes on. Musset is a melancholy writer, whose work is often about lost love. His first published book was a self-expressive translation of Thomas De Quincey's *Confessions of an English Opium Eater*, full of personal digressions and even 'improvements'; Musset re-unites De Quincey and Anne, the lost child prostitute, in a sentimental happy ending, as if he found the original unbearable.

Musset drank for some years at the Café Procope, and at the Café de la Regence, on the corner of the Rue Saint-Honore and the Place du Palais Royal. There is a second-hand account of him in the Goncourt journals:

> Dr.Martin told me yesterday that he had often seen Musset taking his absinthe at the Café de la Regence, an absinthe that looked like a thick soup. After which the waiter gave him his arm and led him, or rather half-carried him, to the carriage waiting for him at the door.

Musset's absinthe drinking was well known. Nearly sixty years after his death, when absinthe was about to be banned, a politician with vested interests named Alfred Girod (from the absinthe manufacturing district of Pontarlier) did everything he could to defend it. It was ridiculous to endanger such a successful French industry. The anti-absinthe lobby claimed it turned men into ferocious beasts, he said – but he had a glass every day, and did he look like a mad dog? Finally, in desperation, he said it had inspired the poetry of Alfred de Musset. How could they possibly ban that?

In his lifetime Musset was made a member of the Académie Française, but he often missed their meetings. When somebody remarked that Musset often *absented* himself, Villemain, the Secretary of the Academy, couldn't resist a bitter pun: you mean to say, he said, that he *absinthes* himself a bit too much.

There is a poem dedicated to Musset by another poet of the time, Edmond Bougeois, about the thin green line between being inspired and being washed up.

> Anxious and grieving, in the smoky enclosure
> Of a café, I dream, and, dreaming, I write
> Of the blue tints of the sun that I love
> When I see its light in a glass of absinthe.
>
> Then the mind scales the highest peaks
> And the heart is full of hope and the scent of hyacinth,
> I write and write, saying; absinthe is holy
> And the green-eyed muse is forever sovereign.
>
> But alas! A poet is still just a man.
> With the first glass drunk, for better writing,
> I wanted a second, and the writing slowed.
>
> The tumultuous waves of thought dried up
> And deserted, my brain became hollow:
> It only needed one glass, and I drank two.

Musset's younger contemporary, Charles Baudelaire, the author of *Les Fleurs du Mal* (The Flowers of Evil), became fixed in the public mind – particularly on the other side of the channel – as vice incarnate. He was more complex than that, and Christopher Isherwood has tried to pin down some of his contradictions. He was a religious blasphemer, a scruffy dandy, a revolutionary who despised the masses, a deeply moral individual who was fascinated by evil, and a philosopher of love who was ill at ease with women. In his *Intimate Journals*

Baudelaire writes, "Even when quite a child I felt two conflicting sensations in my heart: the horror of life and the ecstasy of life. That, indeed, was the mark of a neurasthenic idler."

Baudelaire was a great explorer of the new sensations of urban life, of early 'modernity' and what we might now call alienation and neurosis, extending the domain of art and poetry to cover previously taboo subjects and find a new, strange beauty in them. He was a great exponent of dandyism, considered as an attitude or a philosophy rather than just a matter of clothing. He was also completely unimpressed by the idea of 'progress', hated the banality of modern life, and was inclined to believe in Original Sin. Late in his life he began to fear madness. He tried to give up drink and drugs and took up prayer with a new intensity, praying not only to God but to Edgar Allan Poe (whom he revered, and translated into French), as some people might pray to a saint to 'intercede' for them.

Isherwood writes, "Paris taught him his vices, absinthe and opium, and the extravagant dandyism of his early manhood which involved him in debt for the rest of his life." Baudelaire also translated De Quincey's *Confessions of An English Opium Eater* and wrote his own classic accounts of hashish, opium and alcohol in *Les Paradis Artificiels* and in his essay 'Wine and Hashish Compared as a Means for the Multiplication of the Personality'. Jules Bertaut's *Le Boulevard* includes a picture of Baudelaire rushing into a café, the Café de Madrid, and moving the water jug: "the sight of water upsets me", he says, before sinking two or three absinthes with a "detached and insouciant" air.

Baudelaire wrote nothing specifically about absinthe, and when he writes about alcohol he calls it generically "wine", as in his famous prose-poem 'Drink!' ('*Enivrez-vous*', literally, 'get drunk'):

It is necessary to be drunk all the time. That is everything; it's the only question. So as not to feel the horrible burden of time breaking your back and bending you towards the ground, you must get drunk without respite.

But on what? On wine, poetry or virtue, it's up to you. But get drunk.

And if sometimes, on the palace stairs or on the green grass of a ditch, in the mournful solitude of your room, you wake up, the drunkenness already going or gone, ask the wind, the wave, the star, the bird, the clock, anything that flies and flees, anything that moans and groans or rolls or sings or speaks, ask them what time it is: and the wind, the star, the bird, the clock will answer you: "It is the hour to get drunk! So as not to be the martyred slaves of time, get drunk; get drunk unceasingly! With wine, or poetry, or virtue, as you prefer."

This is not just about alcohol, although various people from Rimbaud to Dowson to Harry Crosby would later behave as if it was. Wine is a symbol, almost like the 'wine' in Persian mystical poetry, and the real issue is about maintaining a state of manic intensity and inspiration that defeats time. The closest parallel is perhaps Walter Pater's conviction that to "burn always with this hard gem-like flame, to maintain this ecstasy, is success in life", in his 'Conclusion' to *The Renaissance*.

When Baudelaire writes of "wine", the poem that is closest to the absinthe poetry of the same era (sounding its distinctive notes of poison, greenness, oblivion, and death) is probably 'Poison' in *Les Fleurs du Mal*, some of which runs

Wine knows how to clothe the most sordid slum dwelling
    In a miraculous luxury
And makes fabulous porticos surge up
    In the gold of its red vapour,
Like a sunset in a hazy sky.

[. . .]

All that is nothing compared to the poison that flows
    From your eyes, from your green eyes
. . .

All that is nothing to the terrible marvel
  Of your saliva that bites,
Which plunges my remorseless soul into oblivion,
  And sets it spinning and swirls it swooning
Towards the shores of death.

Baudelaire is ultimately concerned with something for which
drink and drugs are only symbols or intimations, and he
writes in 'Invitation to the Voyage' that, "Each man carries
within him a dose of his own opium". Drugs, drink and
syphilis caught up with Baudelaire and he died at 46, already
brought low by a stroke. Towards the end he was taken in by
nuns, but they threw him out again for his blasphemies and
obscenities.

   Baudelaire was a seminal figure for the 1890s' poets.
Baudelaire found his artistic materials in the proto-modernist
squalor of the Parisian metropolis, and so Eugene Lee-
Hamilton's luxuriantly wallowing sonnet about him is as
much about the place as the man. It is from his 1894 *Sonnets of
the Wingless Hours*, a title that already suggests time hanging
heavy with Baudelairean *ennui* but enlivened, in this case,
with "vague fumes of musk, with fumes from slums and
slimes" and "the gorgeous iridescence of decay":

A Paris gutter of the good old times,
  Black and putrescent in its stagnant bed,
  Save where the shamble oozings fringe it red,
Or scaffold trickles, or nocturnal crimes.

It holds dropped gold; dead flowers from tropic climes;
  Gems true and false, by midnight masquers shed;
  Old pots of rouge; old broken vials that spread
Vague fumes of musk, with fumes from slums and slimes.

And everywhere, as glows the set of day,
  There floats upon the winding fetid mire
The gorgeous iridescence of decay:
[. . .]

Absinthe comes further into the foreground with Paul Verlaine. He was the figure whose absinthe drinking did most to confirm it as a Bohemian cult, despite the all too visible effect it had on him. Verlaine was widely seen as something of a split personality. On the one hand there was his exquisite poetry – deliberately vague, exquisitely suggestive but impossible to pin down, conjuring evanescent emotional landscapes – and on the other there was the absinthe-soaked horror of his life, which remains genuinely appalling. Verlaine attacked his wife on several occasions, and even tried to set fire to her. He shot and wounded Rimbaud with a revolver, and he attacked his own mother more than once, taking a knife to her at the age of seventy-five because he wanted some money. Later in life he repented the years gone by, and blamed his excesses on absinthe.

For a long time absinthe was a self-conscious part of Verlaine's identity. The playwright Maurice Maeterlinck was in a Belgian railway station at Ghent one day when a train rolled in which must have seemed to have some kind of maniac on board:

> The Brussels train came to a halt in the almost deserted station. A window in a third class carriage opened with a great clatter and framed the faun-like face of the old poet. 'I take sugar with it!' he cried. This was apparently his usual greeting when he was on his travels: a sort of war-cry or password, which meant that he took sugar with his absinthe.

Verlaine was the only child of exceptionally doting parents. His mother had finally succeeded in producing him after a series of miscarriages, and she kept the foetuses pickled in jars in their house, which must have been a little oppressive. One night Verlaine had a furious row with her and smashed the jars. He was rather ugly, and in his teens he became unhappily aware that he was not very attractive to women. One of his teachers remembered, "a hideous mug that reminded one of a hardened criminal", and a friend's mother was horrified to meet him; she thought he was, "like an orang-utan escaped from the Jardin des Plantes".

Verlaine's instability with drink showed itself early on: he frequented Lemerre's bookshop in the Passage Choiseul, one of the Paris arcades, and Lemerre remembered that he never left the bookshop "without pausing for a break in a little café at the end of the passage. There he sometimes drank more than one absinthe, and very often [François] Coppée had great trouble in dragging him away." Verlaine never liked to be dragged away. Another friend from his youth, Edmond Lepelletier, was coming back with Verlaine through the Bois de Boulogne after a night of drinking, when Verlaine wanted to go back to the Pré-Catelan for another drink. Lepelletier tried to restrain him, at which point Verlaine went berserk, unsheathed his swordstick, and chased him for his life.

A spate of bereavements – father, favourite aunt, dearest cousin – worsened Verlaine's drinking. "It was upon absinthe that I threw myself," he wrote of this period later, "absinthe day and night." Marriage seemed to have a stabilising effect for a year or two, but things were already troubled when disaster struck in 1871: Verlaine met Arthur Rimbaud, a teenage poet with whom he became completely obsessed, destroying his marriage. Rimbaud was to give him some of the best and worst times of his life; looking back, after Rimbaud's death, a sympathetic journalist encouraged him to recall the shooting incident. Surely Verlaine must have been relieved to find he had only wounded him? "No," he said, "I was so furious at losing him that I'd have liked to know that he was dead. . . The boy had diabolical powers of seduction. The memory of the days we had spent wandering on the roads, wild and intoxicated with art, came back to me like a swelling tide laden with perfumes of dreadful delight . . ."

Verlaine and Rimbaud went to London in 1872, living in a room in Howland Street, off Tottenham Court Road (now a wasteland of institutional buildings; nothing remains of the eighteenth-century house, which had a commemorative plaque put on it in the 1930s). Verlaine sent his impressions of London to Lepelletier. Things were a little different from Paris: "'We don't have spirits,' replied a maid to whom I put this insidious request: 'One absinthe, if you please, mademoiselle.'" But in due course he discovered Soho, and a French café in Leicester Square, and on a subsequent visit he met his disciple Dowson and went to the Crown.

Rimbaud broke with Verlaine in 1873, which led to the shooting. Verlaine fired two or three shots, hitting Rimbaud in the wrist. They were in Brussels at the time and the wounded Rimbaud still wanted to leave for Paris, so Verlaine and his long-suffering mother accompanied him to the station. Here Verlaine, still in possession of the gun, became so agitated that Rimbaud called the police. Verlaine was initially charged with attempted murder, later reduced to criminal assault, but the real trouble came from the revelation of their relationship. Verlaine was sent to prison. Prison was good for him, at least in as much as he stopped drinking to excess and vowed never to touch absinthe again. He spent most of his time in solitary confinement, and returned to Catholicism. After his release he met Rimbaud once more, who encouraged him to blaspheme and, as Rimbaud put it, he made the ninety-eight wounds of Christ bleed again. Verlaine attacked Rimbaud, who hit back and left Verlaine unconscious; he was found next morning by some peasants.

Verlaine was now reduced to school teaching. He may not have been ideal schoolmaster material, given that he was an alcoholic pederast, but he made a very honourable job of it. Teaching French in the North of England, and in Bournemouth, was one of the more peaceful and stable periods of his life. Things started to slip after he was back in France, teaching English – which he couldn't even speak very well – at the College Notre Dame in Rethel. He fell into a serious relationship with a pupil, Lucien Letinois, who seems to have reminded him of Rimbaud, and he also started drinking again. His teaching was better in the mornings. One of his pupils remembered him slipping into town after the morning classes ended at 10.30 and going to a small bar to refresh himself, where, "he imbibed so many absinthes that he was often incapable of getting back to the school without assistance". He could have been a positive asset to any school that wanted a course in moral turpitude, but as it was the headmaster had to let him go. It was at this period that he wrote to Mallarmé about his miserable life ("Every happiness, except in God, is denied me . . ."), ending his letter in English: "Kindly write sometimes to your gratefully [sic] and so friendly, VERLAINE." Absinthe in front of him, he continued with a postscript: "In haste, on my travels, I happen to be in a tavern . . . Still sugared, confused. Very worried. Excuse all horrors. . ."

From now on he abandoned all hopes of respectability. He received another month in prison for threatening his mother with a knife, despite her protests to the court that he was really a good boy at heart. He settled completely into café life, becoming the presiding celebrity of the Latin Quarter. His poetic reputation was safe – so safe that the police were ordered not to bother him, whatever he did – but his health was beginning to fail. Frequently tramp-like in appearance, he had for some time looked much older than he was, and he suffered from diabetes, cirrhosis of the liver, heart trouble, syphilis, erysipelas, and leg sores. A contemporary witness, Louis Roseyre, was shocked by just what a genuinely squalid sight he was, with his filthy beard and scarf, drunk and surrounded by hangers-on. He was usually accompanied by his 'secretary' a jester-like fool called Bibi-la-Purée, a homeless eccentric who wore a top hat and a huge bouquet in his tattered formal overcoat. Bibi crowned his undistinguished career at Verlaine's funeral, where he stole all the mourners' umbrellas.

The English writer Edmund Gosse has left a more congenial picture of Verlaine at this period, originally published in *The Savoy* in 1896 as 'A First Sight of Verlaine'. Gosse had gone to Paris three years earlier in search for Symbolist poets, which he recounts in the manner of a man looking for rare butterflies in a jungle. "I learned that there were certain haunts where these later Decadents might be observed in large numbers," he writes, and so "I determined to haunt that neighbourhood with a butterfly net, and see what delicate creatures with powdery wings I could catch. And, above all, was it not understood that that vaster lepidopter, that giant hawk-moth, Paul Verlaine, uncoiled his proboscis in the same absinthe-corollas."

Gosse's safari took him to the Boulevard St.Michel, dull in the day but "excessively blazing and gay at night"; "to the critical entomologist the eastern side of this street is known as the chief, indeed almost the only habitat of *poeta symbolans*, which, however, occurs here in vast numbers", (it is, he says, a bit like the eighteenth-century chocolate-house scene in London, where, "chocolate and ratafia, I suppose, took the place of absinthe"†). After three patient days he succeeds in meeting Verlaine, who seems to have been remarkably well-behaved. Instead of looking like a tramp he had a new dark suit and a new white shirt of which he was very proud, shooting the cuffs for Gosse to admire. He spoke in a low "veiled utterance" about the beauties of Bruges, and in particular about the beautiful old lace to be seen there, before reciting his 'Clair de Lune'. Gosse always seems to have found Verlaine on his best behaviour. When he met him in London he was no less obliging. Gosse told him he was like a Chinese philosopher. "Chinese, if you like", replied Verlaine; "but philosopher – certainly not!"

Verlaine made the fortune of the cafés where he drank, notably the Café Francois 1st, where a Belgian artist named Henry de Groux saw him in 1893: "He had his huge and perpetual sly smile . . . He was still sober, but installed in front of a splendid *verte*." This is starting to overlap with the Verlaine of myth, the Verlaine that Bergen Applegate romanticized in *Verlaine: His Absinthe-tinted Song*: "he seems to have staggered out of the pages of Petronius – some vague, indefinite creature, half beast and half man – a veritable satyr . . . "

† Ratafia was a popular almond cordial or liqueur.

1893. A basement café, Place St. Michel, Paris. The air is fetid with tobacco smoke, mixed with the pungent, acrid odour of absinthe. . . The wan, purplish light shed by the gas jets from the walls, mingled with the more ruddy glow from a large oil lamp hanging above the group, throws into his glass some rays of iridescent splendor. Half curiously, half questioningly, his sunken, glowing eyes peer into the greenish opalescent liquid. The look is that of man not altogether certain of his identity – the fixed gaze of a somnambulist taking on a puzzled expression at the moment of wakening. Well might he question, for into that devil's chalice he had poured all his youth, all his fortune, all his talent, all his happiness, all his life.

There is a less indulgent picture of Verlaine in Max Nordau's book *Degeneration*. Nordau analysed 'degeneracy' as a pseudo-clinical malaise affecting European culture, and he found Verlaine to be a prime example. It is not just his "Mongolian physiognomy"† and "madly inordinate eroticism", or even the fact that he is a "paroxysmal dipsomaniac". Above all it is the mystical vagueness and deliberate "nebulosity" of his poetry, with its reliance on rhyme to guide its movements and its frequent failure to make concrete sense. "The other mark of mental debility [is] the combination of completely disconnected nouns and adjectives, which suggest each other, either through a senseless meandering by way of associated ideas, or through a similarity of sound." Nordau finds it to be a case of what we might now call schizoid thinking, although even he has to admit that "in the hands of Verlaine [it] often yields extraordinarily beautiful results", and he praises 'Chanson d'Automne' for its "melancholy magic".

Verlaine was aware of his bad reputation. Sometimes he was defiant: "I have long been considered an absolute monster . . .

† Verlaine's eyes and cheekbones were often described as looking Chinese or Mongolian.

I don't know anyone of mark who hasn't got his halo – in reverse". At other times he was more defensive: "I have ruined my life and I know very well that all the blame is going to be put on me. To that I can only answer that I truly was born under Saturn . . ." At his most contrite he blamed the absinthe, already commemorated at the end of his poem to François Coppée:

Moi, ma gloire n'est qu'une humble absinthe éphémère
Prise en catimini, crainte des trahisons,
Et, si je n'en bois pas plus, c'est pour des raisons.

My glory is only a humble ephemeral absinthe
Taken stealthily, fearful of treasons,
And if I drink no more, I have my reasons.

In his 1895 *Confessions* he repented his involvement with absinthe altogether, giving a memorable sketch of his early drinking:

Yes, for three days after the burial of my beloved cousin I existed on beer, and nothing but beer. When I returned to Paris, as if I were not unhappy enough already, my boss lectured me on the extra day I had taken off and I told him to mind his own damn business. I had turned into a drunkard, and because the beer was bad in Paris, I fell back on absinthe, absinthe in the evening and at night. The morning and afternoon were devoted to the office, where they liked me no better for my outburst; and besides, out of consideration for my mother and my boss, I had to keep them both unaware of my new and deplorable habit.

Absinthe! How horrible it is to think of those days, and of more recent days which are still too near for my dignity and health – particularly my dignity, when I come to think of it.

A single draught of the vile sorceress (what fool exalted it into a fairy or green Muse?): One draught was still amusing: but then my drinking was followed by more dramatic consequences.

I had a key to a flat in Batignolles where my mother and I were still living after my father's death, and I used it to return at whatever hour of the night I chose. I would tell my mother lies as big as my arm, and she never suspected them – or perhaps she did suspect, but forced herself to turn a blind eye to them. Alas! Her eyes are closed for ever, now. Where did I spend the nights? Not always in very respectable places. Stray "beauties" often enchained me with "garlands of flowers", or I spent hour after hour in THAT HOUSE OF ILL FAME described with such mastery by [Catulle] Mendes; I shall speak of it again at the proper time and place. I used to go there with friends, among them the dearly lamented Charles Cros, to be swallowed up in the taverns of the night where absinthe flowed like Styx and Cocytus.

Early one fine morning (though to me it was wretched) I came back, surreptitiously as usual, into my room, which was separated from my mother's by a passage, and undressed quietly and went to bed. I wanted an hour or two's sleep, unmerited although, philanthropically speaking, it was deserved. I was sleeping soundly at nine o'clock, when I should have been preparing for the office and drinking my broth or chocolate. My mother came in, as she always did, to wake me.

She gave a loud exclamation, as if she wanted to laugh, and said (for the noise had woken me):

"For God's sake, Paul, what have you been doing? You certainly got drunk again last night."

The word "again" hurt me. "What do you mean by again?" I said bitterly. "I never get drunk, and yesterday I was less drunk than ever. I had dinner with an old friend and his family; I drank nothing but red water, and coffee without cognac after dessert, and I came back a little late because it was a good way from here. I went to sleep quite peacefully as you can see."

My mother said nothing, but from the handle of the double window she unhooked a hand mirror which I used for shaving: she held it up to my face.

I had gone to bed with my top hat on.

I tell this story with utter shame; later on I shall have to relate many worse absurdities which I owe to my abuse of this horrible drink: this drink, this abuse itself, the source of folly and crime, of idiocy and shame, which governments should tax heavily if they do not suppress it altogether: Absinthe!

—

The other great source of folly, crime, idiocy and shame in Verlaine's life was Arthur Rimbaud. This brilliant but disturbed adolescent from Charleville sent Verlaine some of his poems, and Verlaine was so impressed that he invited the sixteen year-old Rimbaud to come and stay in Paris. He went to meet him off the train with Charles Cros, but they missed each other. Before Verlaine had even returned from the station, the boy genius had already made an appalling impression on Verlaine's wife, Mathilde, and his mother-in-law Madame Maute de Fleurville. Deeply awkward and provincial, Rimbaud was incapable of literary small talk and made up for it by being intensely surly. The main thing anyone could remember him expressing was his sneering hatred for Madame M. de F.'s cherished dog. "Dogs are *liberals*", he said.

Rimbaud was influenced by Baudelaire and by his own study of the occult. He was impressed by Baudelaire's thoughts on dreams: "To dream magnificently is not a gift granted to all men. It is through dreaming that man communicates with the dark dream by which he is surrounded." Rimbaud believed that the writer must be a mystic seer, akin to a medium, and that writing and thinking simply come through us, as dreams do. It is not that we think, but that we watch our thoughts taking place, and not so much that we speak, but that something speaks through us. It is an attitude to the mind that leads directly to automatism and to early surrealism. Individuality and conscious talent were pernicious illusions, like the ego: "I", said Rimbaud famously, "is an other". Rimbaud followed the more extreme tendencies in Baudelaire's writing without any of the reservations that Baudelaire himself had about them. For Rimbaud, it was not enough merely to "be drunk" all the time, as Baudelaire seemed to recommend. He pursued a programme of wilful madness: "The poet must make himself a *seer* by a long, immense, and reasoned *derangement* of all the senses." The faculties had to be opened up: "They must be roused! Drugs, perfumes! The poisons taken by the Sybil!" He was hardly likely to be deterred by the bad reputation of absinthe; on the contrary.

Rimbaud behaved at times like a man possessed. He didn't simply suffer from head lice, for example, but kept them handy to throw at passing priests. He encouraged Verlaine to mistreat and abuse his wife, and seemed determined to destroy their marriage. He disrupted a poetry reading by saying "merde" (shit) at the end of every line, and when the photographer Carjat tried to shut him up, he attacked him with Verlaine's swordstick. Drinking with Verlaine and some friends in the Café Rat Mort†, Rimbaud told Verlaine to put his hands on the table because he wanted to try an experiment. When Verlaine did so, Rimbaud slashed at them with a knife. On another occasion they were drinking with Antoine Cros when Cros, who had been away from the table, noticed his beer was bubbling unpleasantly. Rimbaud had put sulphuric acid in it.

Verlaine's wife Mathilde was distressed by the violent infatuation that had sprung up between Rimbaud and her husband. One day, while they were away travelling together, she found some disturbingly strange letters from Rimbaud in

† The Dead Rat Café, which had crockery bearing a picture of two rats fighting a fatal sword duel, complete with top-hatted rats as their seconds.

Verlaine's desk. She told the Cros brothers about these letters, and Antoine said that in his opinion Verlaine and especially Rimbaud had both become deranged by their absinthe drinking.

Rimbaud's biographer Enid Starkie describes him in the cafés on the Boulevard St.Michel, keeping himself in a more or less permanent state of intoxication. He also liked a café on the Rue St.Jacques called the Academy, as he wrote to his friend Delahaye:

Parmerde, Junish 72

Mon ami,

. . .

There is a drinking place that I like. Long live the Academy of Absomphe, despite the waiter's ill-will! It is the most delicate, the most tremulous of garments – this drunkenness induced by virtue of that sage of the glaciers, absomphe! If only, afterwards, to lie down in the shit!

Around the same time he wrote 'The Comedy of Thirst', a poem which suggests the deliberate self-undoing he sought through drink, quite distinct from the would-be happy drinking practised or attempted by Verlaine. The Comedy of Thirst contains a number of dialogue voices, including 'Friends' in the third section:

Come, the Wines go to the beaches,
And the waves by the millions!
See the wild Bitter
Rolling from the top of the mountains!
Let us, wise pilgrims, reach
The Absinthe with the green pillars

The poet replies:

Me: No more of these landscapes.
Friends, what is drunkenness?

I would just as soon, or perhaps even prefer,
To rot in the pond
Under the horrible scum
Near some floating bits of wood.

The idea of thirst often recurs in Rimbaud's work, partly as a metaphor for desire. As for metaphorical drunkenness, his best known work is probably the 'Drunken Boat', about a voyage of extreme abandonment, oceanic dissolution, and final disillusionment.

. . .

Sweeter than the flesh of hard apples is to children
The green water penetrated my hull of fir
And washed me of spots of blue wine
And vomit, scattering rudder and grappling hook.

And from then on I bathed in the Poem
Of the Sea, infused with stars and lactescent,
Devouring the green azure where, like a pale elated
Piece of flotsam, a pensive drowned figure sometimes sinks
. . .

Rimbaud came to look back on his literary career with disgust. At nineteen he recalled his earlier opinions and deranged experiences in the prose poem, *A Season in Hell*:

. . .

I liked stupid paintings, door panels, stage sets, back-drops for acrobats, signs, popular engravings, old-fashioned literature, church Latin, erotic books with bad spelling, novels of our grandmothers, fairy tales, little books from childhood, old opera, ridiculous refrains, naïve rhythms. . . I believed in every kind of witchcraft.
. . .

I grew accustomed to pure hallucination: I saw quite frankly a mosque in place of a factory, a school of drummers made up of angels, carriages on roads in the sky, a parlour at the bottom of a lake; monsters, mysteries. The title of a vaudeville conjured up horrors before me.

. . .

My health was threatened. Terror came. I used to fall into a sleep of several days, and when up, I continued the saddest dreams. I was ripe for death, and along a road of dangers my weakness led me to the edge of the world and Cimmeria, a land of darkness and whirlwinds.

. . .

He was finished with literature at the age of twenty, and turned to science and commerce, travelling to Africa and becoming a trader in coffee and guns. Verlaine tried to make Rimbaud's work better known, and championed it in his study, *Les Poètes Maudits*. Rimbaud the man was largely forgotten by the time he died. He had effectively disappeared, and many people assumed he had died years earlier. On his deathbed he had extraordinary visions: "columns of amethyst, angels in marble and wood; countries of indescribable beauty and he used, to paint these sensations, expressions of curious and penetrating charm." Having always been violently anticlerical, he seems to have made a bizarre late conversion to Catholicism†. Rimbaud was to be a major influence on the Surrealists, and Breton lauded him in the *Surrealist Manifesto* as "Surrealist in the practice of life, and elsewhere."

† At least, he did according to his sister. It has been disputed.

Chapter Five
Genius Unrewarded

ÉTUDE

SUR LES MOYENS

DE

COMMUNICATION

AVEC

LES PLANÈTES

PAR

CHARLES CROS

EXTRAIT DU *Cosmos* DES 7, 14 ET 21 AOUT 1869.

PARIS

AUX BUREAUX DU *COSMOS*, 62, RUE DES ÉCOLES

ET CHEZ GAUTHIER-VILLARS, 55, QUAI DES GRANDS-AUGUSTINS

1869

Twenty absinthes a day: Charles Cros's 1869 book on communication with other planets. Cros also invented synthetic rubies and the phonograph.

Charles Cros, poet and inventor, seems to have been a genius in the most mainstream sense of the word. In her biography of Verlaine, Joanna Richardson tells us that by the age of eleven Cros was already a gifted philologist, and taught Hebrew and Sanskrit to two professors at the College de France. He waited until he was twenty five before showing the world the automatic telegraph that he had invented, at the Paris International Exhibition in 1867. He also gave his outline of a colour photography technique to the Académie des Sciences, and he invented the phonograph eight months before Edison. In 1869 he published an essay on communicating with other planets. By now he was also publishing poetry, and he had met a woman named Nina de Callias; this was to be the decisive relationship in his life. She had parted from her journalist husband, Hector de Callias, because of his addiction to absinthe, and she now presided over her own intellectual and Bohemian salon, where Verlaine would not only read his poetry but even sing and act in comedy dramas. It was here that Cros met Verlaine in 1867, and they became friends.

Cros and Nina broke up in 1878. He married another woman, but his own absinthe addiction increasingly took him over. He became an habitué of the Chat Noir, a café opened in 1881 by a failed painter named Theodore Salis. Salis also wanted to run a kind of salon: he not only had his waiters dressed in the outfit of the Académie Française, but he personally insulted each customer as they came in. Cros would drink as many as twenty absinthes a day at the Chat Noir, and he died one night in 1888 while finishing a poem. Nina had predeceased him; she died insane in 1884.

André Breton includes Cros in the *Anthology of Black Humour*, and in his biographical entry he reminds us that Cros was also the first man to artificially synthesise rubies. Lacking

the capital and the character to develop his inventions commercially, Cros never made any money from them. He lived
and died in poverty.

Still, Cros has had some unexpected admirers. The American illustrator Edward Gorey had a taste for Cros's writing
and translated some of it. He illustrated Cros's rhyme for
children, 'The Salt Herring', which has something remarkably
bleak under its deliberately silly surface. A rhyme about
nothing, it is the story of a blank white wall against which a
man leans a ladder and bangs in a nail, tying a string to the nail
and then tying a dried herring to the string, which continues
to twist in the wind ever after. Weirdly desolate, like some of
Gorey's own work, it was described by Breton as a feat of
"making the poetic engine run on empty".

Cros's more cynical and sardonic side earns him a place in
Joris-Karl Huysman's *A Rebours*, the original "Yellow Book"
(Lord Henry Wotton lends Dorian Gray a copy of this
yellow-bound book in *The Picture of Dorian Gray*, and Dorian
finds it to be "the strangest book that he had ever read").
Huysman's hero, the ultra-decadent Des Esseintes, keeps a
book by Cros in his extraordinary library and admires Cros's
satirical story 'The Science of Love', "which was calculated
to astonish the reader with its chemical extravagances, its
tight-lipped humour, its icily comic observations."

Cros also figures in Marie Corelli's *Wormwood*, where she
praises him as an underrated genius and notes his recent death,
"surrounded by the very saddest circumstances of suffering,
poverty and neglect". She quotes his poem 'L'Archet' in
full and commends his collection *Le Coffret de Santal* (The
Sandalwood Box). More than that, the unattributed poem
'Lendemain' – the poem that inspires Gaston Beauvais on
his career of "making some dramas" with absinthe and
women – is by Cros.

> With flowers and with women
> With absinthe and with flame
> One can divert oneself a little
> And play a role in some dramas

Absinthe drunk on a winter evening
Lights up in green the smoky soul
And flowers on the loved one
Give a heavy scent before the clear fire.

Then the kisses lose their charm
Having lasted a few seasons;
Back and forth betrayals
Make us part one day without any tears.

We burn letters and bouquets,
And the fire consumes our nest;
And if the sad life is spared
Absinthe and hiccups remain. . .

The portraits are eaten by flames. . .
The twitching fingers tremble. . .
We die from having slept too long
With flowers and with women.

———

Not the least extraordinary thing about Cros's scientific discoveries is that they seem to have been real, which was not always the case with the results of absinthe-fuelled researches. The Swedish playwright August Strindberg spent years in Paris delving into alchemy and other subjects, during a period of increasingly paranoid mental turmoil recorded in *Inferno* and *From An Occult Notebook*.

"I wonder if we shouldn't go out and be bohemian. . ." he suggested to a friend in 1904, "I long for Montparnasse, Madame Charlotte, Ida Molard, absinthe, merlan frit, du Blanc, Le Figaro and [Café Closerie des] Lilas! But! – but!!!" In practice, absinthe hadn't always agreed with him. A few years earlier he had written in his dairy, "Concerning absinthe, several times this autumn I have drunk absinthe with Sjostedt, but always with unpleasant results." He goes on to describe these, with an impressive balance of paranoia and insight: the café "became filled with horrid types" and on the street ragged people "covered with filth as though they had come out of the sewers" appeared and stared at him: "I have never seen such types in Paris, and wondered if they were 'real' or 'projected'." He had, however, seen such people before in London: there were hellish, filthy people teeming at "the mouth of London Bridge, where the throng bears a truly occult appearance".

In addition to alchemy, Strindberg's projects and researches included colour photography, telescopy, "air electricity as motor power", "nickel plating without nickel (transmutation of metals)", "silk from a liquid without silkworms", and much more. Writing later, Delius remembered a time when he believed in Strindberg's scientific genius, even if his insights could be hard to follow. One day Strindberg showed Delius a photograph of Verlaine:

> Paul Verlaine had just died, and Strindberg had in his possession a rather large photo of the poet on his deathbed. He handed me the photo one day and asked me what I saw on it. I described it candidly, namely, Verlaine lying on his back covered with a thick eider-down, only his head and beard visible; a pillow had dropped on the floor and lay there rather crunched up. Strindberg asked me if I did not see the huge animal lying on Verlaine's stomach and the imp crouching on the floor?

Delius wondered if Strinberg was sincere about this, or if he was trying to mystify him. "However," he adds, "I may say I believed implicitly in his scientific discoveries then . . ."

> For instance, Rontgen rays [X-rays] had just been discovered, and he confided to me one afternoon over an absinthe at the Café Closerie des Lilas that he himself had discovered them ten years ago.

Strindberg's biographer, Michael Meyer, cites a number of authorities who believe Strindberg's mental condition was exacerbated or even caused by his chronic indulgence in absinthe.

—

Casting a characteristically jaundiced eye on "the idols of the youth of today", Edmond de Goncourt despatches the top three with a brief character assassination: "Baudelaire, Villiers de l'Isle Adam, and Verlaine: three men of talent admittedly, but a sadistic Bohemian, an alcoholic, and a murderous homosexual."

Long before he became anyone's idol, Villiers de l'Isle Adam had already made a striking appearance in the Goncourt journals, one September evening in 1864:

> "He was a typical literary Bohemian or unknown poet. His hair, which was parted in the middle, kept falling in stringy locks over his eyes, and he would push it back with the gestures of a maniac or an illuminati. He had the feverish eyes of a victim of hallucinations, the face of an opium addict or a masturbator, and a crazy, mechanical laugh which came and went in his throat. Altogether, something unhealthy and spectral. . . He looks as if he were descended from the Templars by way of the Funambules."

Writing of Paris cafés at this period, François Fosca gives a role call of casualties with Villiers de l'Isle Adam at the head: "There were many who had to suffer for their weakness for the Green Fairy: Villiers de l'Isle Adam, Charles Cros, Glatigny, the artist André Gill, and the Communard Eugène Vermesch, whom it led to a padded cell. . ."

Learning that the throne of Greece was vacant, Villiers de L'Isle Adam immediately announced his claim to it by a telegram to *The Times*. This might have seemed to his contemporaries to be exactly the sort of lunatic scheme an absinthe drinker would embark on, but Villiers de l'Isle Adam was in earnest. He gained the support of two of his cousins – one a governor of Siberia, the other the English Lord Buckingham – and eventually went to see the Emperor to discuss his claim. He went heavily made up, bent double, and plastered with foreign medals and decorations (looking, says Goncourt, just like an old broken down King of Greece ought to look). But nothing came of it.

Villiers de l'Isle Adam is particularly remembered for *Axel*, which W.B. Yeats says he studied as if it were a "sacred book". It has also been influentially discussed by the American critic Edmund Wilson, who took it as a key point in the Symbolist rejection of ordinary reality. Gothic and Wagnerian, loaded with Rosicrucian symbolism, *Axel* is the story of Count Axel, who lives in remote and ancient castle in the depths of the Black Forest, absorbed in the study of alchemy. Hidden in the crypt below the castle is a vast treasure, its whereabouts unknown even to Axel. Meanwhile the location of the treasure has been discovered by another Rosicrucian adept, a young woman who has escaped from the convent where her family have placed her. Pressing the secret button on a heraldic death's head in the crypt, she unleashes a torrent of gold, diamonds and pearls.

Although at first she attempts to shoot him, she and Axel fall in love, and she suggests that they should travel together to the fabulous Orient. She paints a lush picture of the East and its heroic possibilities, but Axel's reply is definitive. Her dreams of the Orient are so beautiful, he says, it would be foolish to try and make them real. "If only you knew what a heap of uninhabitable stones, what a sterile and burning soil, what dens of loathsome creatures, those wretched places are *in reality* – although they seem glamorous to you, with memories far away in that imaginary Orient which you carry within yourself." It is in this same speech against the external world and mere reality that Axel utters his most famous line: "Live?" he says, disgusted: "Our servants will do that for us."

It was a favourite line of Lionel Johnson. Unlike most

writers with a taste for aristocratic hauteur, Villiers de l'Isle Adam was a real Count. He died in vastly reduced circumstances, attended by his illiterate mistress. His writing was admired by Mallarmé, Huysmans, and Verlaine, who included him as one of his *poètes maudits*, and by Breton, who includes him in the *Anthology of Black Humour*.

———

Writing in the 1924 Surrealist Manifesto, Breton lists some of his chosen precursors of surrealism and says what they are supposedly surrealist "in". Rimbaud, as we have seen, is proto-surrealist "in life and elsewhere", Jonathan Swift "in malice", the Marquis de Sade "in sadism", and Baudelaire "in morals", followed by "JARRY in absinthe".

Alfred Jarry (1873–1907) was a bizarre figure. His own life was as much of a creation as his stage works, and eventually it became inseparable from them. Dwarfishly short, speaking with deliberately staccato or robotic intonations, and wearing a cape and an enormous stovepipe hat "taller than he was", Jarry immediately attracted attention in literary Paris. He lived in a tiny room at the foot of a dead-end alley off the Boulevard Port-Royal, and the spiral staircase leading up to it was decorated with handprints in blood on the walls. The room was draped with black velvet, filled with owls, and adorned with religious paraphernalia of crucifixes and censers.

Jarry consumed alcohol, absinthe, and ether in appalling quantities, with essentially magical or shamanistic intentions and disastrous results. Something of a misogynist, he was nonetheless a close friend of Madame Rachilde, older novelist and author of *The Marquise de Sade*, and she has left a vivid picture of his drinking:

> Jarry began the day with two litres of white wine, three absinthes followed at intervals between ten o'clock and midday, then at lunch he washed down his fish, or his steak, with red or white wine alternating with further

absinthes. In the course of the afternoon, a few cups of coffee laced with brandy or spirits whose names I have forgotten, then, with his dinner, after, of course, further aperitifs, he could still take at least two bottles of any vintage, whether good or bad. Now, I never saw him really drunk, except on one occasion when I took aim at him with his own revolver, which sobered him up instantly.

Jarry's drink of preference was, notoriously, absinthe, although later – when he ran low on money – he turned to ether, which was even worse. He liked to call absinthe "l'herbe sainte" (the holy herb, punning as "erbsant") and his "holy water". He cultivated a thoroughgoing aversion to the other kind of water; in that respect he was not unlike the American comedian W.C.Fields, who used to say, "How can you drink that? Fish have been fucking in it." "Anti-alcoholics," Jarry said:

> are unfortunates in the grip of water, that terrible poison, so solvent and corrosive that out of all substances it has been chosen for washings and scourings, and a drop of water, added to a clear liquid like absinthe, makes it muddy.

Jarry was never in the grip of water, which seems to have disagreed with him. Somebody once slipped him a glass as a practical joke, and – thinking it was a clear spirit such as *marc* – he threw it back in one. He then pulled, "the most horrible of faces" and was unwell for the rest of the day.

Jarry came to exist in what Rachilde remembers as, "that state of permanent drunkenness in which he seemed to quiver instead of living normally". It was from her that he borrowed the pair of bright yellow high-heeled shoes that he wore to Mallarmé's funeral. For the most part people liked him – Oscar Wilde took to him at once and described him as "most attractive. He looks just like a very nice renter" (rent-boy) – but it is clear that he could be a strain on the nerves. Very pale but ultra-fit, Jarry did almost everything to excess. He was a fanatical cyclist, and he used to race trains on his pushbike (he had a very expensive state-of-the-art racing cycle, a Super Laval 96, which he bought on credit in 1896 and still hadn't finished paying for when he died in 1907). He was also keen on firearms, and used to walk around Paris at night, intoxicated and carrying a pair of revolvers and a carbine rifle. When somebody asked him for a light in the street, he pulled out a revolver and blasted it in their face (it works as a sort of pun in French). Mercifully they weren't hurt. When he was in the country he used to hunt grasshoppers with his revolvers. Once, when he was engaged in target practice against a garden wall and a woman complained that he was endangering the lives of her children, he reassured her that if any did get shot he would help her to make some more.

'The Argonaut's Dinner' chapter of André Gide's novel *The Counterfeiters* contains a scene in which Jarry, drunk on absinthe, fires a revolver at a man in a café. It is inspired by a real incident when Jarry fired at a sculptor named Manolo (he is also reported to have shot at a man named Christian Beck during a banquet). He missed, probably on purpose. Like Wilde, Gide also took to Jarry, and remembers him as he was in about 1895: "It was the best period of Jarry's life. He was an incredible figure whom I also met at Marcel Schwob's, and always with tremendous enjoyment, before he became a victim of frightful attacks of *delirium tremens*."

Gide goes on to remember him as a "plaster-faced Kobald [a kind of gremlin], got up like a circus clown and acting a fantastic, strenuously contrived role which showed no human characteristic". Jarry's terrible, programmatic drinking was ultimately an attempt to break down the distinction between external and psychic reality, and his theatricality also tried to erase the boundaries between art and life, and to fuse the two. Jarry came to identify himself with his monstrous stage creation Père Ubu, the grotesque but comic anti-hero at the centre of his play *Ubu Roi*.

Ubu Roi takes place, "In Poland, that is to say, nowhere", with a minimalist set design that notionally included "palm trees growing at the foot of the bed so that little elephants standing on bookshelves can browse on them." Dimly based on the tragi-comic figure of a teacher that Jarry remembered from his schooldays, Père Ubu is a farcically gross figure who murders his way to the Polish throne – poisoning his enemies with a lavatory brush, which he carries like a monarch's sceptre – and institutes a reign of terror and debauchery. He is finally defeated by the king's son and the Tsar's army, at which point he flees to France, where he promises to commit further outrages. Jarry had performed the play with puppets in his attic as far back as 1888, but it was premiered on stage in 1896, with a set painted by Toulouse-Lautrec.

Toulouse-Lautrec and Jarry knew each other from *La Revue blanche*, an anarchist journal, where Jarry would turn up to the office in a woman's blouse and a pink turban. Both dwarfish, both outrageous, and both *absintheurs*, Jarry and Lautrec seem to have hit it off at once. Lautrec's most recent biographer, David Sweetman, notes that Henri would be the first to die, "but first there was still a lot more drinking and. . . laughing to do, now joined by another doomed figure [Wilde], before illness and the Green Fairy would claim them both."

Sweetman describes the play as, "scatological, outrageous, absurd and just downright crude". The actor playing Ubu came on, wearing an obesely padded costume with a spiral squiggle on the front, and uttered the single opening word "Merdre!" – a personal modification of "merde", perhaps roughly equivalent to "shite". The audience immediately went berserk, and fighting broke out for and against the play. The shambles continued for fifteen minutes or so, before the play could continue.

W.B. Yeats and Arthur Symons were in the audience, and Yeats found the experience profoundly disturbing. He shouted in support of the play, feeling he should back the radicals, but the whole business left a nasty aftertaste. Instead of the more introspective and Symbolist aesthetics that Yeats favoured, he saw in the play something of the harshness, 'objectivity' and ugly vitality that would characterise much of the twentieth century, and perhaps even the rise of totalitarianism. Breton later described the Ubu plays as anticipating "both the fascist and the Stalinist". For Yeats, Ubu was the harbinger of bad things to come: "After us", he wrote, "the Savage God".

It is not obvious from *Ubu*, but Jarry was an immensely erudite individual. Well versed in Latin and Greek classics, his enthusiasms included neo-Platonism, heraldry, and Thomas De Quincey. He had more in common with Yeats than Yeats realised, because Jarry had been touched by the occult revival in nineteenth-century France, and he was well versed in the arcane. He had read seminal French occult writers such as Stanislas de Guaita and Joséphin Péladan, and it is against this background, and the conscious cultivation of hallucinatory states, that Jarry drank absinthe not to stupefy himself but to drive himself mad, beyond rationality.

Jarry sought to live a waking dream. Oscar Wilde had already written of the need to fuse art and life, but Jarry did it with an intensity that looks forward to surrealism rather than back to Wilde. When he was being dragged away after shooting at Manolo he exclaimed, "Wasn't that a beautiful work of literature?" "We can say," Breton wrote, "that after Jarry, much more than after Wilde, the distinction between art and life, long considered necessary, found itself challenged and wound up being annihilated as a principle." After Jarry, said Breton, biography seeps unstoppably into literature: "The author imposes himself in the margins of the text ... [and there is] no way to rid the finished house of that workman who's taken it into his head to fly a black flag over the roof."

More than just the fusion of art and life, often seen as the central project of avant-gardism, Jarry had a potentially more disturbing project to fuse dreaming and waking. Arcane and esoteric as much as avant-garde, Jarry stands – as Roger Shattuck says – in the tradition of Jean-Paul Richter, Rimbaud and especially Gérard de Nerval, whose professed end was to "direct his dream". As Breton would later write "I believe in the future reconciliation of those two states, which seem so mutually contradictory, of dream and reality, in a kind of absolute reality, of super-reality." Jarry tried to take the liquid shortcut.

Jarry's thinking on these subjects is visible in his novel *Days and Nights*, about an absinthe-drinking conscript named Sengle who deserts from the French army. Jarry himself had been conscripted, but was released again for "precocious imbecility". Sengle's desertion is not only literal but metaphorical; he is profoundly absented in spirit, having gone 'away' by escaping into himself.

The days and nights of the title are reality and dream. Jarry writes that Sengle, following Leibniz, "believed above all that there are only hallucinations, or only perceptions, and that there are neither nights nor days (despite the title of this book, which is why it was chosen) and that life is continuous." It is continuous in the same way that consciousness is seen as continuous – and as being all that there is – in *The Tibetan Book of the Dead*, a book that Jarry might have liked; it wasn't translated until after his death†.

Preceding this passage (in the chapter entitled 'Pataphysics') Sengle's thoughts have taken on a distinctly magical – or psychotic – colouring. He finds that his thoughts can control the outside world: "Sengle came to believe, on the strength of testing his influence on the behaviour of small objects, that he had the right to assume the probable obedience of the world at large." Playing dice, intoxicated with absinthe and brandy, he finds he can control the dice, predicting to his opponent what they will do and envisaging it in his mind's eye before it happens.

---

† Jarry also quotes a Chinese legend which he had found in a thirteenth-century book translated by the Marquis Hervey de St Denys, the Orientalist and writer on dream-control. It concerns the Leao people and their 'flying heads', which detached themselves at nightfall and flew away, returning at morning.

Sengle is walking in the forest with his friend Valens, feeling "in a state of mind as if he had taken hashish" and experiencing a hallucinatory sensation of his soul having detached itself from his body and flying like a kite in the air, attached only by a fragile thread. The idea of the 'astral body' is referred to in the same chapter.

Jarry's external life was not proceeding as smoothly. Poverty had him in its grip. He fished his own food out of the Seine, partly from eccentricity (he dyed his hair green as well) but also from necessity. He was now in cramped and dingy lodgings at 7 rue Cassette, which he called Our Grand Chasublerie because there was a manufacturer of ecclesiastical vestments on a lower floor. On the mantelpiece was a stone phallus, a gift from Félicien Rops, covered with a purple velvet skullcap. Jarry's ceiling was so low that even at his height his head brushed it. Other people had to stoop. The bed had no legs – he said low beds were coming back into fashion – and he wrote lying flat on the floor. As Roger Shattuck reports, "It was said that the only food that could be eaten conveniently in the place was flounder."

Jarry's drinking was unabated; if anything it was worse, because now he turned to ether when he couldn't afford absinthe. Keith Beaumont quotes a late Jarry prose work in which the hero, Erbrand, is in a final descent not unlike Jarry's own:

> he drank alone and methodically, without ever succeeding in reaching a state of drunkenness, and without any hope of becoming what it is fashionable these days to call an alcoholic: his doses were too huge for them not to slide over his cells as a river filters through an eternal and indifferent bed of sand and disappears. . .
>
> And he drank the very essence of the tree of knowledge at 80 proof. . . and he felt at home in a Paradise regained. . .
>
> But soon he could drink no more in the darkness, since for him there was no longer any darkness, and no doubt like Adam before the Fall. . . he could see in the dark. . .
>
> And he often went without food, because one cannot have everything at once and drinking on an empty stomach does more good.

Erbrand's 'seeing in the dark' sounds less like acuity of sight than hallucination; perhaps it is the kind of 'seeing in the dark' that can be done while floating in an isolation tank.

Finally, Jarry became very ill, and had to be attended by what he called "merdcins" ("docturds"). Drinking on an empty stomach does more harm, and Jarry's health was worsened by starvation. It is often said that what kills alcoholics is not just the drink but the lifestyle that goes with it, and this was true in Jarry's case. He wrote to friend that "the rumour has been put about . . . that Père Ubu [that is, of course, Jarry himself] drank like a fish. I can admit to you, as an old friend, that I had somewhat lost the habit of *eating* and that was my only illness."

To Madame Rachilde he wrote, "We must rectify the legend – for Père Ubu, as I am called, is dying not of having done too much drinking, but of not having always had enough to eat." He also told her, characteristically, that he believed the brain functioned after death during its decomposition, and that it was these dreams that constituted Paradise. Jarry's last request was for a toothpick. They brought him one just in time and he was delighted, dying almost immediately afterwards.

Roger Shattuck's brilliant chapter on Jarry in his book *The Banquet Years* is aptly and succinctly entitled 'Death by Hallucination'. Jarry leaves behind him not only his own work but a growing legacy of his admirers, 'The College of Pataphysics'. The *Société des Amis d'Alfred Jarry* publishes a Jarry journal entitled *L'Etoile-Absinthe*.

———

Not everybody who drank absinthe was a highly acclaimed genius, as we shall see in the next chapter. Alphonse Allais' prose piece 'Absinthe' looks at its effect on that quintessential turn-of-the-century figure, the struggling man of letters. Allais, a friend of Cros and Verlaine, was an oddball comic writer who has the distinction of painting the first completely monochrome colour-field pictures. It was often said that contemporary artists couldn't paint, so Allais and some others – mostly writers, not artists – formed the Salon des Incoherents, whose members *really* couldn't paint. Allais's masterpieces include a white rectangle, 'Anaemic Young Girls Going to their First Communion in a Blizzard' (1883) and his entirely green canvas of 1884, 'Some Pimps Lying in the Grass Drinking Absinthe'.

'Absinthe' is an early stream-of-consciousness piece, following the progressive intoxication and changing perceptions of a struggling writer sitting on a boulevard during 'L'Heure Verte', surrounded by the great urban mystery of other people.

'ABSINTHE'

Five o'clock.

Rotten weather. Grey sky. . . dreary, mind-chilling sort of grey.

Oh, for a short, sharp shower to get rid of all these stupid people milling around like walking cliches. . . Rotten weather.

Another bad today, dammit. Devilish luck.

Article rejected. So politely, though:

'Liked your article. . . interesting idea. . . nicely written. . . but not really in the style of the magazine, I'm afraid. . .'

Style of the magazine? Magazine's *style*?? Dullest magazine in the whole of Paris! Whole of France.

Publisher preoccupied, distrait, mind elsewhere.

'Got your manuscript here somewhere. . . yes, liked your novel. . . interesting idea. . . nicely written. . . but business is very slow at the moment, you see. . . already got too much stuff on our hands. . . ever thought of writing something aimed more at the market? Lots of sales. . . fame. . . honours list. . .'

Went out politely, feeling stupid:

'Some other time, perhaps.'

Rotten weather. Half past five.

The boulevards! Let's take to the boulevards. Might
meet a friend or two. If you can call them friends.
Load of worthless. . .But who *can* you trust in
Paris?

And why is everyone out tonight so *ugly*?

The women so badly dressed. The men looking so
stupid.

'Waiter! Bring me an absinthe and sugar!'

Good fun, watching the sugar lump melt very quietly on
its little filter as the absinthe gradually trickles over it.
Same way they say a drip of water hollows out
granite. Only difference, sugar softer than granite. Just
as well, too. Can you imagine? Waiter, one absinthe
and granite!

Absinthe on the rocks! That's a good one, that's a good
one. Very funny. For people who aren't in a hurry –
absinthe and granite! Nice one.

Sugar lump's almost melted now. There it goes. Just
like us. Striking image of mankind, a sugar
lump. . .

When we are dead, we shall all go the same way. Atom
by atom, molecule by molecule. Dissolved, dispersed,
returned to the Great Beyond by kind permission of
earthworms and the vegetable kingdom.

Everything for the best then. Victor Hugo and the
meanest hack equal in the eyes of the Great God
Maggot. Thank goodness.

Rotten weather. . .Bad day. Fool of an editor.
Unbelievable ass of a publisher.

Don't know though. Perhaps not so much talent as keep
telling self.

Nice stuff, absinthe. Not the first mouthful, perhaps. But
after that.

Nice stuff.

Six o'clock. Boulevards looking a bit more lively now.
And look at the women!

A lot prettier than an hour ago. Better dressed, too. Men
don't look so cretinous either.

Sky still grey. Nice mother-of-pearl sort of grey.
    Rather effective. Lovely nuances. Setting sun
    tingeing the clouds with pale coppery pink glow.
    Very fine.

'Waiter! An absinthe and anis!'

Good fun, absinthe with sugar, but can't stand around all
    day waiting for it to melt.

Half past six.

All these women! And so pretty, most of them. And so
    strange, too.

Mysterious, rather.

Where do they all come from? Where are they all going
    to? Ah, shall we ever know!

Not one of them spares me a glance – and yet I love
    them all so much.

I look at each one as she passes, and her features are
    so burnt on my mind that I know I will never
    forget her to my dying day. Then she vanishes, and
    I have absolutely no recollection what she looked
    like.

Luckily, there are always prettier girls following
    behind.

And I would love them so, if only they would let me!
    But they all pass by. Shall I ever see any one of them
    again?

Street Hawkers out there on the pavement, selling
    everything under the sun. Newspapers. . . celluloid
    cigar-cases. . . cuddly toy monkeys – any colour you
    want. . .

Who *are* all these men? The flotsam of life, no doubt.
    Unrecognised geniuses. Renegades. Eyes full of
    strange depths.

A book waiting to be written about them. A great book.
    An unforgettable book. A book that everyone would
    have to buy – everyone!

Oh, these women!

Why doesn't it occur to just one of them to come in and
    sit down beside me. . . kiss me very gently. . . caress

me. . . take me in her arms and rock me to and fro
just as mother did when I was small?
'Waiter! An absinthe, neat. And make it a big one!'

Chapter Six
From Antiquity to the Green Hour

L'Absinthe by Apoux: lechery, buffoonery, and death.
Copyright Roger-Viollet.

Like so many things that end badly, the story of absinthe begins well. In the ancient world the absinthe plant – *artemisia absinthium*, or wormwood – was widely known as one of the most valuable medicinal herbs. The Ebers Papyrus, an Egyptian papyrus from 1600 B.C., recommends wormwood as a stimulant and tonic, an antiseptic, a vermifuge, and a remedy for fevers and period pains. Pythagoras thought that wormwood leaves in wine would ease childbirth, and Hippocrates also recommended it for period pains, as well as anaemia and rheumatism. Galen recommended it for fainting and general weakness, while the Roman naturalist Pliny believed it was good for the stomach, for bile, and for digestion in general, and Dioscorides, writing in his *De Materia Medica*, considered it a good antidote for drunkenness†.

Apuleius writes that the plant was first given to the centaur Chiron by the goddess Artemis, hence its name, and it is with the Greeks that it gets its more widespread modern name, from *apsinthion*; "undrinkable", because of its bitterness.

Paracelsus, the Renaissance alchemist and physician, rediscovered the Egyptian practice of using wormwood against fevers, particularly malaria, while Nicholas Culpeper's seventeenth-century *English Physician* offers a trove of unreliable information:

> Wormwood is an herb of Mars. . . hot and dry in the third degree. Wormwood delights in Martial places, for about forges and iron works you may gather a car load of it. It helps the evils Venus and the wanton boy produce. It remedies the evils choler can inflict on the body

† This might seem almost ironic, but it is more reasonable than it sounds, as we shall see in Chapter Eleven.

of a man by sympathy. Wormwood, being an herb of Mars, is a present remedy for the biting of rats and mice. Mushrooms are under the dominion of Saturn, if any have poisoned himself by eating them, Wormwood, an herb of Mars, cures him, because Mars is exalted in Capricorn. Suppose a man be bitten or stung by a martial creature, imagine a wasp, a hornet, a scorpion, Wormwood. . . gives you the present cure.

Better yet, Culpeper tells us that it will prevent both drunkenness and syphilis, free virgins from "the scab", and cure melancholy in old men, although it will also make covetous men splenetic.

Wormwood had always been found reliable for getting rid of intestinal worms in humans and animals, and it would also repel moths – like its relative, camphor – and kill insects. The fifteenth century *Saint Albans Book of Hawking* recommends wormwood juice to kill mites on a hawk: "Take the Iuce of wormewode and put to ther thay bei and thei shall dye." Tusser's 1580 *Husbandrie* rises to instructive rhyme:

Where chamber is sweeped, and wormwood is strowne,
No flea for his life dare abide to be knowne.

What is more,

It is a comfort for hart and the braine,
And therefore to have it is not in vaine.

Wormwood is not the only insecticide that has been used for making drinks; in 1950s America, the "Mickey Slim" cocktail was comprised of gin with a minute quantity of DDT. This was thought to give the drink an extra 'kick', and give the drinker a jittery or shaky effect that some people found pleasant. We shall see the logic of this, and its relation to absinthe, in Chapter Six.

On a more pleasantly psychotropic note, wormwood was associated with visionary dreams. It was once believed that on

St.Luke's Day a person could see their "heart's desire" if they drank a concoction of vinegar, honey, wormwood and other herbs. Lady Wilkinson writes in her 1858 *Weeds and Wild Flowers* that:

> An old belief continues to be connected with the circumstance of the dead roots of wormwood being black, and somewhat hard, and remaining for a long period undecayed beneath the living plant. They are then called 'wormwood coal'; and if placed under a lover's pillow they are believed to produce a dream of the person he loves.

———

There is an account that wormwood "grew up in the winding track of the serpent as she departed from Paradise", and the Book of Revelations features the descent of the bitter star from heaven, after the Seventh Seal has been opened. "And the name of the star is called Wormwood: and the third part of the waters became wormwood; and many men died of the waters, because they were made bitter." In Russia, the name for wormwood is "chernobyl", lending a distinctly apocalyptic note to the Chernobyl nuclear disaster, while in the French bible it is simply called "absinthe".

Rue is probably the most bitter plant known, but wormwood comes a close second. This is due to a compound called absinthin ($C_{30}H_{40}O_6$), which has a bitterness detectable at one part in 70,000. Pliny records that after Roman chariot races the victor would be given a wormwood drink, as a reminder that even victory has its bitter side. This bitter quality has given wormwood a long metaphorical career in connection with things "grievous to the soul" as the Oxford English Dictionary has it. "The sight of other people's good fortune is gall and wormwood to a vast number of people", for example, or "It was wormwood to the proud spirit of Agrippa to be treated as a mere astrologer".

There is a hard edge to several of the instances cited in the O.E.D., like Benvenuto's, "Absinth and poyson be my sustenance", from his 1612 *Passenger's Dialogues*. John Webster's Jacobean tragedy *The White Devil* includes an exchange between Vittoria and the Machiavellian Flamineo, who has caused the death of Vittoria's husband, murdered his own brother, and driven his mother mad with grief:

Vittoria: Ha, are you drunke?
Flamineo: Yes, yes, with wormewood water; you shall tast
   Some of it presently.

It is a characteristically Jacobean exchange, of the sort that usually leads to maniacal laughter and a stage covered in corpses. As one of John Ford's characters says in another Jacobean play, "There's wormewood in that laughter."

———

There were a number of wormwood drinks before absinthe proper. "Absynthites" or wormwood wine, made by steeping leaves in wine rather than fermenting them, was drunk in the Renaissance just as it had been in Greek and Roman times; it is described in Morwyng's 1559 *Treasure of Evonymous* and Cooper's *Thesaurus* of 1565. Wormwood water or *eau d'absinthe* was widely recommended for stomach aches, and there was also wormwood beer, known as "purl". Samuel Pepys drinks this in his *Diary*, while visiting a seventeenth-century London brothel, and in the nineteenth century Robert Southey records it as being drunk at All Soul's, Oxford: "Their silver-cups. . . are called ox-eyes, and an ox-eye of wormwood is a favourite draught there. Beer with an infusion of wormwood was to be had nowhere else."

Absinthe as we know it today is thought to have appeared only at end of the eighteenth century. It is sometimes dated to 1792, invented, so the story goes, by a Doctor Pierre Ordinaire. Fleeing the French revolution, the monarchist

Ordinaire settled in a Swiss village called Couvet. Here he supposedly found wormwood growing wild, cooked up his own special recipe, and never looked back. When he died in 1821 his highly alcoholic concoction was already known as La Fée Verte, and it was regarded in the local region as a tonic. It is now known that two sisters, the Henriod sisters, were already making absinthe before Ordinaire arrived, although some versions of this story have Ordinaire giving them the recipe.

When a man named Major Dubied discovered the product he found that it cured indigestion, improved the appetite, and was good for fevers and chills. He was so impressed that he bought the recipe from the Henriod sisters and started manufacturing it himself. In 1797 his daughter married a man named Henri-Louis Pernod, and the Pernod drink dynasty began. Before long Dubied moved his operations from Switzerland to France, to save on import duty. He had an absinthe factory at Pontarlier, in the Jura region bordering Switzerland. As the drink became more popular, daily production increased exponentially from 16 litres to 408 litres to 20,000 litres. Competitors sprang up, and by the time absinthe was banned there were no less than twenty-five distilleries in the small town of Pontarlier.

Absinthes varied in quality. The best were distilled, using grape alcohol, while the inferior ones were simply macerated, or had vegetable essences added to industrial alcohol. Typically, dried wormwood (*artemisia absinthium*, or *grande absinthe*) anise and fennel would be steeped overnight in alcohol. This mixture was then boiled to produce the distillate of alcohol combined with steam distilled terpenoids from the herbs. For further refinement more herbs could then be added, such as '*petite absinthe*' (*artemisia pontica*), hyssop, and lemon balm, and it could then be filtered. It could also be double-distilled, for greater smoothness and integration of contents. Processes and recipes varied, but the salient point is that strong alcohol is not created in the making of absinthe, as it is with whisky or brandy: instead, alcohol, wormwood and other herbs are simply added together, with varying degrees of refinement. The traditional green colour comes – or did come, initially – from chlorophyll, which is faded by light, hence the need for shady green bottles.

The Pernod factory was a model of efficiency, hygiene, and good industrial relations, and by 1896 it was producing a staggering 125,000 litres a day. Things ran smoothly until one Sunday, August 11th 1901, when the factory was blasted by lightning. There was so much alcohol on the premises that it took days to put the fire out, while bottles melted and exploded in the heat. It would have been far worse had one of the workers not opened the giant reservoirs of inflammable absinthe into the adjoining river, the Doubs, flavouring it for miles. Barnaby Conrad relates the unexpected benefits of this for geological research. A Professor Fournier believed that the River Loue, thirteen miles from Pontarlier, was connected to the River Doubs by an underground channel and he had tried to prove this by putting a fluorescent substance into the Doubs and tracing its progress, but without much result. Now, standing by the River Loue three days after the lightning had struck the Pernod factory, he saw the water turn that familiar milky yellow-green colour, and he could smell the alcohol fumes coming from the river, "like a drunkard's breath".

—

Absinthe drinking received a great boost with the French colonial wars in North Africa, which began in 1830 and peaked in 1844–47. French troops were given a ration of absinthe to protect then from malaria and other fevers, and to kill bacteria in their drinking water, fending off dysentery. This was felt to work so well that it became a part of French army life, from Madagascar to Indo-China. At the same time, however, the French army in North Africa became accustomed to cases of delusional insanity, known as *le cafard*. French colonists and expats in Algeria also took to absinthe drinking, and Arabs wanting to get some black-market absinthe could sidle up to a French soldier and hint that their camel had worms.

The colonial association was to be an enduring one: years later, as a publicity stunt, Monsieur Ricard the pastis tycoon rode a camel down the Champs Elyseés. When French soldiers of the *Bataillon d'Afrique* returned to France, they took their taste for absinthe home with them. Covered in glory from a largely successful war, the "Bat d'Af" made absinthe drinking a dignified and even glamorous sight on the café terraces of the Paris boulevards. Soon the habit spread into civilian life, from the military to the bourgeoisie, and the golden age of absinthe began; a shortlived period before it was seen to be a problem. People would later look back to this time nostalgically, after the character of absinthe had changed, and remind each other how it had been.

Absinthe drinking was one of the defining features of Parisian life under the Second Empire, the reign of Napoléon III that lasted from 1852 to his downfall with the Franco-Prussian war of 1870. After the revolutions of 1848 had been suppressed, the bourgeoisie ruled with a vengeance and great fortunes were made and lost on the volatile stock market. It was a gilded era of opera, high class prostitution, and conspicuous consumption.

The respectable bourgeois custom of absinthe drinking became almost universal. It was supposed to sharpen the appetite for dinner. The time between five and seven o'clock was *l'heure verte*, the green hour, when the smell of absinthe would be carried on the early evening air of the Paris boulevards. Given the strength of absinthe – Pernod, probably the most respectable brand, was 60 per cent alcohol or 120 degrees proof, almost twice the strength of whisky – drinking it was also a pleasantly ritual way of shutting down the day and getting into evening mode. The idea, originally, was to have just the one.

To some extent people were protected from absinthe abuse at this period by the strict times laid down for drinking it. To have absinthe before dinner was entirely acceptable, or even to have one before lunch, but to try and drink it all night would be an abject *faux pas*, and waiters would raise their eyebrows. Despite that, alcoholism was clearly a risk right from the start, and one that would increase as people developed a taste for the drink. Novelist and man of letters Alphonse Daudet blamed absinthe drinking for the spread of alcoholism in nineteenth-century France, and he complained to Dowson's friend Robert Sherard that "Before those wars [the Algerian wars] we were a very sober people. " Sherard goes on to observe that because the semi-respectable absinthe drinker was ashamed to be seen drinking too much, he would soon learn to keep moving from one café to another:

> He takes his first drink at one café, his second somewhere else and his tenth or twelfth at a tenth or twelfth other café. I know a very distinguished musician who used to start off at the Café Neapolitain and finish up at the Gare du Nord. . .

Sherard points out that some absinthe contained up to 90 per cent pure alcohol, three times as much as brandy.

> It is, moreover, an insidious drink, and the habit of consuming it grows upon its victim, who sooner or later has to abdicate all willpower in the control of his passion. . . As a matter of fact, one has observed the usual effects of absinthism, the hoarse, guttural absinthe voice, the wandering, glazed absinthe eye, the cold and clammy hand. . . in people who have never drunk a glass of absinthe in their lives. Various *amers*, or bitters, even the supposed harmless vermouth, will, in due course, if taken in excess, conduct their man to epilepsy, paralysis and death. Absinthe gets its work done more speedily.

Alcoholics were always going to find absinthe congenial, but it soon began to attract a wider circle of converts, and its changing image has a particular bearing on three other groups: artists and Bohemians, women, and finally the working classes.

The English writer H.P.Hugh gives a vivid report of the Green Hour in Montmartre. It already two hours long, but when it shades into the world of Bohemia it can last all night.

As the night closes in you watch with fascination the gradual streaks of light that crawl out, as avenue after avenue is lighted up, and the whole city is lined out in fire at your feet. The red sails of the Moulin Rouge swing round, the flash light from the Tour Eiffel touches the Sacre Coeur and whitens the thousand year old church of Saint-Pierre. The other Montmartre awakens while the quiet inhabitants of the hill go to sleep. It is a strange grey study in nature, this midnight Montmartre. It is the doing and the done, and the done and the doing. Artists with hope before them, poets with appreciation of some girl only, and side by side with these the hurried anxious faces of unkempt women and tired-eyed men.

The sickly odour of absinthe lies heavily on the air. The "absinthe hour" of the Boulevards begins vaguely at half-past-five, and ends just as vaguely at half-past-seven; but on the hill it never ends. Not that it is the home of the drunkard in any way; but the deadly opal drink lasts longer than anything else, and it is the aim of Montmartre to stop as long as possible on the *terrasse* of a café and watch the world go by. To spend an hour in a really typical haunt of the Bohemians is a liberal education. There is none of the reckless gaiety of the Latin Quarter, but at the same time there is a grim delight in chaffing at death and bankruptcy.

Almost from the start there was a strong affinity between Bohemia and absinthe, the most powerful and seemingly cerebral of drinks. Bohemia had always had a grim and stressful side; it wasn't so much a place as a career stage; the stage of the less well known or struggling writers and artists who might one day end up in the Académie Française, but might equally end up in the asylum, the charity ward, or the morgue. For many Bohemians this stage could continue almost permanently, or until something broke. After Henri Murger, author of *Scènes de la vie de Bohème*, died in 1861 at the age of 39, one of the Goncourt brothers wrote in their journal:

> It strikes me as the death of Bohemia, this death by decomposition, in which everything in Murger's life and the world which he depicted is combined: the orgies of work at night, the periods of poverty followed by periods of junketing, the neglected cases of pox, the ups and downs of an existence without a home, the suppers instead of dinners, and the glasses of absinthe bringing consolation after a visit to the pawnshop; everything which wears a man out, burns him up, and finally kills him. . .

Absinthe was unquestionably the career drink of intellectuals and artistic wannabes. As Flaubert said of the writing life:

> Being a dramatist isn't an art, it's a knack, and I've got hold of the knack from one of the people who possess it. This is it. First of all you have a few glasses of absinthe at the Café du Cirque. Then you say of whatever play is being discussed: "It's not bad, but it needs cutting", or "Yes, but there's no play there."

Above all, said Flaubert, you must never actually write a work of your own: "Once you've written a play. . . you're done for."

Flaubert also gives a nicely mundane spread of Parisian clichés about absinthe when he writes an entry for it in his *Dictionary of Received Ideas*, which runs simply:

> ABSINTHE: Exceedingly violent poison. One glass and you're dead. Journalists drink it while writing their

articles. Has killed more soldiers than the Bedouins. Will
be the destruction of the French Army.

No doubt some journalists really did drink it while writing
their articles.

Absinthe was, "the Green – or 'Green-Eyed' – Muse". It
was described as being the genius of those who didn't have
any genius of their own, but the death of any real genius for
those who did. Any number of French satirical cartoons from
the period play with this cliché of absinthe and inspiration
(although – in the manner of most nineteenth-century cartoons – few of them are actually funny). "It's astonishing", says
one, "I've drunk four absinthes and I still haven't got the
quatrain for my sonnet. . . Garcon! An absinthe!" Another
depicts the great Montmartre poet 'Vert-de-Gris', who goes
to look for beautiful inspirations in a café, equipped with a
little frame cut from cardboard. He puts this up against his
absinthe glass, and peers through it while he pours the water
in, believing that he is watching the tumults of Niagara Falls.
One satirical drawing tells the sad story of 'The Decadent',
who only goes to the café so that he can make his study of
manners for the book he has been researching for ten years.
Unfortunately he can't take his fifteen absinthes without
becoming completely drunk; the next day, he remembers
nothing, and that is why he has to go back to the café every
night. Saddest of all is the dishevelled looking artist who has
no money left after his seventh absinthe, because he knows it
is only after the eighth that genius arrives.

Chapter Seven
Before the Ban

William Orpen's magnificent pen and ink drawing *The Absinthe Drinker*. The top hat may have seen better times.

In the course of their often grim depiction of Bohemian life, the Goncourt journals include some particularly grisly accounts of absinthe intoxication. Leon Daudet tells Goncourt about his mistress, a woman named Marie Rieu who was nicknamed Chien Vert, or 'Green Dog' (and became the model for Sapho in Daudet's novel of the same name). Daudet, writes Goncourt, was:

> talking about Chien Vert and his affair with that mad, crazy, demented female. . . a mad affair, drenched in absinthe and given a dramatic touch every now and then by a few knife-thrusts, the marks of which he showed us on one of his hands.

Plenty of drinks are routinely mentioned in the journals – wine, beer, champagne – but it is the references to absinthe that have an almost Gothic quality, like this glimpse into The Absinthe Hotel, a once great house named the Chateau Rouge:

> which has become a filthy hotel where the very bed-room of Henri IV's mistress has been turned into the 'Mortuary': the room where several layers of drunkards are piled one on top of another until the time comes for them to be swept out into the gutter. A hotel where the proprietor is a giant in a blood-red jersey with a couple of blackjacks and an armoury of revolvers always within reach. And in this hotel, strange down and outs of both sexes, including an old society woman, an *absintheuse* who 'puts away' twenty-two glasses of absinthe a day – that dreadful absinthe tinted with sulphate of zinc. . .

And this particular story gets even worse: we're told the woman's son, a respectable barrister, was unable to get her away from the absinthe, and killed himself out of disgrace and despair.† No less Gothic is this uncanny, flesh-creeping extract from 1859:

My mistress was lying there beside me, dead drunk with absinthe. I had made her drunk and she was sleeping. Sleeping and talking. Holding my breath, I listened. . . It was a strange voice which aroused a peculiar emotion akin to fear, that involuntary voice bursting forth in uncontrolled speech, that voice of sleep – a slow voice with the tone, the accent, the poignancy of the voices in a boulevard drama. To begin with, little by little, word by word and recollection by recollection, as if with the eyes of memory, she looked back into her youth, seeing things and faces emerge, under her fixed gaze, from the darkness in which the past lay sleeping: "Oh yes, he loved me all right!. . . Yes. . . they used to say that his mother had a look. . . He had fair hair. . . But it wouldn't work. . . We'd be rich now, wouldn't we?. . . If only my father hadn't done that. . . But what's done is done. . . only I don't like to say so. . ."

There was something terrifying about bending over that body, in which everything seemed to be extinct and only an animal life lingered on, and hearing the past come back like a ghost returning to a deserted house. And then, those secrets about to emerge which were suddenly held back, that mystery of unconscious thought, that voice in the darkened bedroom, all that was as frightening as a corpse possessed by a dream. . .

———

† J.-K.Huysmans also describes the Chateau Rouge in his 1898 novel *La Bièvre et Saint-Severin*.

Paris in the later nineteenth century was awash with substance abuse of one kind or another. Strawberries soaked in ether were a smart dessert, and morphine was popular with society women: silver and gold-plated hypodermic syringes could be obtained at upmarket jewellers. Alexandre Dumas complained that morphine was fast becoming "absinthe for women", which is vivid but not quite accurate; the real absinthe for women was absinthe.

Henri Balesta describes women taking to absinthe drinking as early as 1860, catching it like a disease: "Absinthomania is in effect basically contagious; it is from the man that the sickness is transmitted to the woman. Thanks to us, there are absintheuses." And they are brazen about it, too; look on the boulevards, says Balesta, and you will see the absintheuses have as much *hauteur* as the absintheurs.

Changing manners meant that women were now able to drink in cafés, and absinthe was a modern drink; in its way it was as modern for women as cigarette smoking, or riding a bicycle. Doris Lanier cites an advertisement featuring a young *demi-mondaine* holding up a glass of absinthe and announcing that it is one of her minor vices.

An increasing number of adverts from the period show liberated women drinking absinthe and even smoking at the same time, while contemporary paintings tell a different story, with worn-out looking women staring blankly into the middle distance over their glass. Doctor J.A.Laborde wrote in 1903:

> Woman has a particular taste for absinthe and if she intoxicates herself rarely with wine and alcohol, it has to be recognised that in Paris at least, she is frequently attracted by the aperitifs and, without risk of exaggeration, I would say that this intoxication has been for several years as common among women as among men. It is possible to state that clear cases of chronic absinthism occur in women at the end of eight, ten months, or a year in young women and even young girls of eighteen to twenty years old.

A *New York Times* correspondent reported that cirrhosis of the liver was increasing among French women, and explained their drinking as "merely part of the general tendency of the female to imitate the male, other aspects. . . being the boyish bob, the masculine cut in clothing, and the readiness with which they take to cigarettes."

The same correspondent, Sterling Heilig, notes a tendency for women to drink absinthe neat, which he explains as a reluctance to drink too much fluid; these women are wearing corsets, and they want to avoid bloating themselves. It may be true. The immediate 'straight to the brain' hit of absinthe is also comparable to the often noted affinity that many women have for cigarettes, and the clean taste of absinthe – outside the normal spectrum of fermented drinks – may have been part of the appeal for people who were not otherwise great drinkers of beer, wine or spirits. Even a glass of white wine can taste unclean after absinthe, so it fosters its own particular taste in the same way as mentholated cigarettes.

In his memoirs of life in Montmartre, Francis Carco writes that, "Absinthe has always accentuated certain traits of the capricious temperament, of dignity, of obstinacy, of buffoonery, particularly in women." Many people thought there was more at stake than that, as realistic anxieties about alcoholism fed into the prevailing fear of 'degeneration', which can be found in writers as varied as Max Nordau, Marie Corelli, and Zola. Sterling Heilig sums up the problem in sensational terms:

> What the doctors fear the most is from the ladies drinking. . . absinthism, in particular, is said to create a special race, both from the point of view of the intellectual faculties and physical characteristics. This race, the doctors say, may very well continue for a limited time, with all its physical deformities and vicious tendencies, even for several generations, but, exposed in every sort to accident and malady, given over to impotence and sterility, the race soon disappears. The family dies out.

There is a less crazed picture of female absinthe drinking in Zola's 1880 novel *Nana*, which traces the career of a Second Empire *demi-mondaine* on the make. Away from the glittering world that she inhabits professionally, Nana is now indoors with her lesbian friend Satin.

> She would chat away for hours, pouring out endless confidences, while Satin lay on her bed in her chemise, with her feet higher than her head, smoking cigarettes as she listened. Sometimes, on afternoons when they were both in the dumps, they would treat themselves to absinthe, 'to help them forget' as they put it. Satin did not go downstairs or even put on a petticoat, but simply went and leant over the banisters to shout her order to the concierges's little girl, a kid of ten who, when she brought up the absinthe in a glass, would look furtively at the lady's bare legs. Every conversation led up to a single subject: the beastliness of men.

Unglamorous, *déclassé*, frowstily intimate, this private absinthe drinking provides a telling contrast to Nana's more public champagne drinking career with men.

Equivocal but calm – unlike the anti-absinthe hysteria that was to mount by the end of the century – Zola's picture bears comparison with the two most famous representations of absinthe drinking by painters, Manet and Degas. These pictures retain a certain inscrutability, and if they have more than that in common it is a deliberately prosaic and unglamorous quality.

Edouard Manet's famous picture *The Absinthe Drinker* (1859) was his first major painting, starting his career off on an odd foot. His model was an alcoholic rag-picker named Collardet, who frequented the area around the Louvre. Manet thought he had a strange dignity about him, and even a kind of nobility. Manet had already been interested in drunkenness as a subject when he was studying painting under Thomas Couture. He invited his teacher to come and see his painting when he had finished it, but the response can't have been what he was hoping for. "An absinthe drinker!" said Couture, "And they paint abominations like that! My poor friend, you are the absinthe drinker. It is you who have lost your moral faculty."

It is a strange picture, with its top hat and its odd jaunty foot, and it wasn't only Couture who hated it; it went down badly with almost everybody. When Manet submitted it to the Salon in 1859, it was promptly rejected, spearheading a revolution in sensibility that would lead to the establishment of the Salon des Refusés four years later. Its aesthetics owe something to Manet's friend Baudelaire, who believed it was necessary to find new kinds of beauty and heroism in the 'Modern' squalor of the contemporary metropolis, as in his poem 'The Wine of the Ragpickers'. The top hat itself has something Baudelairean about it; Manet had depicted Baudelaire in a similar top hat. The original painting lacked the glass of absinthe, which Manet painted in later to add emphasis. The Absinthe Drinker was one of four related works that Manet referred to as "the philosophers". Manet later put his absinthe drinker into the background of another picture, The Old Musician. As for the real man, Collardet, he was so pleased with being painted that he became a persistent nuisance at Manet's studio.

William Orpen's 1910 picture *The Absinthe Drinker*† is like a junior relative of the Manet, with its top-hat and in particular the odd angle of the foot, which looks like a reference to the earlier work. More Gothic than the Manet, with its cobwebby shading, it still catches an air of decayed contentment. Orpen was a great admirer of Manet, and the year before he had painted a picture entitled *Homage to Manet*.

Orpen's other great absinthe picture, his 1912 *Café Royale*, contains no less than five glasses of absinthe discreetly dotted

† See p. 113.

about. If his *Absinthe Drinker* was a homage to Manet, then the *Café Royale* is his homage to Degas, Orpen's other great influence and enthusiasm: the photographic-style composition, with people coming and going at the edges, has a particularly Degas-like quality. The man sitting at the back is Oliver St.John Gogarty, who appears in James Joyce's *Ulysses*. He is drinking an absinthe with a glum-looking Nina Hamnet, the famous model: she lived on to be a derelict character in 1950s Soho, still telling people, "Modigliani said I had the best tits in Europe". As for the caryatid columns and mirrors, they are just as Enoch Soames might have known them.

Edgar Degas's famous picture *L'Absinthe*, originally entitled *Dans un Café* (1876), with its miserable looking couple, was even more unpopular than the Manet. It has been suggested that the man of the pair is Verlaine. He is not, but there is still a resemblance, which may have influenced the composition of three later photographs of Verlaine by Jules Dornac, sitting behind a white marble table with his back to a mirror. The man in the painting is a friend of Degas called Marcellin Desboutin, who was an artist himself and had studied under Couture. Desboutin is not even drinking absinthe: the brown drink in front of him has been identified as black coffee in a glass tumbler, a so-called 'Mazagran'. The absinthe drinker in this case is the woman, an actress and model named Ellen Andrée, and it is her blank, inscrutably burned-out expression that gives the painting its power. The two figures are dislocated from each other and bleakly isolated in a way that suggests the work of Edward Hopper. The viewer could be forgiven for feeling "if this is Bohemia, you can keep it".

The café they are in is La Nouvelle Athènes, which stood at 9 Place Pigalle. It is vividly remembered by George Moore as the place of his education. "I did not go to either Oxford or Cambridge," he says, "but I went to the Nouvelle Athènes":

> With what strange, almost unnatural clearness do I see and hear – see the white face of that café, the white nose of that block of houses, stretching up to the Place,

between two streets. I can see down the incline of those two streets, and I know what shops are there; I can hear the glass door of the café grate on the sand as I open it. I can recall the smell of every hour. In the morning that of eggs frizzling in butter, the pungent cigarette, coffee and bad cognac; at five o'clock the fragrant odour of absinthe. . .

The usual marble tables are there, and it is there we sat and aestheticized till two o'clock in the morning.

The popularity of La Nouvelle Athènes as a Bohemian venue was due to Desboutin himself, who had led his cronies there from a café called the Café Guerbois. Barnaby Conrad adds that despite his wretched appearance Desboutin – who had at one time been very rich – was an ardent monarchist, with the most courtly manners. Desboutin's biographer Clement-Janin was annoyed at the reputation this painting gave his subject, and he denied that Desboutin was an absinthe drinker: the title should, he said, really have been *La Buveuse d'Absinthe et Marcellin Desboutin*.

Degas's picture caused controversy after it made its way to England, where Ronald Pickvance has traced its career. It was bought by a collector named Henry Hill, who lent it to a Brighton exhibition in 1876. The sober and neutral catalogue entry read only *A Sketch at A French Café* , and the Brighton Gazette critic called it "The perfection of ugliness. . . The colour is as repulsive as the figures; a brutal, sensual-looking French workman and a sickly looking grisette; a most unlovely couple." As Pickvance says, it is the figures which are causing the repulsion "not the absinthe, which hasn't yet been spotted."

It went quietly back into Hill's collection after the exhibition, and didn't cause any disturbance until it was sold at Christies in 1892. It now appeared as Lot 209, *Figures at a Café*, and the public hissed at it as it sat on its easel. Nonetheless it was bought, and in 1893 it was lent to the Grafton Gallery, a new gallery which aimed to rival the Grosvenor (the 'greenery-yallery' gallery). Now the picture was simply entitled *L'Absinthe*, giving the critics their cue. At first they were largely favourable, after a fashion: "The big head of the man", said the *Pall Mall Budget*, "a romantic, easy-going dreamer, is dashed in with a touch of instantaneity worthy of the greatest master." And as for his companion:

> The woman, apathetic, heavy-lidded, and brutish, absolutely indifferent to all things external, nods to the warm languor of the poison. Her flat, shuffling feet tell all the tale. Every tone and touch breathes the sentiment of absinthe.

A major critic of the day, D.S. MacColl, described it as "the inexhaustible picture, the one that draws you back, and back again." It was in response to MacColl that the bricks started to fly. The *Westminster Gazette* critic – "The Philistine", as he signed his pieces – wrote that any one who valued dignity and beauty would never be induced to consider *L'Absinthe* to be a work of art. Sir William Blake Richmond weighed in to attack it as too 'literary': "*L'Absinthe* is a literary performance. It is not a painting at all. It is a novelette – a treatise against drink. Everything valuable about it could have been done, and has been done, by Zola."

Sickert, in contrast, felt that, "much too much has been made of 'drink', and 'lessons', and 'sodden', and 'boozing' in relation to the picture", and that it should simply have been called '*Un homme et une femme assis dans un café*'. The lesson he had in mind was probably that of George Moore, who must have recognised the setting, and could have said something more interesting than, "What a slut! The tale is not a pleasant one, but it is a lesson." As for the lesson, it could be almost anything: in one of the many parodies the picture has attracted, it is, "I'll never use that dating agency again."

MacColl summarized the opposition to the picture as the "French poison" view versus the "temperance tract" view. He later met Degas in Paris and found him stung by the response to the picture, to which he would never have given such a flamboyant title as 'L'Absinthe'. He objected to being attacked by the press and being said to paint, as he put it, "*comme un cochon*" (like a pig).

As for Ellen Andrée, she was far less miserable than she looks in the picture. Barnaby Conrad cites an interview she gave to Felix Feneon, over forty years later:

> My glass was filled with absinthe. Desboutin has some-thing quite innocuous in his. . . and we look like two idiots. I didn't look bad at the time, I can say that today; I had an air about me that your Impressionists thought 'quite modern', I had chic and I could hold the pose as they wanted me to. . . But Degas — didn't he slaughter me!"

———

In France, absinthe began to change its public character, par-ticularly after it became a favourite drink of the working classes. In Zola's 1877 novel *L'Assommoir*, a character named Boche remembers a man he used to know: "a joiner who had stripped himself stark naked in the rue Saint-Martin and died doing the polka — he was an absinthe drinker." Around 1860 absinthe had started to leave Montparnasse and spread from the bourgeoisie and the Bohemians to the workers, and it was from then on that it started to be regarded as a threat to society.

Commenting on the "most grave" problems of "con-tamination" (whereby bourgeois habits spread to workers) a Doctor Legrain wrote in 1903: "I am an old Parisian; I've lived in Paris for 43 years. I've seen very clearly the first invasion of the aperitif with the bourgeoisie, and it is only much later, in the last fifteen or twenty years, that I have seen the workman consume it in his turn." Doctor Ledoux, five years later, has a similar story to tell:

> Our fathers still knew the time when absinthe was an elegant drink: on the café terraces, old Algerian warriors

and bourgeois idlers consumed that louche beverage with the aroma of mouthwash. The bad example was set from on high, and little by little absinthe democratised itself.

A certain Professor Achard knew exactly what was happening: it was all down to the improvements that had been made to the conditions of the working classes, particularly the increase in wages and the reduction of the working day to only eight hours; consequently they had "more time and money to waste on drink".

A far more likely factor was the change in price between absinthe and wine. In its respectable heyday absinthe had been a relatively expensive drink, but the cost dropped over the years, especially with the appearance of cheaper and nastier brands. In particular, the ravaging of the French vineyards by phylloxera in the 1870s and again in the 1880s made wine more expensive. It had a double effect in this respect, because absinthe manufacturers who had previously used grape alcohol now turned to industrial alcohol, making absinthe cheaper still. At 15 centimes, a glass of absinthe was about a third the price of a loaf of bread; a bottle of wine might be a franc (100 centimes). Absinthe was cheapest of all in bars like the ones around Les Halles, for market workers, where you could stand and drink absinthe for only 2 sous (10 centimes). In rock bottom bars like Le Père Lunette there were no tables or chairs: nothing but the zinc counter.

A new object begins to appear in the iconography of absinthe pictures: the workman's toolbag, lying idle by the café table. *La Mère*, an 1899 painting by Jules Adler, shows a miserable looking woman carrying a child in her arms as she hurries past two men drinking at a café. She seems to be averting the child's gaze, as if one of the sottish looking men might be its father. One of them is evidently making a point to the other, raising his hand in laboured emphasis in the manner of a ponderous drunk. The open toolbag sits under the table. On the window of the café is written 'Absinthe 15 centimes a glass'. A slightly later cartoon in *Le Rire* shows a similar bag – somewhere between a cricket bag and a leather satchel, still carried by railway workers – lying idle beside another table. This time the table's dishevelled inhabitant, who is sunk a bit lower in his chair than he should be, is settling down to get his head round one of life's mysteries: "absinthe kills you but it makes you live."

It kills you, but it makes you live. It is the distinctive two-sided rhetoric that develops around addictive drugs, with the idea that they come to supply everything but lead to ruin. Trying to explain the fascination of surgery, a doctor told the Goncourt brothers that, "you get to the point where nothing matters but the operation you are performing, the science you are practising. It's so beautiful. I sometimes think that I should stop living if I couldn't operate. It's my absinthe." And on the other side of the addiction coin, Zola's *Nana* contains a grim warning in the figure of Queen Pomare, the aged ex-courtesan. Satin tells Nana the story:

> Oh, she had been such a splendid girl once, who had fascinated all Paris with her beauty. And such go, and such cheek – leading the men about by their noses, and leaving great notabilities blubbering on her staircase! Now she was always getting drunk, and the women of the district gave her absinthe for the sake of a laugh, after which the street urchins threw stones at her and chased her. Altogether it was a real come-down, a queen falling into the mud! Nana listened, feeling her blood freeze.

———

One of the first people to get on the absinthe case was Henri Balesta, in his 1860 book *Absinthe et Absintheurs*. For the most part Balesta's sensationalistic and cautionary work is taken up with case histories that might have come from nineteenth-century engravings and temperance tracts. A father introduces his little six year old daughter – who is already grieving for the death of her mother – to absinthe in order to comfort her, and inadvertently makes her an addict. After she dies from absinthism, he hangs himself. Another absinthe drinker brings misery on his whole family, and finally encounters a prostitute who turns out to be his daughter.

Balesta observes that "absinthomania" is not "a vice peculiar to the rich and idle" (something which within a few years would need no pointing out); "the man of the people, the workman, has not been spared its ravages." He also made the prescient point that working-class absinthe abuse blighted wives and children and damaged whole families, in a way that middle-class Bohemian self-destruction tended not to.

Was absinthe worse than other types of alcohol? We can look at the pharmacology later – and consider why Van Gogh drank turpentine – but debate continued on this subject. Absinthe was widely perceived as a poison, and it was associated with ruin in general and insanity in particular. The 1865 *Dictionnaire de Médecine*, edited by Littre and Robin, listed absinthism as a variety of alcoholism but emphasised that the results were due to something other than alcohol.

Doctor Auguste Motet had been examining *absinthistes* in a Paris asylum, and in 1859 he published his findings as, *Considérations générales sur l'alcoolisme et plus particulièrement des effets toxiques produits sur l'homme par la liqueur absinthe*. He concluded that absinthe was worse than other drinks, producing hallucination and delirium. Louis Marce of the Bicêtre Hospital gave essence of absinthe to animals, with predictably dire results, and the conclusive breakthroughs in establishing absinthism as a disease distinct from alcoholism came with Marce's former student Valentin Magnan.

Magnan's work was reported, somewhat sceptically at first, in the London *Lancet* of March 6th 1869. Magnan had given essence of wormwood to a guinea pig, a cat and a rabbit, all of which went rapidly from excitement to epileptic-type convulsions. "It is not the first time we have had to notice discussions on this subject", said *The Lancet*, "and to comment upon the inadequacy of the evidence produced in order to prove that absinthism, as met in the Parisian world, is something different from chronic alcoholism." Magnan is reported in *The Lancet* again on Sept 7th 1872, this time with less scepticism. He has now succeeded in isolating an "oxygenated product" from absinthe, which has proved "powerfully toxic": it has caused a large dog to suffer violent epileptic attacks, ending in death, with "an extraordinary rise in temperature from 39 centigrade to 42." In 1903 a Doctor Lalou demonstrated that the substance principally responsible for the toxicity of absinthe's essential oil was thujone.

The slang "Charenton Omnibus" – there was a large lunatic asylum at Charenton – had become current for absinthe from around 1880. It was now firmly associated with madness, and "*Absinthe rend fou*" (absinthe drives you mad) became a well known temperance warning. Statistics were produced to show that a person was no less than 246 more times more likely to become insane from drinking absinthe than other forms of alcohol, and a French temperance leader, Henri Schmidt, described it as "truly 'madness in a bottle'".

By now the writing was on the wall for absinthe, but the drinkers were undeterred. People had been getting quite drunk enough in 1874, when French consumption stood at 700,000 litres a year, but by 1910 it had increased to thirty six million litres a year. Absinthe had become a proletarian vice associated with epilepsy, epileptic offspring, tuberculosis, neglected children, and spending the food money on drink: a popular anti-absinthe song of the period rhymes "misère" with "proletaire", which says it all. This is absinthe at its most powerfully unglamorous, as one of the opiates of the people. A Jacques Brel song, 'Jean Jaures', about the assassinated socialist leader, looks back and asks what our grandparents had to live for, "between absinthe and High Mass". And the spectre of degeneration was never far away from the contemporary discussion, either:

The French medical authorities are overwhelmed by this slow but sure poisoning of the population. The race is degenerating; the stature of men is lessening; in some places soldiers up to standard height are difficult to find;

the minimum height in the army has had to be lowered. Absinthism is much more pernicious than alcoholism; its influence on the brain is particularly bad. In the last thirty years the number of lunatics has increased threefold. In Paris, at the hospital where such cases are especially nursed, statistics show that nine out of ten are due to absinthe poisoning.

—

Absinthe may have "democratised itself", but as the century came to a close Bohemia drank on, undeterred by popular competition. Absinthe has a special place in the mythology of French painting and, as we all know, it was the favourite drink of the creature that Lawrence Alloway has nicely identified as "that late nineteenth century Bohemian monster, the aristocratic dwarf who cut off his ear and lived on a South Sea Island."

Born into an aristocratic family who suffered badly from in-breeding, Henri de Toulouse-Lautrec was not a true dwarf – he was about five feet tall – but his legs were stunted and his head disproportionately large, making him seem shorter than he was. Having started out painting sporting subjects, Lautrec found his real metier in his mid-twenties, when he started to paint and draw the music halls, theatres, cafés, and low-life of Paris, particularly the Montmartre area and the Moulin Rouge. In the course of his work he revolutionized poster design and at the same time immortalized figures such as La Goulue (The Glutton, once known as Louise Weber), who was the Moulin Rouge's star can-can dancer.

Gustave Moreau described Lautrec's pictures as "entirely painted in absinthe", and Julia Frey gives an account of Lautrec's acclimatisation to it:

At the end of the day, Henri would hobble from the atelier down the curved rue Lepic. . . He liked to go in the twilight to *étouffer un perroquet* (literally: choke a parrot – a Montmartre expression meaning to down a glass of green absinthe, commonly known as a *perroquet*). . . It is ironic to see the parrot of Henry's childhood, his infant emblem for evil which had haunted his sketchbooks, reappear in the form of a liqueur – a symbol of his downfall. The image of the diabolical parrot and, by extension, the evil green of absinthe, seemed to have a special importance for him, even in his art. He later said to a friend, 'Do you know what it is like to be haunted by colours? To me, in the colour green, there is something like the temptation of the devil.'

Lautrec became a notoriously heavy drinker, and his preferred mixture was a lethal combination of absinthe and brandy known as an Earthquake (*Tremblement de Terre*). "One should drink little but often" was Lautrec's prescription, and to help him maintain this regime he possessed a hollow walking stick that contained a supply of absinthe; precision made, this alcoholic's *vade mecum* contained half a litre, and even unpacked a little glass. Lautrec also put goldfish in the water jug when he gave dinner parties, Alfred Jarry style.

"No, I assure you, Dear Madame, I can drink safely," he once remarked, "I'm so close to the ground already." But drink and fast living took their toll on Lautrec, who was also suffering from syphilis. He could at times be rude and boorish, his temper was unpredictable, and his tendency to drool on his chin grew worse. He also started to get very drunk on small quantities of alcohol, in the classic manner of terminal alcoholism. Worse than that, paranoia – soon to be the subject of Yves Guyot's monograph, *L'absinthe et le délire persécuteur* – had begun to set in.

Lautrec started to see things such as a beast with no head, and the elephant from the Moulin Rouge began to follow him about. It can't have been as funny as it might sound. He saw dogs everywhere, and he now slept with his absinthe cane to defend himself in case he was attacked by policemen in the night. Ernest Dowson knew Lautrec slightly, and on the 1st March 1899 he ended a letter to Leonard Smithers with some sad news from Paris: "Toulouse-Lautrec you will be sorry to hear was taken to a lunatic asylum yesterday".

Lautrec was confined in a private asylum at Neuilly at the end of February 1899. There are varying accounts of how he got there: he either collapsed in the street with delirium tremens, or he was kidnapped by two asylum staff on the orders of his mother. Once in the asylum – an expensive private clinic in an eighteenth century mansion – he was not free to leave, and the rights and wrongs of his imprisonment were debated in the newspapers. Lautrec was unlucky enough to have an early version of electro-shock treatment, but despite that his mental health improved in the asylum, largely because he was prevented from drinking. On his release he started drinking again; at first more discreetly, with the help of his absinthe cane. He finally died peacefully from drink and syphilis at his family home in 1901, aged 36, with his father in attendance. Ever the sporting aristocrat, the old Count had started hunting flies round the room by flicking his elastic laces at them. "Old fool", said Lautrec – and they were his last words.

———

If people like Toulouse-Lautrec needed to be protected from themselves, it was even more true of the lower orders. It is perhaps surprising that absinthe lasted as long as it did, given the extraordinary publicity that was now ranged against it. The final impetus for the ban came with the First World War, and the fear that beer-drinking Teutons would annihilate the decadent, absinthe-drinking French. The distinction between their drinking habits had already been widely noted in connection with France's catastrophic defeat in the Franco-Prussian War. A 1914 French propaganda postcard in Marie-Claude Delahaye's collection shows an attractive woman sitting at a café table, holding up her absinthe to admire it and wearing a Prussian helmet, the classic *pickelhaube* with the ornamental spike on top the Ruritanian eagle crest on the front. The clear message is that absinthe and the Boches on the same side. The banning of absinthe would mark the end of an era, and all the more so because it coincided with the war: just as the 1960s are often reckoned to have lasted until around 1974, so the nineteenth century really lasted until the First World War.

Absinthe makes its last great appearance in art, just before the ban, in Pablo Picasso's 1914 cubist sculpture *Absinthe Glass*. It had already figured in Picasso's work during his 'Blue Period' of 1901–1903. Picasso had gone to Paris in 1900 with his friend Carlos Casagemas, but in February 1901 Casagemas committed suicide. For the next couple of years Picasso's pictures were predominantly melancholy studies of poverty and depression-ridden subjects, painted in tones of blue and green. Absinthe-drinking seems to figure in these pictures as an instance of addiction, angst and psychic extremity. It is the 'hope of the hopeless', and an emblem of terminal Bohemianism, although it also has more positive connotations in Picasso's work. Absinthe fitted in with a generally Baudelairean tradition of low-life urban and café subjects and, in particular, Picasso associated it with Alfred Jarry. He was fascinated by Jarry and tried to emulate him in several respects, which included drinking absinthe and carrying a revolver.

Woman Drinking Absinthe of 1901 features a woman dressed in blue sitting at a table in the corner of a red café, with a glass of absinthe before her. She is clasping herself with her abnormally long, expressively distorted arms and unusually large hands, one hand supporting her chin and the other snaking up her arm towards her shoulder. She looks at once rapt and troubled. *Woman Drinking Absinthe* has a somewhat post-impressionist quality, like the work of Gauguin. In *The Absinthe Drinker* of the same year, the painting has become rougher and more blurred with bolder, thicker brushstrokes on the table top and a distinctive speckling on the woman's clothing. The picture as a whole is darker, with a small warm light in a distant window, while the composition is intensely concentrated down a line that runs from the woman's peaky, crimson-lipped face through the hand and spoon to the glass of absinthe.

Two Women Seated in a Bar of 1902 features the two women sitting on bar stools with their bare backs to the viewer. On the surface just beyond them, the viewer can see a glass of absinthe. The two figures have a heavy sculptural plasticity, and their dresses and the wall are absinthe coloured. It is a relatively calm composition, but feelings of angst come to the fore again with *The Poet Cornutti (Absinthe)* of 1902–3. The haggard and sparsely bearded Cornutti is sitting beside a woman at a café table, like the two figures in the Degas picture. Cornutti's hands are expressively long and thin, and there is a touch of controlled craziness in his feline face, which has a slightly Chinese quality. On the table are the spoon, carafe and glass of absinthe. A note added to the back of the picture by Picasso's friend Max Jacob explains that Cornutti was an ether addict who died in obscurity.

Picasso's Blue Period came to an end in 1903, and absinthe doesn't significantly figure in the happier period which succeeded it, the so-called Rose Period. But with Picasso's Cubist works, absinthe is back again. Now, in these far more intellectual, less emotional works, the objects are fragmented into facets as if seen from several directions at once, and absinthe bottles are now used, without any melodrama or angst, as basic props for structural dissection, along with guitars, tables and chairs. *The Glass of Absinthe* (1911) is a classic work of analytical cubism, although the viewer would be hard pressed to say where the glass of absinthe actually is. It is presumably all over the picture, along with what might be a spoon and a book. *Bottle of Pernod and Glass* (1912) is easier to read, with bottle, glass and table all clearly visible, and other works include bottles of 'Ojen' anisette and 'Anis del Mono'.

This attention to brand names has an almost proto-Pop quality, although nobody can agree what it means. Things are clearer when Picasso paints the soup and stock brand, Bouillon Kub, which is probably a pun on Kubism. It may be significant that Picasso's absinthe is part of a more urban and synthetic 'Modern' world, as opposed to the apples and wine bottles in the work of painters such as Matisse and Cezanne. Like many artists, Picasso was caught up in art wars, and his hated rival around 1907 was Matisse, who he said was worse than absinthe: Picasso encouraged his friends to go around writing "*La peinture de Matisse rend fou!*" (Matisse's painting drives you mad) on walls, twisting what was by then the old cliché "*Absinthe rend fou!*"

Picasso's absinthe masterpiece is his '*Absinthe Glass*' sculpture of 1914, a painted bronze in an edition of six, all of which were painted differently. Brooks Adams has discussed this glass in a virtuoso piece of interpretation. By way of a doomy opening comparison, Adams quotes Gertrude Stein's *The Autobiography of Alice B. Toklas* on the feel of Paris light just after the First World War had begun, when the Battle of the Marne was under way and things looked bad for France. Stein's friend Alfred Maurer remembers being in a cafe:

> I was sitting said Alfie at a café and Paris was pale, if you know what I mean said Alfie, it was like a pale absinthe.

Adams comments: "That absinthe conveys the vacuum, peculiar light, weather, and vibrations of Paris in a state of imminent siege and reflects its hallucinatory power as symbol for the end of an era."

Picasso had just published some pictures of a cubistically deconstructed guitar and violin in a little magazine edited by Guillaume Apollinaire, *Les Soirées de Paris*. The magazine only had fourteen subscribers, and after Picasso's instruments appeared, thirteen of them wrote in and cancelled their subscriptions. Undeterred, Picasso embarked on the absinthe glass, which has a stable, glass–like base but an opened out, sliced up body. On top rests a real absinthe spoon and a painted bronze sugar cube: "insouciant, crowning touches", says Adams, "like a Wallenda high wire routine, they're brilliant but dumb." As for the subject, Adams sees it as a bomb thrown at high seriousness, an emblem of Picasso's youth and a passing era's excess, and a defiant celebration of the now clearly endangered drink. More sombrely, "Since absinthe is ultimately fatal, all of Picasso's *Glasses* qualify as sculptural *memento mori*". The speckling on several of them recalls the speckled painting on Picasso's *Absinthe Drinker* picture, but one glass in the series is largely black, apart from some stippling on the edges and the inside. This one, for Adams:

> recalls the Satanic lull of absinthe taking effect, beginning to light up the body. Black conveys the vacuum produced by absinthe, and stippled colours conjure up its magic, tranquilizing effect. The verbal equivalent for Picasso's twinkling colour is *la fée verte*, green fairy – a common French phrase for absinthe.

Adams goes on to suggest that by painting each glass differently, Picasso is celebrating the individual's freedom of choice in alcoholic consumption, and moreover that the open form of the sculptures suggests Picasso's open attitude to drug control.

The glasses have also been seen to contain references to, among other things, a face, a woman with a hat, and the crucifixion. Symbolism aside, anybody who has ever toyed with an absinthe glass and spoon, resting the spoon on the glass, will feel the sheer sculptural fascination that the subject must have held for Picasso, with its different materials assembled in different planes. The sculptures also play with three orders of representation: the spoon is actually real, the sugar cube is a realistic counterfeit, and the glass is diagrammatic. Whatever their complexities and ramifications, the six glasses certainly represented an endangered object, as Picasso knew. Germany declared war on 13th August 1914, and on 16th August the Minister of the Interior took emergency measures to prohibit the sale of absinthe. In March 1915 the Chamber of Deputies at last voted to prohibit absinthe not just from sale, but from manufacture. Absinthe was finally banned.

Chapter Eight
After the Ban

Victor Berlemont preparing an absinthe in Soho's French Pub,
London, 1939. Photo copyright Hulton–Getty

Nostalgia being what it is, absinthe was no sooner gone than at least some people started to remember it with affection. Having allegedly brought Parisians to the brink of terminal degeneracy and racial extermination before the ban, after the ban it could be remembered as the recipe for good conversation. Barnaby Conrad cites Robert Burnand on the disappearance of absinthe as a symptom of cultural decline:

> The spirit of the boulevard is dead. . . Where will one find again the time to stroll, to daydream, to chisel a thought, to launch an arrow?. . . Absinthe, the magical absinthe of the green hour, whose jade flower blossomed on every terrace – absinthe poisoned the Parisian in a delicious way, at least giving him fertile imagination, whereas the other cocktails sickened one without exaltation.

But absinthe was gone for good, or at least for the twentieth century; even pastis was banned by the Vichy government in 1940, and not allowed back until 1949. In place of absinthe came a newer, jazz-age, American-style cocktail culture, an early step in the Americanisation and globalisation of Paris. Gradually the French forgot absinthe.

James Joyce remembers it in his 1922 *Ulysses* (retrospectively set one day in 1904) where absinthe drinking figures as part of the young Stephen Dedalus's aesthetic character and Continental aspirations, like his "Latin Quarter hat". His Parisian memories include the "green fairy's fang" and "froggreen wormwood", and a bout of absinthe drinking with his student cronies throws up the Latin toast:

Nos omnes biberimus viridum toxicum diabolus capiat posteriora nostra

(We will all drink the green poison and the devil take the hindmost). Later Leopold Bloom has to apologise for Stephen, because he's been drinking the "greeneyed monster". Absinthe is remembered again in the great swirling dream of *Finnegans Wake*, with Paris once more a major association, when "Brother Intelligentius" is "absintheminded, with his Paris addresse" [sic].

———

In America, meanwhile, absinthe had developed very specific cultural meanings: absinthe is more Gothic, doomy and wicked in America than anywhere else. It is possible that the American sense of absinthe was influenced by the fact that absinthe has a more than passing similarity to paregoric, a bygone opiate panacea that consisted of a 90% alcohol base, anise oil, camphor, and tincture of opium; like absinthe, paregoric was mixed with water and turned cloudy.

A short story published in 1930, Coulson Kernahan's 'Two Absinthe-Minded Beggars', presents two young men who have read about Parisian life and feel they need to research further into absinthe. After all, they are, "literary men, or hope to be, and one day we may give the world a work of art in which we shall have to picture an absinthe-addict, or the effect of absinthe upon the taker, and our knowledge ought to be first-hand." They want to learn the secret of Verlaine's inspiration, and they want to experience the "magical" effect of absinthe in lifting the mood. They order their absinthe:

> The waiter. . . set before each of us a tumbler half-filled with a thinnish liquid of some sort. Within the tumbler, as within a receptacle – we wondered whether he was about to show us a conjuring trick – stood a wine glass,

also filled, but to the brim, with a liquid of some sort, which was viscous. . . and which, by the look of it, might have been gum. Then bowing, the waiter withdrew, and we two children, who fancied ourselves men of the world, were left wondering what in the same world we were next supposed to do.

They have to ask the waiter, who makes no reply but proceeds silently with the business:

[he] said nothing, but, lifting the wine-glass, first tilted and finally inverted it over the tumbler until the gum-like liquid had oozed heavily and stickily – to writhe, snake-like, and smoke-like, in nacreous curls, coils, and spirals, until the two liquids within the tumbler, in combining, assumed the colouring and the cloudiness of an opal. I did not like the look of the stuff, and by the heavy and drugged smell, felt sure I should dislike the taste. "It is an unholy looking dope," I said. The stealthiness with which the thicker liquid curled, coiled, and spiralled itself around the thinner liquid made me think of a python enfolding and crushing its victim.

They order repeatedly, hoping to feel the exhilaration that they have been promised, but all they experience is despondency. Aside from whatever literary merit it might or might not have, Kernahan's story offers a 1920s picture of the 'two glasses' method described by George Saintsbury, and a fanciful picture of absinthe as liquid evil. This is not how absinthe clouds; Kernahan's description is more like watching milk in tea. Absinthe is not thicker than water but thinner and lighter, being mostly alcohol, so that by adding water slowly it is possible to have the lower half of the liquid opaque and the upper half translucent.

Kernahan's fantastically Expressionist description of absinthe is half Chinatown and half Dracula's Castle: the bowing of the silent waiter; the unholy-looking "dope";

the predatory behaviour of the python liquid as it ravishes the innocent water in the glass; the evil attributes of viscosity and ooze; and above all the uncannily familiar visual imagery of curling, coiling and spiralling in tendrils. It is like the movie poster for Roman Polanski's *Chinatown*, with its wickedly sinuous smoke. Kernahan gives us absinthe as Sax Rohmer might have described it in one of his Doctor Fu Manchu books.

An earlier story, 'Over an Absinthe Bottle' by William Chambers Morrow, is no less lacking in literary merit but considerably more morbid. A mysterious stranger invites a starving young man to have some absinthe with him, and play dice in a restaurant's private booth. The stranger is flush with money and keen not to draw attention to himself, and it transpires that he is a bank robber on the run. He sends the young man to the bar for their drink, and they continue to play dice. When the police open the door of the booth, they find both men sitting there, dead.

Edgar Allen Poe had been an absinthe drinker, as part of his more general alcoholism, and he would drink a mixture of absinthe and brandy with his publisher John Sartain, who was himself a heavy absinthe drinker. Poe managed to give up alcohol altogether for a short spell towards what was to be the end of his life, but he was encouraged to relapse by some friends and died shortly afterwards in Washington College Hospital suffering from hallucinations and delirium tremens.

Aside from morbidity, the signification of absinthe in America was also very much associated with the image of New Orleans. It was a place where the somewhat decayed elegance of French-American culture, with its peeling stucco and sinuous wrought-iron balconies, met the swampland wickedness of Louisiana. Doris Lanier discusses the culture of New Orleans at length in her book, *Absinthe: Cocaine of the Nineteenth Century*. Absinthe was not a particularly widespread drink in America outside of New Orleans, but it was made better known by a popular song, 'Absinthe Frappé', with lyrics by Glenn McDonough:

At the first cool sip on your fevered lip
You determine to live through the day,
Life's again worth while as with a dawning smile
You imbibe your absinthe frappé.

This is understood to be happening first thing in the morning. Absinthe Frappé, absinthe with crushed ice, was a speciality of the Old Absinthe House. A 1907 article in *Harper's Weekly*, 'The 'Green Curse' in the United States', blamed McDonough's lyric (sung to Victor Herbert's "catchy air") for making absinthe more popular, and claimed that it was known to be "almost as fatal as cocaine in its blasting effects upon mind and body."

Writing in his superb study of American literary alcoholism, *The Thirsty Muse*, Tom Dardis notes during his discussion of Eugene O'Neill that absinthe was regarded as the most extreme terminal point in intoxicating drinks. O'Neill, writer of *The Iceman Cometh*, attended Princeton for a single inglorious academic year in 1906–7, where he liked to shock his fellow students with his drinking. "Social drinking", says Dardis, "was largely confined to beer and wine, while the harder stuff was regarded as the proper comfort for people these students thought of as bums. When the shock of his whisky drinking had worn off, O'Neill determined to show his friends the effects of absinthe, widely regarded in those days as the ultimate in its power to intoxicate":

After persuading Louis Holladay, a Greenwich Village friend, to bring a bottle of the infamous fluid to the Princeton campus, O'Neill consumed enough of it to throw him into a frenzy of violence in which he destroyed virtually all the furniture in his room. He had been searching for his revolver; when he found it he "pointed it [at Holladay] and pulled the trigger. By good fortune it was not loaded." Two of his classmates recalled that "O'Neill had gone berserk. . . It took three to pin him to the floor where he shortly collapsed and was put to bed."

What may have begun as a pose became a serious problem later, but O'Neill confronted his alcoholism and substantially gave up drinking, although he was still far from happy with life and relied instead on quantities of chloral hydrate and Nembutal. He composed his own epitaph for his tombstone, to be chiselled below his name:

THERE IS SOMETHING
TO BE SAID
FOR BEING DEAD

———

Before America's ill-advised general Prohibition in 1919, concerns about absinthe in particular had already led a Senate committee to conclude it was "indeed a poison" and the Senate voted in 1912 to prohibit "all drinks containing thujone", ahead of the French ban. Americans famously continued to drink, and for a while at least absinthe and pastis must have been a healthier alternative to bathtub gin, with an added Southern elegance and a renegade quality in defiance of a Washington directive. Dardis cites a friend of William Faulkner on the party scene in the 1920s, remembering life in the Vieux Carré quarter of New Orleans: "The favourite drink at that time was Pernod, made right there in New Orleans and it cost six dollars a bottle. We made it up in great pitchers for all our parties."

Elizabeth Anderson, wife of the short story writer Sherwood Anderson, wrote "There was a great deal of drinking among us, but little drunkenness. We all seemed to feel that Prohibition was a personal affront, and that we had a moral duty to undermine it. . . . The great drink of the day was absinthe, which was even more illegal than whisky because of the wormwood in it. . . It was served over crushed ice, and since it did not have much taste of alcohol that way, it was consumed in quantities."

The American writer who has written most persuasively and evocatively about absinthe's real merits as a drink is undoubtedly Ernest Hemingway. Hemingway's enduring contact with absinthe, long after the French ban, came from his experience of Hispanic culture in Spain and Cuba. Absinthe was never outlawed in Spain, and Pernod shifted operations to Tarragona when the French ban descended. Some of the best absinthes currently available are Spanish, and English writer Robert Elms has written atmospherically about his encounter with absinthe in the early 1990s in Barcelona's notorious Barrio Chino†.

Hemingway was always a heavy drinker, and Dardis notes that for a long while Hemingway seemed to have a special talent for drinking, "despite occasional signs that all was not as benign as it might appear". In 1928 he suffered the first of a long series of self-inflicted accidents when he pulled the chain in his apartment's hallway lavatory; at least, he pulled *a* chain, and brought the glass skylight down on top of himself. It left a lifelong scar on his forehead. It is not clear what part alcohol played in this and various other accidents, says Dardis, but Hemingway "seems to have been drinking before virtually all of them".

When Hemingway lived in Florida he was able to obtain his absinthe from Cuba, where he owned a house and fished. Barnaby Conrad quotes a 1931 letter in which Hemingway writes "Got tight last night on absinthe and did knife tricks. Great success shooting the knife underhand into the piano." As for the damage, he liked to claim "the woodworms did it", and Conrad nicely notes the comic transposition of "wormwood", which may be unconscious on Hemingway's part.

Hemingway spent a lot of time in Spain, where he was a great devotee of bullfighting. In his bullfighting book, *Death*

† See end of book.

in the Afternoon, he explains why he gave up bullfighting himself: "it became increasingly harder as I grew older to enter the ring happily except after drinking three or four absinthes which, while they inflamed my courage, slightly distorted my reflexes."

Hemingway's great paean to absinthe comes in his Spanish Civil War novel, *For Whom The Bell Tolls*. Robert Jordan is an American guerrilla leader on a mission to blow up a bridge, and one of his few comforts is absinthe, the "liquid alchemy" which can replace everything else, and which can even stand as a part-for-the-whole drop of the better life he has known in Paris:

> . . . one cup of it took the place of the evening papers, of all the old evenings in cafés, of all chestnut trees that would be in bloom now in this month, of the great slow horses of the outer boulevards, of book shops, of kiosks, and of galleries, of the Parc Montsouris, of the Stade Buffalo, and of the Butte Chaumont, of the Guaranty Trust Company and the Ile de la Cité, of Foyot's old hotel, and of being able to read and relax in the evening; of all the things he had enjoyed and forgotten and that came back to him when he tasted that opaque, bitter, tongue-numbing, brain-warming, stomach-warming, idea-changing liquid alchemy.

Jordan is drinking with Pablo, an untrustworthy member of his partisan band who finds absinthe too bitter. "That's the wormwood," Jordan explains "In this, the real absinthe, there is wormwood. It's supposed to rot your brain out but I don't believe it. It only changes the ideas. You should pour water into it very slowly, a few drops at a time." Later comes Hemingway's definitive judgement: whisky with water is "clean and thinly warming":

> But it does not curl around inside of you the way the absinthe does, he thought. There is nothing like absinthe.

Hemingway's writing about absinthe is notable for its absolute authenticity, right down to the way that Robert Jordan feels a "delicate anaesthesia" on his tongue. The other notable American absintheur, Harry Crosby, was as much in love with the idea of absinthe as with the reality, just as he was taken with the idea of Baudelaire.

Crosby was a young millionaire American who travelled around 1920s Europe with his wife Caresse (formerly the first ever Girl Scout in America) and their dogs Narcisse Noir and Clytoris. They made their base in Paris, with a flat on the Ile St.Louis, and set up the renowned Black Sun Press at 2 rue Cardinale. Crosby was an extraordinary mix of vitality, naivety and extremity, and he has been mythologised as part of Twenties American Paris by Malcolm Cowley in *Exiles Return*. Together, Harry and Caresse – who had been called Polly Peabody when she met him – embarked on an extraordinary and ultimately disastrous work of self-creation together: "We can", Harry told her, "become very cultured and improve ourselves."

In theory Crosby was blessed with almost everything – looks, money, intelligence, a beautiful wife – but he was a deeply disturbed young man, obsessed with decadence and death, who wore a black flower in his lapel and tried to live his life according to Oscar Wilde's *Picture of Dorian Gray*. Clearly unbalanced to begin with, he had been made worse by a traumatic experience in World War One (during which he won the Croix de Guerre) when an ambulance that he was driving took a direct hit from a cannon shell, leaving Crosby miraculously unscathed beside his dying co-driver.

In his marvellous biography of this tragic but more than faintly absurd character, *Black Sun*, Geoffrey Wolff quotes from Crosby's list of words that he pre-assembled for future use in his poems, demonstrating the influence, as Wolff says, of Baudelaire, Huysmans, Poe and Wilde:

absurd, bleak. . . chaos. . . desolate. . . disconsolate, disil-
lusion, envenomed. . . entangled. . . fragrant, feudal,
fragment, gnarled. . . grandeur, heraldic. . . illusion. . .
idolatry. . . labyrinth. . . legend, lurid. . . mediaeval, mysterious, macabre, merciless, massacre, nostalgia. . . obso-
lete, orchid. . . primeval. . . perfume, pagan, phantom. . .

And so they went on. Much of Crosby's trouble came from an
over-indulgence in Baudelaire, particularly Baudelaire's desperately miserable poem 'Spleen IV'. It is not hard, says Wolff,
to see how this must have affected Crosby: "He recognized its
beauty, shining like a black pearl in a cup of dead-green
absinthe."

Crosby bought black irises for Baudelaire on the anni-
versary of his birth, and in 1925 he wrote a sonnet, the
work of a latterday Enoch Soames, notable (says Wolff) for its
"preposterous, *outré*, unmotivated gloom"

> I think I understand you Baudelaire
> With all your strangeness and perverted ways
> You whose fierce hatred of dull working days
> Led you to seek your macabre vision there
> Where shrouded night came creeping to ensnare
> Your phantom-fevered brain, with subtle maze
> Of decomposed loves, remorse, dismays
> And all the gnawing of a world's despair.
>
> Within my soul you've set your blackest flag
> And made my disillusioned heart your tomb,
> My mind which once was young and virginal
> Is now a swamp, a spleen filled pregnant womb
> Of things abominable; things androgynal
> Flowers of Dissolution, Fleurs du Mal.

Crosby published it in his book *Red Skeletons*, illustrated by
the belatedly decadent artist Alastair (Hans Henning Voigt,
who had already been working with John Lane at the Bodley
Head). This featured poems such as 'Black Sarcophagus',

'Futility', 'Desespoir', 'Orchidaceous', 'Dance in a Madhouse' and 'Necrophile', and it attracted the praise of a now ageing Arthur Symons ("a strange originality, something macabre, violent, abnormal, sinister, and also – 'shadows hot from hell' "). But Crosby came to feel that the whole book – with its epigraphs from Wilde and Baudelaire, and Alastair's Beardsleyesque illustrations – was too derivative, and he blasted his remaining copies to pieces with a shotgun.

Conrad comments astutely that for Crosby, the drink of Baudelaire, Wilde, Lautrec, Rimbaud and others "was worth *an ocean of associations*, a morbid green paradise" [my emphasis]. Crosby's diaries contain some atmospheric references to absinthe. One day in 1927 he met Caresse at the Gare du Nord, and he records her "running down the platform carrying two ponderous volumes of Aubrey Beardsley and two bottles of absinthe." Always a great bibliophile, Crosby found some rare and curious things in bookshops: in 1928,

I went and procured in a bookshop a bottle of very old absinthe (it was a choice between this or an erotic book with pictures of girls making love) and the man in the bookshop recommended Ramuz *Le Guérison de Maladies* [The Cure of Ills] but as I already had the Guérison to all maladies i.e. the absinthe I did not buy the book but went instead to an apothecary's where I bought two empty bottles marked hair tonic into which I decanted the absinthe. . .

Harry graduated from absinthe to opium, which was finally his drug of choice. A friend remembers that Harry and Caresse kept their opium, which looked like a pot of blackberry jam, in her toy chest, and that shortly before the opium appeared "there was a Verlaine jag with absinthe, so we had a great deal of absinthe around the flat."

The Crosbys knew Hemingway, who introduced Crosby to James Joyce, and Harry seemed to be progressing beyond decadence. He joined the board of the avant-garde periodical *transition* and his press – having published books by Poe and

Wilde – became more Modernist, publishing work by Joyce, Hemingway, Hart Crane and D.H.Lawrence. But Crosby was still obsessed by death, and his last diary entry includes the credo "one is not in love unless one desires to die with one's beloved."

One evening in December 1929, Crosby was due to meet Caresse and his mother, and then go on to dinner and the theatre with the poet Hart Crane, whom Harry had earlier introduced to absinthe. Instead he met his current mistress, Josephine Bigelow – who, interestingly enough, looked remarkably like him – at the Hotel des Artistes in New York. They took their shoes off and lay on the bed fully clothed for a while, then Crosby shot her through the temple and lay there for a couple of hours as the sun went down, before shooting himself between the eyes. Ezra Pound wrote that Crosby had died from "excess vitality", and that his death was "a vote of confidence in the Cosmos." Perhaps it was, but it is hard not to feel that the Curse of Literature helped to do him in as well.

———

Remaining illegal in America after the war, absinthe was largely a memory of old New Orleans until it gained a new identity through the Gothic subculture: one of the best recent absinthe pages on the Internet is run by a woman named Mordantia Bat. Absinthe figures in Anne Rice's 1976 vampire novel *Interview with the Vampire*, but not in quite the way one might expect. It is not, in this case, good for vampires. Claudia, who has plans of her own, has found and drugged two angelic orphans to provide Lestat with blood, but he is stricken after drinking it:

> " 'Something's wrong with it,' he gasped, and his eyes widened as if the mere speaking were a colossal effort. He could not move [. . .] He could not move at all. 'Claudia!' He gasped again, and his eyes rolled towards her.

" 'Don't you like the taste of children's blood. . .?' she asked softly.

" 'Louis. . .' he whispered, finally lifting his head just for an instant. It fell back on the couch. " 'Louis, it's. . . absinthe! Too much absinthe!' he gasped. 'She's poisoned them with it. She's poisoned me. Louis. . .' He tried to raise his hand. I drew nearer, the table between us.

" 'Stay back!' she said again. And now she slid off the couch and approached him, peering down into his face as he had peered at the child. 'Absinthe, Father,' she said, 'and laudanum!'

" 'Demon!' he said to her. 'Louis. . . put me in my coffin.' He struggled to rise. 'Put me in my coffin!' His voice was hoarse, barely audible. The hand fluttered, lifted, and fell back.

Bad stuff.

In Francis Ford Coppola's 1992 *Dracula*, Gary Oldman's Count falls in love with Jonathan Harker's fiancée Mina, who reminds him of his long dead love. Wearing a distinctly West Coast pair of shades, he follows her to an MTV version of Victorian London. After talking to her in the street, they go to a drinking parlour with a table for two and a bottle of absinthe, with which the Count performs the spoon and sugar ritual. "Absinthe is the aphrodisiac of the soul", he tells Mina: "The Green Fairy who lives in the absinthe wants your soul – but you are safe with me." Coppola's prop department had surpassed themselves to borrow a particularly fine absinthe spoon for its blink-and-you-miss-it appearance on the screen. The spoon, with a sinuous plant motif, belongs to Marie-Claude Delahaye, a key figure in the French revival of interest in absinthe†.

---

† It is now in Madame Delahaye's absinthe museum at Auvers-sur-Oise, along with the props department letter. The spoon can be seen on p.232 of her book *L'Absinthe: Histoire de la Fée Verte*.

By now the idea of absinthe was finding its place within a San Francisco and West Coast tendency towards a kind of kinky Victorianism, with substances to match. In 1994 *Newsweek* magazine reported that "in the lofts and garrets of the Pacific Northwest, artistic types looking for inspiration in a glass are beginning to dust off the drugs their forefathers made famous." Opium, opium tea, and laudanum were all reportedly making a comeback alongside absinthe, accompanied by clothing that the London *Times* called "Victo-grunge". And in the same year, young New Orleans based Goth writer Poppy Z. Brite published her story, 'His Mouth Will Taste of Wormwood' in the collection *Swamp Foetus*:

> "To the treasures and pleasures of the grave," said my friend Louis, and raised his goblet of absinthe to me in drunken benediction.
>
> "To the funeral lilies," I replied, "and to the calm pale bones." I drank deeply from my own glass. The absinthe cauterised my throat with its flavour, part pepper, part licorice, part rot. It had been one of our greatest finds: more than fifty bottles of the now-outlawed liqueur, sealed up in a New Orleans family tomb. Transporting them was a nuisance, but once we had learned to enjoy the taste of wormwood, our continued drunkenness was ensured for a long, long time. We had taken the skull of the crypt's patriarch, too, and now it resided in a velvet-lined enclave in our museum.
>
> Louis and I, you see, were dreamers of a dark and restless sort. We met in our second year of college and quickly found that we shared one vital trait: both of us were dissatisfied with everything.

Not everyone has been impressed with Brite's writing (although you could forgive her a lot for the title 'Are You Loathsome Tonight?') but I did once see a girl on the London Underground, possibly a tourist, dressed in a black lace dress and combat boots and reading *Swamp Foetus* with every appearance of rapt satisfaction.

Absinthe moved further into mainstream counter-culture with the 1997 video for the track 'The Perfect Drug' (available in a 'Domination Mix' and an 'Absinthe Mix') by dark and doomy S/M oriented U.S. band Nine Inch Nails, in which Trent Reznor is seen preparing absinthe amid Edward Gorey-style landscapes, and perhaps regretting having murdered a girl. Along with Nine Inch Nails, Gothic rocker Marilyn Manson is also said to buy crates of absinthe from the United Kingdom. Underground 'absinthe clubs' were alleged to be springing up in D.J.Levien's absinthe pulp fiction *Wormwood*, a fictional state of affairs only possible because absinthe remains illegal in America. Its legal status caused speculation when Presidential wife Hillary Clinton was photographed in Prague with a glass of absinthe in front of her. Did she actually drink any, people wondered, or was it a neat counterpart to her husband's trick of 'not inhaling?'

———

In Britain, meanwhile, absinthe meant something very different. Absinthe was never banned in Britain, largely because, as we have seen, it remained a drink for intellectuals, and never showed signs of becoming popular with the masses as it had in France; it never became a '*problem*'. Instead it continued quietly within the cocktail drinking culture of the 1920s, much to the disapproval of a 1930 writer in the medical journal *The Lancet*. In his article 'Absinthe and Absinthe Drinking in England', C.W.J.Brasher opens by noting that his readers may be unaware that absinthe – banned in France, Belgium, Switzerland, Italy, Germany and Bulgaria – is still imported into England.

Dr.Brasher cites three well-heeled gents who, reading slightly between the lines, are evidently being treated for dipsomania:

I have been informed by a member of an exclusive London club that when a cocktail is ordered it is customary to inquire whether a "spot" shall be added – that "spot" being absinthe. Another London clubman states that "the cocktail 'with a kick in it' is often ordered by the more hardened cocktail drinker" and that "kick" is obtained by the addition of an extra quantity of the basic spirit. . . of the cocktail or of a variable amount of absinthe. A third patient states that "when in my club a cocktail is ordered, the waiter inquires 'with or without?' – i.e. with or without absinthe."

Brasher proceeds to review the case against absinthe in some detail, largely from French sources, adding a few scary flourishes of his own.

Brasher's views on absinthe are close to those of the French, but there is a more moderate English view when Evelyn Waugh's brother Alec gives a glimpse of cocktail-era drinking in his book *In Praise of Wine*. He recalls drinking absinthe in the Café Royal's Domino Room:

> I took it with appropriate reverence in memory of Dowson and Arthur Symons, Verlaine, Toulouse-Lautrec, and the Nouvelle Athènes. I only drank it once for I loathed the taste of it. In those days you ordered a dry martini 'with a dash', a dry martini was half gin and half vermouth and a dash was not Angostura bitters but absinthe. Even thus diluted I thought it ruined the cocktail. But I daresay I should like it now.†

In Evelyn Waugh's 1928 novel *Decline and Fall*, absinthe figures as a comic symbol of a life that is both 'fast' and more

† Waugh also raises the interesting empirical point that absinthe seems to double the power of drinks taken after it. This is a widely noticed phenomenon, and it used to be said that "absinthe is the spark which explodes the gunpowder of wine". Drink writer H. Warner Allen warned of this so-called "potentiating" effect, "Those who experiment with absinthe will do well to remember that it has the curious property of doubling the effect of every drink that is taken after it, so that half a bottle of wine at the meal which follows it will be equivalent to a whole bottle."

than a little rotten. Expelled from Oxford for indecent behaviour (of which he is entirely innocent), the earnest young Paul Pennyfeather slides into a chain of bizarre misadventures which begin with a horrible school-teaching job and end with a prison sentence. He is sent to prison after becoming involved with Margot Beste-Chetwynde, whose seemingly gracious lifestyle turns out to be funded by an Argentine prostitution business, The Latin-American Entertainment Co Ltd. Perhaps the reader should have seen a sleazy end on the cards after Margot is described as "gazing into the opalescent depths of her *absinthe frappé*", especially as it seems to have been mixed by her worldly ten year old son.

Absinthe plays a grimly comic role in another Waugh novel, *Scoop*, this time by virtue of its extremity. William Boot, journalist for the Fleet Street paper *The Beast*, is drinking some "genuine sixty per cent absinthe" with a gloomy Dane named Olafsen:

> ". . .What are you drinking, Eriksen?"
> "Olafsen. Thank you, some grenadine. That absinthe is very dangerous. It was so I killed my grandfather."
> "You killed your grandfather, Erik?"
> "Yes, did you not know? I thought it was well known. I was very young at the time and had taken a lot of sixty per cent. It was with a chopper."
> "May we know, sir," asked Sir Jocelyn sceptically, "how old you were when this thing happened?"
> "Just seventeen. It was my birthday; that is why I had so much drunk. So I came to live in Jacksonburg, and now I drink this." He raised, without relish, his glass of crimson syrup.

Olafsen is bad news when he is drunk.

> "When I was very young I used often to be drunk. Now it is very seldom. Once or two time in the year. But always I do something I am very sorry for. I think,

perhaps, I shall get drunk tonight," he suggested, brightening.

"No, Erik, not tonight."

"No? Very well, not tonight. But it will be soon. It is very long since I was drunk."

The confession shed a momentary gloom. All four sat in silence. Sir Jocelyn stirred himself and ordered some more absinthe.

There is less of this drily comic British reasonableness in the authentic and evocative accounts of expat drinking given by Malcolm Lowry, an Englishman in Mexico, and Samuel Beckett, an Irishman on the continent. Lowry was an alcoholic for all of his adult life, suffering, as he once put it, from "delowryum tremens" during the "Tooloose Lowrytrek" of his existence. Asking a friend, "Do you mind if I have a swig of your cooking sherry?" and finishing the bottle was relatively normal behaviour for Lowry: he also drank aftershave, and he once drank a whole bottle of olive oil in the sad hope that it was hair tonic. He saw elephants in Soho and vultures on his washbasin, and he shook so badly that he had to improvise a pulley system to get a drink to his mouth.

In Lowry's 1947 Mexican novel, *Under The Volcano*, a minor character named Monsieur Laruelle drinks anis because it reminds him of absinthe: "his hand trembled slightly over the bottle, from whose label a florid demon brandished a pitchfork at him." The main mention of absinthe comes during an evocative strew of details, suggesting the drinking life as a phantasmagoric whirl of ill-spent time:

The Consul dropped his eyes at last. How many bottles since then? In how many glasses, how many bottles had he hidden himself, since then alone? Suddenly he saw them, the bottles of aguardiente, of anis, of jerez, of Highland Queen, the glasses, a babel of glasses – towering, like the smoke from the train that day – built to the sky, then falling, the glasses toppling and crashing, falling

downhill from the Generalife Gardens, the bottles breaking, bottles of Oporto, tinto, blanco, bottles of Pernod,
Oxygénée, absinthe, bottles smashing, bottles cast aside,
falling with a thud on the ground in parks, under
benches, beds, cinema seats, hidden in drawers at
Consulates . . .

'Oxygénée' was a famous brand of absinthe, advertised by a
picture of a florid-looking man in a state of robustly chubby
well-being, with the improbable slogan "*C'est ma santé*" ("It's
my health").

The whirling effect of Lowry's list is comparable to the
young Samuel Beckett's evocation of drinking on the Continent in his early novel, *A Dream of Fair to Middling Women*,
where the same brand rates an incidental mention: "Money
came from the blue eyes of home, and he spent it on concerts,
cinemas, cocktails, theatres, aperitifs, notably these, the potent
unpleasant Mandarin-Curaçao, the ubiquitous Fernet-Branca
that went to your head and settled your stomach and was like
a short story by Mauriac to look at, Oxygénée. . ." It is very
different from his equally evocative account of another quality
of drunkenness back home, drinking "all the stout that helped
to bloat the sadness of sad evenings."

After the Second World War, with the jazz-age cocktail era
long gone, absinthe had an even lower profile in Britain, sur-
viving as little more than a faint cliché about the Nineties or
Paris. In some childish cartoons about "the art look" that
Swinging Sixties art dealer Robert "Groovy Bob" Fraser did
when he was at his prep school, one of them is captioned "the
old Bohemian hardened by many years of drinking absinthe,
and cafés of Montmartre." Given that Fraser (already noted as
"lacking in team spirit") was aged about ten at the time,
he was even then showing the promise of a not altogether
wholesome career†.

---

† Smooth and charismatic, Fraser was once London's grooviest art dealer.
He hung out with the Rolling Stones, and it is Fraser who appears
handcuffed to Mick Jagger in Richard Hamilton's print *Swingeing London*

Absinthe (Albanian absinthe, no less) is also mentioned as a humorously horrible beverage in Kingley Amis's novel *The Biographer's Moustache*. It is clear that if absinthe has been earnestly Gothic and doomy in the USA, it has had a persistently comic aspect in England, where extremity and excess are seen differently, and wickedness is to some extent funny, as are foreigners, artiness, and exaggerated sophistication. From Enoch Soames to Robert Fraser there has been something funny about absinthe in Britain for much of the twentieth century: despite its real merits as a drink, you can't help feeling that Tony Hancock might have liked a glass.

[sic] after they were busted for drugs together in 1967. His curriculum vitae also included a one night stand with Idi Amin. Fraser was known for his taste in modern art, and for the trail of unpaid bills his gallery left behind it. He became a heroin addict, and by the time of his death from AIDS in 1986 he was largely forgotten.

Chapter Nine
The Absinthe Revival

Night of the demon: *The Absinthe Demon* by Jacques Sourian, 1910.
Copyright ANPA, Paris.

The recent absinthe revival has its origins in the collapse of the Iron Curtain, and Czechoslovakia's 1987 'Velvet Revolution', which led to the opening up of Prague to young Westerners. London-based musician John Moore, one time guitarist with the Jesus and Mary Chain and latterly a member of Black Box Recorder, first encountered absinthe in Prague in 1993:

> One winter, as I stood in a Prague bar, studying the bottles, I noticed one that looked particularly inviting. Filled with emerald green liquid, it looked like it could inflict damage. It was absinthe. I knew a little about absinthe but had never expected to try it. Like most people, I thought it had been banned and gone forever. [. . .]
> The first effects were almost immediate. It felt like it had been injected rather than swallowed. There was no slow build up, no gradual seeping into the bloodstream. Armed with a glass of water, I finished the rest and then ordered another glass. A friendship had begun.

The "absinth" Moore had discovered, spelt without the final 'e', was a Czech Bohemian brand called Hill's. Compared to the old French absinthe, Bohemian absinthe is a different animal altogether: it is much less aniseedy, it doesn't go cloudy with water, and it has its own novelty ritual preparation with flame, which was never done in France. In this instance Bohemia is a place rather than a state of mind, although any confusion between the two can have done the product's image no harm.

The Hill's distillery business, Hill's Liquere, was set up by Albin Hill in 1920, producing a range of spirits. Business boomed and in the 1940s the company opened a second factory: wartime Czech drink rationing was based on the volume of liquid rather than the strength of alcohol, so it made sense for drinkers to buy absinth and dilute it. But with the onset of post-war communism, Hill's prosperity came to an end. The distillery was confiscated, and by 1948 official production of absinth had ceased. In 1990, however, with the return of a free market economy, Albin Hill's son Radomil began producing absinth once again.

John Moore wrote an engaging piece on absinthe for the groovy London slacker mag *The Idler*, which appeared in the Winter 1997 issue. In addition to a brief history and a sound overview, the piece contains a couple of points likely to pique readers' interest: first, says Moore,

> The addition of sugar gives the drinking of absinthe a ritualistic feel, similar to using intravenous drugs. Both involve spoons, fire and a little patience: similar means to a not completely dissimilar end.

And secondly, "as far as I can remember, I have never had hallucinations while drinking it, but it does produce incredibly vivid dreams. They are invariably surreal and obscene."

The most significant part of the piece, however, may have been the little box at the end:

> Since coming across it by accident in 1993, I have had a steady supply, thanks to friends and Mr Hill himself. Call the Idler if you are interested in importing it.

It was *The Idler*'s own founders, as it turned out – editor Tom Hodgkinson and art director Gavin Pretor-Pinney – who would share Moore's interest in importing it. In late summer 1998 the three of them met businessman George Rowley, who had experience in importing Czech beers and spirits and had been thinking of importing Hill's, with whom he had already made separate contact. Radomil Hill urged them to form a single company before he would deal with them commercially, and so 'Green Bohemia' was founded. In time their absinthe importing would become so successful that *The Idler* men would have little time for producing the very excellent *The Idler*, letting it dwindle from a regular magazine to an occasional annual that finally reappeared after a longish break. Long known to be dangerous, absinthe had nearly killed *The Idler*.

Absinthe was re-launched in Britain in December 1998, attracting widespread and excitable Press coverage. "Now", wrote the broadsheet *The Guardian*, "to the horror of alcohol awareness campaigners, a British company has secured an importation contract with a tiny Czech distillery after discovering that the drink was never formally prohibited in this country." The *Daily Mail*, the most respectable of the tabloids, ran a shock-horror story which compared absinthe to using vodka, cannabis and LSD all at the same time, much to the gratification of Green Bohemia. "You can't buy that kind of publicity", said a happy Mr Hodgkinson.

Green Bohemia's formidably hip publicity machine was able to run pieces on its 'Hall of Fame' celebrity customers, including their first ever customer, American actor Johnny Depp. In Britain to shoot the movie *Sleepy Hollow*, Depp wanted to get some absinthe to drink with Hunter S. Thompson, whom he had played in the film of *Fear and Loathing in Las Vegas*. Suede launched their 1999 album Head Music with absinthe at London club China White, and other music industry customers ran the gamut from rapper Eminem to Goth Marilyn Manson. *Select* magazine ran a regular feature called 'Our Absinthe Friends' which invited bands to get drunk on absinthe – supplied by Moore – and then recorded their ramblings as they fell to pieces.

———

Suddenly people were thirsty for the word absinthe, with a distant cultural memory of it as "mysterious, tantalising, the quintessential decadent *fin-de-siècle* drink". But in other respects Hill's success was surprising, since it was an open secret that it was not particularly pleasant. "Horrible" said one attempted drinker: "a powerfully cloying smell and taste of marshmallows, combined with flavours of cough mixture, herbs and vanilla essence, and fierce alcohol." *The Times* described it tasting of "aquavit on steroids with a hint of singed hair, leaving a strong anaesthetic aftertaste like eating a million of those round pink Liquorice Allsorts everyone avoids." "I have never drunk Vosene shampoo before," said a *Daily Telegraph* journalist in Prague, "but it must be pretty close to this."

A drinker in Prague hit the spot with a revealing comment about Bohemian-style absinthes "You drink absinthe to get drunk quickly – only a masochist would add water and make it a long lasting drink" (good French-style absinthe, in contrast, makes an excellent long drink). Faced with the facts that Hill's is both intensely intoxicating and intensely unpalatable to most people, the logical answer was to drink it mixed and masked. Green Bohemia embarked on a groovy promotion of cocktail culture, publishing recipes for newly invented cocktails containing Hill's, such as the 'Psycho Surfer', the 'Green Rose', the 'Flaming Absinthe Passion', the 'Six Pack', the 'Vincent Van G', the 'China Blue', 'The Bohemian' and various other luxury horrors, several of which were particularly popular in the North of England.

Intoxication was the key, leaving Green Bohemia to strike a careful balance. On the one hand they were genuinely responsible, and issued a guideline that no drinker should be served with more than two absinthes in one night (a directive without precedent in the drinks industry). And on the other hand, everyone knew what the point was. Who drinks to stay sober? Actor Keith Allen, asked for his opinion of Hill's at Green Bohemia's Groucho Club launch, reportedly laughed like a maniac and announced, "It works!"

The French and Swiss were not so amused by the so-called absinthe revival in Britain. "This English [i.e. Czech] stuff isn't absinthe", said French absinthe expert Francois Guy. His family had started making absinthe at Pontarlier in 1870, and he now runs a distillery – of other drinks, absinthe still being illegal in France – and an absinthe museum there. "It's disgusting, alien rubbish. How dare they steal our name?" "It is worse than lamentable", said Jocelyn Parisot, a manager at the Guy factory: "If Baudelaire and Rimbaud had to drink that Czech stuff, they would be turning in their graves."

One of the most formidable French critics was Marie-Claude Delahaye, France's foremost authority on absinthe, who in 1994 opened The Absinthe Museum at Auvers–sur–Oise, where Van Gogh is buried. Delahaye's interest in the subject began when she found a strange pierced and plant-shaped spoon in a Paris flea market in 1981 – an absinthe spoon – and she began collecting absinthe related items, leading to several books on the subject. These have been oriented towards collectable artefacts and paraphernalia (she was already the author of a book on babies' milk bottles) as well as to poets and artists. Something of the appeal of absinthe bric à brac for her, as she explains in her book *Histoire de la Fée verte*, is to recapture the unhurried and leisurely quality of bygone absinthe drinking, whether in a café or under shady trees in the Midi within, "*un climat de farniente, de douceur de vivre.*"

Delahaye objected strenuously that Czech 'absinth' was not the real thing, leading Green Bohemia to launch a French-style absinthe with her co-operation in July 2000. Unlike Hill's, this brand – La Fée, with the distinctive eye on the bottle – is more than pleasant enough to make a long drink just with water. ("Cloudy, green, full of the flavour of anise and really quite delicious if you like that sort of thing. . . It is very, very like Pernod except it is stronger and not yellow.") Nothing if not a purist, Delahaye has strong reservations about mixing it with anything else.

The launch of La Fée – again at the Groucho Club, like the launch of Hill's – was accompanied by lavish publicity. The masterstroke of marketing was The Absinthe Bus, a classic London double-decker (a circa 1960 'Routemaster', with the open platform and stairway at the back) painted green. This new incarnation of the Charenton Omnibus toured as far afield as the North of England and the major cities of Scotland, where the harder and more Russian-style drinking culture had already made Hill's popular, introducing punters to the smoother style of La Fée. Fitted with a well-appointed lounge-style cocktail bar upstairs, the absinthe bus announced various destinations at the front including 'Oblivion' and the more optimistic 'Utopia'.

Green Bohemia sponsored the drinks bash after the 2000 Turner Prize – the year that Wolfgang Tillmans won – taking the winner and runners up to a party at Shoreditch Town Hall and plying them with La Fée. Damien Hirst had already been reported as an absinthe enthusiast, and was said to be considering a series of absinthe-inspired works.

Absinthe was now at the cutting edge of millennial party culture, and it had come to mean becoming intoxicated as easily and quickly as possible. It was a development that would have seemed strange to the drug culture of the late Sixties and early Seventies, when the enjoyment of alcohol, especially by the young, was regarded as rather squalid. But now absinthe's allegedly drug-like properties gave the E-generation an alibi to enjoy getting drunk.

Green Bohemia's upbeat and witty public image strategies promoted absinthe as the spirit of "freedom." This neatly combined the new freedom of post-Iron Curtain Prague, and laissez-faire economics, with the disinhibiting effects of getting totally inebriated (a kindred spirit drink, Pernod, had already been advertised with the equally neat slogan of "Free the spirit"). Absinthe continues to go from strength to strength in the UK, where the absinthe scene has spanned a similar social mix to 'Brit Art', i.e. proletarians larging it and public school wide boys moving and shaking the whole business. Unlike the more Gothic significations that cling to absinthe in America, the British absinthe revival is by far the most positive image that absinthe has ever had.

———

There were only a few dissenting voices from all this jollity, one of them being Nicholas Monson, forty-three year old heir to the 11th Baron Monson. Old Etonian Monson became embroiled in a drink-driving case in 1999 after drinking two glasses of absinthe in a Chelsea bar, and duly lost his licence. But he was prepared to fight against the verdict and appeal, "on the grounds that bars shouldn't be serving poison without a warning." "The Government should make absinthe illegal", said Monson, whose father is President of the Society for Individual Freedom. "This drink has been proven to send people absolutely doolally." Monson admitted drinking two but said he couldn't remember if he might have had three, and compared absinthe's impact to mixing double strength vodka with cannabis. His barrister claimed Monson had a legitimate case, "because he is entitled to expect when he goes on to a licensed premises and is served a drink that he is not going to be 'poisoned'. This drink clearly has mind altering properties."

The Home Office had already tested absinthe to determine whether its allegedly hallucinogenic properties made it illegal under the 1971 Misuse of Drugs Act, and found that they did not. "It is no more dangerous than any other substance that can be misused", said a spokesman. From one angle, the Government had reason to be grateful to the absinthe importers. Since taxation is not only a way of raising money but also a means of discreet social control, the exceptional alcoholic strength of absinthe has merited a discouraging and punitive tax rating, with around sixteen pounds out of a forty pound purchase price going to the State.

Despite the revenue involved, Home Office Minister George Howarth told journalists that the reappearance of absinthe was a "cause for deep concern" and that "We shall be keeping a very close eye on this to see if sales take off." The crucial issue – the one which had already led to its banning in France and its non-banning in Britain – was whether it would spread to the working classes, the 'lager louts' of the popular press, or even to the 'glue sniffers' and solvent abusers. Meanwhile, underlining Green Bohemia's laissez-faire principles, importer Tom Hodgkinson went as far as to say that part of the "fascination" of absinthe, and indeed one of its "principal attractions", was that in drinking it "one is cocking a snook at New Labour's nanny culture." Tony Blair, the British Prime Minister, was reported in the *Daily Telegraph* to have let it be known that "he is keeping a close eye on the matter and if it becomes popular, he will ban it."

Chapter Ten
The Rituals of Absinthe

The safest way to prepare an absinthe: a sonnet by 'Valentin'.
Copyright Marie-Claude Delahaye.

Like opium smoking, Holy Communion, and the Japanese tea ceremony, the word "ritual" often recurs when people talk about absinthe: "the ritual sets it apart"; "the beauty of the ritual"; "There is a certain romance in the ritual. The ritual always draws people back to it." As we have seen, John Moore noted "a ritualistic feel, similar to using intravenous drugs" when he encountered absinthe in Prague, while George Saintsbury relished "the ceremonial and etiquette which make the proper fashion of drinking it delightful to a man of taste."

Absinthe rituals have involved both fire and water. The recent revival was accompanied by a fire ritual from Prague, for drinking East European absinthe. A shot of absinthe is poured into a glass, and a teaspoonful of sugar is dipped into it. The alcohol-soaked sugar is lit with a match, and allowed to burn until it bubbles and caramelises. The spoon of melted sugar is then plunged into the absinthe and stirred in, which often has the incidental effect of setting the absinthe alight. An equal measure, or more, of water is then poured in from a jug or a second glass, dousing any flame. Setting the absinthe alight in the glass has the effect of slightly toning down its excessive alcoholic strength, which can only be a good thing for the premises serving it, but the main feature of the whole affair is simply its novelty. It also recalls American fraternity drinking customs with flaming Southern Comforts and the like. There is altogether little to be said for this performance, and it would have been regarded as an abomination in nineteenth-century France.

The classic method involves absinthe and water. When water is added to a good absinthe it can be seen to go cloudy, or to "louche" as the French has it (literally to become unclear, with connotations of suspicion and ambiguity). The absinthe whitens and becomes opaque when the water upsets the balance of alcohol and herbal matter, making the essential oils precipitate out of the alcoholic solution into a colloidal suspension. This "louche" was highly valued by absinthe drinkers, and to meet the demand for it makers of bad absinthe would add poisonous additives such as antimony to enhance the effect.

Broadly, a measure of absinthe was poured into an absinthe glass, which – in its most standard form – flares upwards from a round foot, like an ice cream sundae glass, and typically has a fat bead instead of a wine-glass style stem. A special pierced spoon was then balanced across the glass, with a lump of sugar on it; and cool water was poured over the sugar and into the glass. As an old Pernod advert instructed drinkers, "Pernod Fils' absinthe can be taken with or without sugar; pour it into a large glass, add iced water very slowly; to sugar it, use the spoon as shown in the picture." It is straightforward enough, but this simple act was capable of an extraordinary degree of minor refinement and savoir faire.

First of all comes the correct paraphernalia. The pierced spoon came in enough elegant varieties to fill whole books for collectors, and more obscure devices were also available to hold the sugar, such as little towers or funnels that sat on top of the glass. The glasses also varied, some of them having the pleasing refinement of an egg-like cavity at the base to measure the correct dose of absinthe ('dose' being another word that recurs when people talk of absinthe: a drug-like word that nobody would use for whisky). Glasses could also be acid etched to the dose level, or marked in some other way.

A jug of water would be to hand, sometimes brand-named, and in some establishments a tap 'fountain' would be on the bar. The jug would have a thin spout, to permit a fine enough trickle. And it is from now on that the narcissism of minor differences really comes into play, although the essence of the whole business – to cut a long story short – is really just about not sploshing the water in all at once.

It would have been an insult for the waiter to prepare a keen absintheur's absinthe. The judicious preparation was half the pleasure, as the drinker reached and approved the exact degree of opalescence in the glass. Careful dripping would allow the drinker to watch individual drops make smoky trails in the drink, with the same concentration that some people put into blowing smoke rings. The drinker could, in the language of the day, *frapper* or *étonner* the absinthe (knock on it or even surprise it, like a living thing), or indeed *battre* it (beat it) by letting the drops one by one fall from on high, all having the effect, eventually, of diluting it.

Dripping water on it from on high was something of an affectation. A contemporary cartoon shows an old French colonial, wearing only his trunks, his medal and his pith helmet with a little flag on top, sitting before a table with his absinthe on it. Up in the tree above him is a little African boy, wearing a fez, who drips water from a bottle drop by drop into the absinthe. By contrast Charles Cros, in 'La Famille Dubois', has a character – after anouncing that it's half past four and time to talk – put an absinthe before his friend and pour a thin stream of water into his glass while explaining how to prepare a good absinthe: "There is no need to pour it from on high (that's just a preconception). It must go gently, gently, and then all at once *flouf!* One has a *purée parfaite.*"

Height may have been optional, but slowness was the essence of the performance. Raymond Queneau's *The Flight of Icarus* drags the instructive pouring of absinthe out to several pages, as the beginner learns not to just drown it†. There is another atmospheric account in Marcel Pagnol's *The Time of Secrets*, where, unusually, it is something of a family affair:

The poet's eye suddenly gleamed.

Then, in deep silence, began a kind of ceremony.

He set the glass – a very big one – before him after inspecting its cleanliness. Then he took the bottle, uncorked it, sniffed it, and poured out an amber-coloured liquid with green glints to it. He seemed to measure the dose with suspicious attention for, after a

† Included in Appendix One.

careful check and some reflection, he added a few drops.

He next took up from the tray a kind of small silver shovel, long and narrow, in which patterned perforations had been cut.

He placed this contrivance on the rim of the glass like a bridge, and loaded it with two lumps of sugar.

Then he turned towards his wife: she was already holding the handle of a 'guggler', that is to say a porous earthenware pitcher in the shape of a cock, and he said:

'Your turn, my Infanta!'

Placing one hand on her hip with a graceful curve of her arm, the Infanta lifted the pitcher rather high, then, with infallible skill, she let a very thin jet of cool water – that came out of the fowl's beak – fall on to the lumps of sugar which slowly began to disintegrate.

The poet, his chin almost touching the table between his two hands placed flat on it, was watching this operation very closely. The pouring Infanta was as motionless as a fountain, and Isabelle did not breathe.

In the liquid, whose level was slowly rising, I could see a milky mist forming in swirls which eventually joined up, while a pungent smell of aniseed deliciously refreshed my nostrils.

Twice over, by raising his hand, the master of ceremonies interrupted the fall of the liquid, which he doubtless considered too brutal or too abundant: after examining the beverage with an uneasy manner that gave way to reassurance he signalled, by a mere look, for the operation to be resumed.

Suddenly he quivered and, with an imperative gesture, definitely stopped the flow of water, as if a single drop more might have instantly degraded the sacred potion.

The dose of spirit is often said to be around 30 ml (according to the *British Medical Journal*) or one fluid ounce, according to most American authorities (an ounce being fractionally less, at 27.5 ml; the British measure 1/5 of a gill comes just between the two at 28.5 ml). If anything, this seems to err on the side of caution and to be based on the modern single spirit measure. I own an absinthe glass, of standard size and form, which is marked to take around 75ml, or a generous double, and this seems a more natural measure, given the eventual volume of diluted fluid shown in contemporary pictures of absinthe glasses in use.

The traditional proportion of water was somewhere around five or six to one, but it varied to taste. Pernod 51 is brand named for the 5:1 ration, but 4:1 has been recommended, and La Fée recently advised between six and eight to one. One of the highest proportions has been prescribed by Barnaby Conrad, talking to an American newspaper in 1997: "one to two inches of absinthe. . . the proportion of absinthe to water should be about 1:2 . . . it should be drunk slowly. And put on period music, like Satie or Ravel, to get in the mood." A ritual indeed, complete with a full psychic setting.

—

All this fetishistic fuss about the dripping of water meant that the preparation of absinthe was not only a pleasure in itself but a decorous affair involving something like skill, in which it was possible to make mistakes. Semi-professional advice was fortunately at hand in the form of "absinthe professors", particularly in little seedy dives, who hoped to be treated to a drink in return for their judicious advice and assistance.

There is an odd sidelight thrown on this social aspect of the absinthe ritual by Henri Balesta, in *Absinthe et Absintheurs*, with its Zolaesque case histories. Amid all the horrors of his book – exaggerated, but perhaps not unfounded – there is an interesting picture of the "professors". By late morning,

> the professors of absinthe were already at their station, yes, the teachers of absinthe, for it is a science, or rather an art to drink absinthe properly, and certainly to drink it in quantity. They put themselves on the trail of the

novice drinkers, teaching them to raise their elbow high and frequently, *to water their absinthe artistically*, and then, after the tenth little glass, with the pupil rolled under the table, the master went on to another, always drinking, always holding forth, always steady and unshakeable at his post." [my emphasis]

Peer-group pressure makes the novice drink, so it is important to do it properly:

It is a solemn trial for the amateur. This is the moment to show himself, to take his place in the esteem of others, to gain the good opinion and respect of his contemporaries. Waiter, an absinthe "panachée". Good!!!.

What a moment for the beginner! He is going to realize the dream of two years. He raises his glass slowly, looking for the last time at the contents, then raises it to his lips. He is going to drink. He drinks. The desire is satisfied, the dream realised. Absinthe is no longer a myth to his palate. Ugh! How awful it is, says the poor devil to himself, making a face, and yet everyone drinks it. But he is being watched. Delicious, this absinthe, very novel, I have never drunk anything like it, he exclaims with a delighted expression, which is indeed against his heart and against his stomach. The second swallow goes better. The third is better yet.

In every circle of young men one finds a veteran whose speciality is "making the absinthe". As soon as he picks up the carafe, the conversations are suspended, the pipes go out, all eyes are on the absinthe-maker, following all the details of the operation to which he devotes himself without missing a single one. The waiter himself, hands behind his back, a four-sous-tip smile on his lips, puts on a good show and nods approvingly. The absinthe-maker, feeling himself the point of cynosure of all eyes, secretly enjoys the admiration that he inspires and strives to be worthy of it. He holds the carafe in a free and easy manner, raising it up to eye level with an elegant sweep of the arm, then he lets fall the water drop by drop into the glasses with a judicious slowness, in such a way as to gradually effect the combination of the two liquids.

There it is, the shibboleth of the absinthe drinker: it is by the greater or lesser degree of chic with which he carries off this delicate operation that the connoisseurs can distinguish the real absinthe professional. . . unfortunately for the inexperienced novice. The waiter himself assists in the task of forming an opinion on the customer; he shrugs his shoulders with an air of pity and takes on the most scornful tone he can manage to murmur, "What a joker! He doesn't even know how to make an absinthe."

———

The language of absinthe drinking opens up the modus operandi of absinthe further, and reveals more ways of preparing it. Not only did you strangle a parrot, and take a one way trip on the Charenton omnibus, and not only did you *frapper* and *étonner* and *battre* the absinthe. More than that, you could have a *pure*, an absinthe without sugar (or much less commonly without water; 'neat'), which is not to be confused with a *purée*, or an absinthe with only a little water and so strong it was like soup, and particularly like *purée des pois*, pea soup, which was low and military slang for a thick absinthe.

The standard or definitive absinthe was the *absinthe au sucre*, but there were minor variations. Une *absinthe anisée* was an absinthe with extra anis, while *une bourgeoise* or *une panachée* was an absinthe with extra anisette cordial. An *absinthe gommée* was sweetened with the addition of gomme syrup, and both the gomme and anisette additions were reckoned to make *une suissesse,* 'feminising' the absinthe (a Swiss woman being sweeter than a *suisse*, or Swiss man). Absinthe could be sweetened with orgeat, at roughly a teaspoon of orgeat per shot of absinthe, and a *Vichy* was absinthe and orgeat in equal quantities, plus the usual amount of water. Absinthe plus orgeat was known in military slang as a "Bureau Arabe" (the "Arab Department", responsible for colonial affairs) the idea being the sweet and the hard, like the iron fist in the velvet glove, or perhaps even the "nice cop/nasty cop".

The name of the *tomate* was less sinister, since it was simply a red drink made with absinthe and a few drops of grenadine, plus the usual water. An *absinthe minuit*, or midnight absinthe, is absinthe with white wine, while the *absinthe vidangeur*, or scavenger's absinthe, is absinthe with red wine. The *minuit* is quite a drinkable combination, but the *vidangeur* is more the stuff of desperation. Toulouse-Lautrec was tragically fond of the *tremblement de terre*, or 'earthquake', which is absinthe and brandy, and another combination which could be safely given a wide berth is the Crocodile. This was one third rum, one third absinthe, and one third *trois-six*†, the recipe coming from a Polish anarchist in the ill-fated Paris Commune.

Nineteenth-century French absinthe culture was not a cocktail culture, and real absinthe is not widely suitable as a cocktail drink, due to the strength of the aniseed flavour. Nonetheless absinthe cocktails were popular in 1920s England. The absinthe martini, as prepared by Anthony Patch in F. Scott Fitzgerald's *The Beautiful and the Damned*, was half gin and half vermouth with a 'dash' or 'spot' of absinthe ("for a proper stimulant"), and W. J. Tarling's *Café Royal Cocktail Book* of 1937 contains numerous cocktails with a dash of absinthe. Those in which it figures more substantially include the Creole (one third absinthe, two thirds sweet vermouth), the Duchess (one third Martini dry vermouth, one third martini sweet vermouth, one third absinthe), the Glad Eye (one third peppermint, two thirds absinthe), the Macaroni (one third martini sweet vermouth, two thirds absinthe) the Pick Me Up (one third cognac, one third martini dry vermouth, one third absinthe), and the Monkey Gland (two thirds dry

† "Trois-six": this was a 36 proof grape spirit, i.e. a rough brandy, as in Baudelaire's poem 'Une Béotie Belge'.

gin, one third orange juice, two dashes absinthe, two dashes grenadine). The "Absinthe" itself is a more classical drink, and in Tarling's book it consists of half absinthe and half water, with a dash of syrup and a dash of Angostura bitters, shaken into a cocktail glass.

There is a more spectacular absinthe cocktail to be found in the cyber-journal *Proust Said That*, when the writer recalls his days of drinking absinthe in South East Asia on military service, circa 1985. Since absinthe is illegal in the USA, it is also prohibited for US service personnel elsewhere in the world.

My first absinthe experience was in a strobe-lit, over-amplified GI bar on Okinawa. What I drank was not the 'Green Fairy' of the Belle Epoque but the 'Purple Haze' of Koza City: a dangerous mix of gin, absinthe, violet and sweet and sour that we'd drink after recon missions to wash the radio chatter out of our heads. Japan is one of the few places on earth where you can still buy absinthe over the counter, but as a US national with a top secret clearance, I was theoretically risking my job every time I ordered a drink. [. . .]

Different bars in the vill all served their own varia-tions on the basic Purple Haze formula, with escalating adjectives to let you know how much absinthe was allegedly in the mix: Regular, Super, Special, Extra, etc. My friend Takeo at the Rock House Purple Haze (actual bar name) created a worst-case-scenario he called the Big Fire, a warhead-like drink crowned by a mushroom cloud of absinthe that took up two-thirds of the glass. Surprisingly tasty, extraordinarily strong, and oddly beautiful under the black lights, upstairs on Gate Two Street. . .

Absinthe with Sprite or 7–Up has also had its followers, both in New Orleans and London, but it lacks the pleasures and comforts of a ritual.

There are two classic preparations left, one with ice and one with water. Absinthe with ice was more popular in America than France, and particularly in New Orleans, where the classic *absinthe frappé* consisted of a jigger of absinthe poured into a glass of cracked ice. An absinthe spoon, or a special small glass with a hole in it, was then placed over the glass with a lump of sugar in the usual fashion, and water was slowly dripped on to it, frequently from a 'fountain' – a special tap device, sometimes mounted on an obelisk – on the bar top. Finally it was stirred with a spoon and strained. The last classic method, little practised now, is the 'two glasses' method described by Saintsbury and Kernahan. A small glass of absinthe is placed inside a larger empty glass, and water is slowly poured into the small glass making the liquids mix and overflow. When the absinthe has been displaced to the extent that the small glass contains only clear water, the liquid in the larger glass is ready to drink.

The final word on the preparation of absinthe should go to 'Valentin', the pen name of Henri Bourette, who wrote a sonnet on the subject that was illustrated by more than one cartoonist. Valentin slowly describes the whole performance in all its exaggeratedly judicious care, ending, "Finally, to crown these unparalleled attentions / Very delicately, take the glass, and then / Throw, without hesitation, the whole lot out of the window."

Chapter Eleven
What Does Absinthe Do?

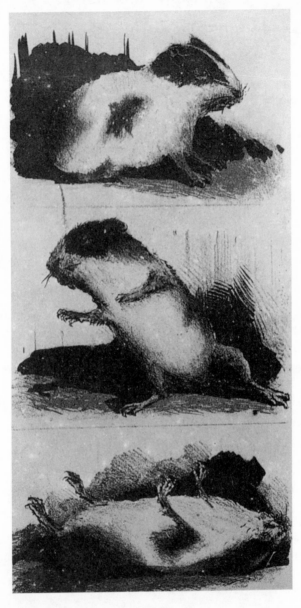

Before and after: a guinea pig under the fatal influence of absinthe, in a cautionary demonstration for French soldiers. Copyright Roger-Viollet.

Ritual aside, what was all the fuss about? What does absinthe do, and how? At the heart of the absinthe legend, beyond decadence and Bohemianism and doom, is the idea that it is supposed to provide a different quality of intoxication. It is sometimes referred to, with varying degrees of imprecision, as a drug, a narcotic, or even a hallucinogen. In moderate doses it was associated with inspiration, "new views and unique feelings", and a peculiarly 'clear' form of intoxication, a "euphoria without drunkenness".

Modern American users, often of homemade wormwood absinthe, seem to confirm this: they report that, "Besides the obvious alcohol buzz, there is a peculiar euphoric cloud – not a fuzzy, mind-numbing cloud as with other 'narcotics'. You don't stare at the walls; you stare beyond the walls"; there is a "euphoric feeling. . . not like alcohol or marijuana. You have a clarity that you don't have with those two." More enthusiastically still, "It brings one to a more clear concise focal point of the conscious mind, while leaving open a sort of pet door to the subconscious if you will, for thoughts and ideas to come in and at the first sip after going through the ritual preparations. . . all the world is poetry."

Those three absinthe enthusiasts – all women, curiously enough – may have a more elegant style than the *Clinical Toxicology Review* (the organ of the Massachussets Poison Control System), but the common denominators are clearly recognisable:

Users noted the 'double whammy' of absinthe intoxication: ethanol inebriation as well as a distinctly different effect (euphoria, sense of well-being, mild visual hallucinations) attributable specifically to the wormwood. Absinthe drinking imparted a cheerful mood and sharpened sense of perception, accounting for both its attraction and the psychological dependence to [sic] its effects remarkable among chronic users.

———

The intoxication is real, but people continue to argue how far it is simply due to alcohol. A journalist in Prague met a drinker who claimed that dripping tiny balls of flaming sugar into his absinthe increased absinthe's "hallucinatory power" by raising its temperature – which is a particularly rich claim since the brand in question contains virtually no wormwood at all. Anecdotal reports on the powers of Hill's ("produces dreams which are incredibly vivid and invariably obscene", for example) are interesting in this light, because in effect it contains almost nothing but alcohol, which may be an underestimated substance.

Absinthe intoxication may involve something like a placebo effect, or more precisely an ambivalent area comparable to the way that cannabis intoxication is recognised by psycho-pharmacologists to be a "learned experience", in line with cultural expectations. Tom Hodgkinson's charming account of absinthe intoxication falls into this area, and gives some idea of the wit that made Hill's so popular in Britain. Your cheeks glow, says Hodgkinson, and a "laid back, giggly drunkenness takes hold". But more than that:

> The other effect – no less important perhaps – is that by simply drinking it you can fancy yourself as a dissolute Bohemian poet in late 19th-century France, trading quips with Baudelaire before knocking off a few stanzas. You would then thrash your mistress, laughing maniac-ally before throwing yourself on the brass bed shouting "I want to die!"

Heady stuff; no wonder staying in is the new going out. Hodgkinson continues:

184

And if you think you start talking bollocks after a few beers, wait until you hear the unutterable nonsense you come out with after two or three absinthe cocktails. As one drinker pointed out, absinthe produces high quality bullshit of the artistic variety, while lesser drinks will only cause a lower class of rubbish to be spouted.

—

Ingestion of absinthe may result in a peculiar quality of intoxication, but it also led to a peculiar and recognizable syndrome, *absinthisme*, which began to be noticed in the 1850s. Sufferers were confused, intellectually slow, and prone to paranoia and horrifying hallucinations. Research gained momentum after Auguste Motet's 1859 thesis 'On alcoholism and the poisonous effects produced in man by the liqueur absinthe', followed by the researches of Marce and Magnan. To recap from Chapter Seven: Magnan, after studying the epileptic states found in absinthe drinkers, found that while alcohol alone would make animals drunk and finally kill them, only wormwood would make them excited and then give them epileptic-type convulsions.

Emile Lancereaux offers a grim picture of absinthism in 1880, describing how the sufferer would experience shimmering lights and terrifying hallucinations. Lancereaux's absintheur might see bloodthirsty animals; stand on the edge of great abysses, terrified of falling; have crawling-insect-style skin irritations; hear wailing, screaming and threats; and have a generalised feeling of being insulted and persecuted (absinthe paranoia was also the subject of Yves Guyot's 1907 monograph, *L'absinthe et le délire persécuteur*).

While no one had quite discovered how absinthe produced its effects, the received opinion on absinthism by now was that it was a distinct sub-category of alcoholism, and that although the alcoholic content of absinthe was higher than almost any other drink, something else was responsible for its terrible effects. Lancereaux, as summarized in the British *Lancet*, "was convinced that the essential oils of absinthe and of the other ingredients of the liqueur were far more toxic than the alcohol in which they were dissolved." More than that, "the attraction that this liqueur exercises on women even more than on men, [is] on account of the essential oils which it contains". Lancereaux made an analogy with the wretchedness of perfume drinkers, whose taste for eau-de-cologne, lavender water, and Parma violets extract is due not just to alcohol but to "the highly toxic essential oils contained in the perfumes"; "Many of these perfume drinkers are women and some of them become addicted to morphine, heroin and cocaine."

Wormwood, of course, had long been the chief suspect. As far back as 1708, Johan Lindestolophe's *De Veneris* ('On Poisons') had warned clearly, from the personal experience of Lindestolophe and his colleague Stenzelius, that continued use of wormwood will cause "great injury to the nervous system". Around the end of the nineteenth century its active ingredient finally came under closer scrutiny. In 1900 a German chemist called Semmler had proposed the correct structure of thujone, although he originally called it tanacetone, because his starting material was tansy oil. It was clear that this was identical with the thujone of another German chemist named Wallach. Thujone occurs in a variety of plants, but it was named for its presence in thuja oil, an essential oil that can be distilled from *Thuja occidentalis* (white cedar) and other conifer trees of the arbor vitae group. Thujone occurs in various homely kitchen herbs, and it is identical not only to the tanacetone of tansy but the salvanol found in sage.

In 1903 Dr.Lalou determined that thujone was largely responsible for absinthe's effects, linking it to other essences such as those of tansy, sage, hyssop, fennel, coriander, and anis. Thujone is a terpene, closely related to menthol – which pure thujone smells like – and camphor: Vicks Vapor rub contains thujone and other terpenes. Tetra-hydra-cannabinol (THC), the active ingredient of cannabis, is also a terpene, as is myristicin, found in nutmeg. A number of absinthe's other ingredients – also convulsant and epileptic in sufficient concentration – contain their own terpenes such as hyssop (pinocamphone) and fennel (fenchone).

Today thujone is classified as a convulsant poison. Around the time of the First World War scientists had already recorded its effect on the nervous system in some detail, without tracing the detailed cause of that effect. It causes excitement of the autonomic nervous system, followed by unconsciousness and convulsions. The involuntary and violent muscular contractions are clonic (rapid and repeating, with intervening relaxation) to begin with, and then tonic (continuous and unremitting). Large enough doses will cause seizures followed by death. Convulsions deliberately induced by camphor and thujone were studied in the 1920s as a model for epilepsy, and they were also used, before the advent of electro-convulsive therapy, to treat schizophrenia and depression.

And now – keeping in mind the pine-fresh, moth-repelling, mentally stimulating odour of camphor, thujone, and other terpenes – it is time to consider the case of Vincent Van Gogh.

———

Vincent Van Gogh (1853–1890) has long been mythologised as a vital part of the creature we met in Chapter Seven, "that late 19th-century Bohemian monster, the aristocratic dwarf who cut off his ear and lived on a South Sea island." In fact Van Gogh was far from Bohemian – he was a deeply religious and lonely individual, who lived among the poor and tried to help them, getting nothing but kicks in the teeth for his efforts – but he has ended up as one of absinthe's most spectacular victims.

Van Gogh became obsessed with the expressive and purely symbolic values of colour, instead of trying to catch real visual impressions, thereby paving the way for Expressionism. In his 'Night Café', for example, with its distorted perspective and its predominant greens and yellows, he said he had "tried to express, as it were, the powers of darkness in a low public house by soft Louis XV green and malachite, contrasting with yellow-green and harsh blue-greens, and all this in an atmosphere like a devil's furnace, of pale sulphur."

Toulouse-Lautrec is said to have introduced Van Gogh to absinthe, and in 1887 Lautrec did a pastel portrait of Van Gogh with a glass of absinthe in front of him. In the same year Van Gogh painted his still life 'Absinthe', featuring a glass of absinthe and a water decanter. Writing in the *British Journal of Addictions*, W.R.Bett paints a lurid mid-twentieth-century picture of absinthe drinking and its alleged effects on Van Gogh's work. The Marie Corelli-style intensity of Bett's account can be judged from his inset pen-portrait of Lautrec:

> the satyric figure of a dwarf with enormous head, huge fleshy nose, repulsive scarlet lips, black bushy beard, myopic malevolent eyes. . . He leans for support on a tiny cane. He stands by a dustbin polluting the night with its hideousness – symbol of filth and putrescence. He sits down at a marble table, eagerly welcomed by those who have wasted life, and now life wastes them: drinking absinthe with hopeless hopefulness. The fairy with the green eyes has enslaved their brains, has stolen their souls. He pollutes the night with foul-mouthed obscenities – symbol of filth and putrescence.

The extremity of Van Gogh's life and – in a particularly literal sense – his vision, has led commentators to go beyond the fashion for romanticized psycho-biography and into the realms of the purely clinical. It has been variously suggested that Van Gogh's brushwork and his treatment of colour and light are the result of schizophrenia, epilepsy, glaucoma, porphyria, digitalis poisoning, and toxic psychosis: the latter being caused by absinthe, as Albert J.Lubin argues in his 1972 psycho-biography *Stranger on the Earth*. Van Gogh's work has been a gift for the, "What Was He On?" school of art criticism. Wilkins and Schulz have argued that the oddly distorted perspective of 'The Night Café' "may have been influenced by visions he experienced at the beginning of an epileptic seizure", and indeed by "absinthe, one of the artist's habitual indulgences. . . known to affect the occipital lobe, which controls vision."

Van Gogh became increasingly unstable and suffered half a dozen psychotic crises in the last two years of his life, at least some of which seem to have been brought on by drinking. His friend Gauguin tried to help him, but found him difficult. One evening they were both drinking absinthe when Van Gogh suddenly threw his glass at Gauguin; next day came the infamous incident when he cut off part of his left ear and delivered it to a prostitute. (As for Gauguin, he was a happier and more robust character: one day in 1897, after receiving a cheque in the post from his Paris dealer, he wrote to a friend from Tahiti "I sit at my door, smoking a cigarette and sipping my absinthe. . . without a care in the world.")

Van Gogh's mental state worsened, and he experienced epileptic fits and hallucinations. He was drinking cognac and absinthe heavily, and among other bizarre behaviour he tried to drink turpentine. This has led to a persuasive article by Wilfred Neils Arnold, pivoting on the fact that thujone is a terpene. Arnold suggests Van Gogh developed an evident affinity for substances with chemical connections to thujone, notably pinene and thujone's twin-sister camphor, which he was also dosing himself with. He wrote to his brother Theo, "I fight this insomnia with a very, very strong dose of camphor in my pillow and mattress, and if ever you can't sleep, I recommend this to you." Arnold reminds his readers that camphor is identical in structure to thujone, with similar pharmacodynamics, and further points out that a contemporary analysis of camphor oil found that it contained pinene and other terpenes in addition to the camphor itself.

Around the same time Van Gogh was visited by his friend Signac, who had to restrain him from trying to drink about a quart of turpentine essence from the bottle. As Arnold says, this has usually been regarded as simply demented, but turpentine contains a large amount of pinene and other terpenes. More than that, says Arnold, it might have amounted to a *pica*

– an eating craze, of the kind sometimes found in pregnant women – which would shed light on some of Van Gogh's oddest acts in his last two years, such as his attempts to eat his paints, which were previously regarded as absurd and unrelated to anything.

Porphyria – a metabolic disease, often congenital, which can cause intermittent mental illness – has also been suggested as one of Van Gogh's problems. It is believed that "Mad" King George III suffered from intermittent porphyria. Thujone has other pharmacological actions in addition to its direct effects on the nervous system, and one of these is that it inhibits porphyrin synthesis. It does this so well, in fact, that it has been used in animal experiments to create an experimental model of acute intermittent porphyria. A 1991 article in the *British Medical Journal* by Loftus and Arnold suggested that Van Gogh had acute intermittent porphyria, a hypothesis which makes sense given the porphyrogenic effect of the terpenoids.

Not that any of this explains Van Gogh's art, but it might say something about his life, which, by all accounts, grew increasingly unbearable. With his visionary mind and his evidently exacerbated nervous system, Van Gogh derived great pleasure from contemplating the stars, and he had written to his brother Theo:

> to look at the stars always makes me dream, as simply as I dream over the black dots of a map representing towns and villages. Why, I ask myself, should the shining dots of the sky not be as accessible as the black dots on the map of France? If we take the train to get to Tarascon or Rouen, we take death to reach a star. One thing undoubtedly true in this reasoning is, that while we are *alive* we *cannot* get to a star, any more than when we are dead we can take the train.

On the 27th of July, 1890, Van Gogh took a gun with him when he went out to paint, and that afternoon he shot himself.

A search party found him after he failed to show up in the

evening, and he died two days later, ushering in one of the most bizarre episodes in his affinitive relationship with thujone, the substance he craved and which seems to have ruled his life to some extent. He was buried in a local cemetery, and an ornamental tree for the grave was provided by his friend Dr Gachet. The tree Gachet chose was a "flame tree", or thuja tree, later to be identified as the definitive source of thujone. Fifteen years later – the short lease on the grave having expired – Van Gogh was disinterred to be buried with his brother Theo. When the casket was uncovered it was found that the roots of the thujone tree had completely entwined around it, like the last frame in one of those 1950s horror comics; it was, a witness reportedly said, "*as though they held him in a strong embrace*".

Not only was Van Gogh's body moved, but also the tree, which was transplanted to Dr Gachet's garden. The tree still survives.

—

Thujone has been getting its tentacles around more people with the practice of recreational wormwood abuse, which has been established in the States for some years. Obscure drugs were a part of hippy "head" culture (as in "head shops", which would sell cigarette papers, perspex water pipes, beads, T-shirts, psychedelic postcards and drug-oriented "comix" – there were several of these shops in the Portobello Road area of London, where they dragged on well past their heyday).

In 1973 Adam Gottlieb published *Legal Highs*, a handy little compendium well in tune with the banana-smoking tenor of its times. This was, after all, a period when somebody was said to have died after injecting peanut butter. Most of these things remained legal because nobody except a fool would ever think of taking them, but after an alphabetical catalogue of herbal horrors (random quote: "Effects: Vomiting, intoxication and increased heartbeat, followed by three days of drowsiness or sleep") we finally come to Wormwood. The active ingredients are given as "Absinthine (a dimeric guaianolide), anabsinthin, and a volatile oil mainly consisting of thujone". Curious heads are advised that the bitter essential oil, extracted into alcohol, can be combined with Pernod or anisette to make absinthe, and that the effects are narcotic. They are also warned that it may be habit-forming and debilitating, and that thujone may cause stupor and convulsions . It was available as a dried herb from the Magic Garden Herb Company in California, and in the form of Woodley Herber's dried wormwood Absinthe mixture, "sold only for historical reference".

A culture of home-made absinthe drinking has recently gained momentum in America: at its simplest by steeping wormwood leaves in vodka or Pernod. "Kurt", on the Internet, reports soaking about two ounces of wormwood in alcohol and angostura bitters, then adding an ounce of oil of anise and leaving the mixture for five days. Far from getting drunk, says Kurt, "One shot was enough to really wake me up, and provided two hours of vivid imagination and a euphoric stimulation. . . I felt very creative and invigorated, but at the same time intoxicated. Vision was slightly distorted (more noticeable in darkness). There was a euphoria and stimulation that had a very unique feel. And this was all due to the absinthe, since the amount of alcohol consumed was under one ounce." Kurt grows fond of his "tincture of wormwood" drink (and he goes on to try more evolved recipes, with parsley, fennel and anise), but he finally concludes that his memory seems to be deteriorating badly, even after he has stopped drinking it. He signs off with "I'll keep y'all informed (if I can remember!)".

And as far as one can tell, he's not been heard from since. More recently wormwood oil has become available on the Internet as a "herbal dietary supplement", although it is not clear what your diet is supposed to be lacking. Wormwood is not known for its vitamins. It also comes with assurances that it has been organically grown, which ought to be the least of anyone's worries. At least one high quality brand is beautifully packaged, with a label that bears a close relation to a sibling brand of wormwood-free pastis: so close, in fact, that punters might well sense an invitation to put the two together. Absinthe in America is now associated with the Gothic and Witchcraft sub-cultures, the latter being quietly solicited by wormwood oil marketing. We are told that absinthe was reputedly first prepared by witches, with some interesting etymologies: the Anglo-Saxon word *wermode* means "waremood" or "mind preserver", and *wermod* is Old English for "spirit mother".

Wormwood oil has also been available for massage and aromatherapy, and it made the headlines in 1997 when a man almost died after drinking some. After becoming intrigued by what he read about absinthe on the Internet, a thirty-one year old Boston man obtained some wormwood oil online from an aromatherapy supplier. He drank only a fraction of an ounce, but was found later at home by his father in an "agitated, incoherent, and disoriented state." Paramedics noted tonic and clonic seizures with "decorticate posturing", and in the emergency room he was "lethargic but belligerent". In addition to seizures he suffered acute kidney failure, followed by heart failure on the second day of hospitalization.

He survived, after spending more than a week in hospital, and the three Washington doctors who treated him published his case in the *New England Journal of Medicine*, expressing concern about the availability of toxic substances over the Internet. The case was widely reported and, perhaps unfairly, the man became famous for his stupidity. But in fact his correspondence with the proprietor of *www.gumbopages.com* – an excellent web-site devoted to New Orleans, which achieved a great deal of unwanted publicity after the doctors claimed its "About Absinthe" section was where the man might have read about absinthe – shows him to be a perfectly intelligent, articulate and thoughtful individual.

I am the one who drank the wormwood oil. . . I believe you were unlucky to be mentioned, but that is all it is – bad luck, a subject whereof I know what I speak.

And I agree with you that to blame the Internet is hysterical and perhaps disingenuous.

There was no confusion in my mind [between wormwood oil and absinthe]. My mistake was in being reckless with my math[s] and taking far too much.

I am sorry for any pain this has caused you.

It is very different from the public face of the case. As one American newspaper reminded readers at the time, "Absinthe. . . has been banned in most countries for decades because it is – doh! – poisonous."

Even the most knowledgeable of amateur absinthe enthusiasts are not immune to accidental wormwood poisoning. One of the three women quoted at the beginning of this chapter reports a bad experience with home-made absinthe:

> I tried adding wormwood essence to a recent batch. . . worked very well. . . but I didn't think about the additional wormwood and drank a bit more than I should have. . . got very ill. Was also seeing "trails" and got rather anxious. So yes, I have experienced the hallucinatory effects of it. But getting to that point is quite dangerous.

———

There have been a number of comparisons between absinthe and cannabis – absinthe has been called "the liquid joint". There are cultural reasons why people might want to believe this, but it also goes back to a now superceded 1975 article, 'Marijuana, absinthe and the central nervous system', by del Castillo *et al.* The authors claimed striking similarities between the psychological effects reported by users of absinthe and marijuana, basing this in part on a 1971 *Playboy* feature on absinthe by Maurice Zolotow, who told his readers that absinthe was "one of the best and safest aphrodisiacs ever invented by the mind of man".

colleagues pointed out that both thujone
...inol are terpenoid, with a similar
...nd proposed that they produce their
...ts by acting on the same receptor in the
...l that this supposed overlap was interest-
...and sociological point of view, which
...e true. But the effects of absinthe and
...t. Although cannabis can cause short
...etimes as a result of anxiety attacks, it is
...and ultimately a stupefiant. Thujone, in
...t, ultimately a lethal over-stimulant and a

...n a remote and mountainous region of
Afghanistan, Eric Newby observed his horses frequently stop-
ping to eat wormwood, "*artemisia absinthium*, a root for which
they had a morbid craving". The result of this was that they
became "extremely frisky, possibly due to some aphrodisiac
quality possessed by the root *absinthium* on which they
continued to gorge themselves". Rats are also stimulated by
thujone, to the extent that in one experiment it seemed to
make them more intelligent: Pinto-Scognamilio, back in
1968, showed that thujone made rats more active, and even
seemed to increase the learning abilities of slower rats. He also
raised a more important and ominous point, which is that the
dosage of thujone has a cumulative effect, referring to an
earlier experiment which found that rats accumulated about
5% per day of the daily dose. By the thirty-eighth day they were
beginning to have convulsions, which takes us back to
nineteenth-century Paris. Small regular doses evidently could
accumulate in the body to produce toxic, psychoactive,
hallucinatory effects.

So how does thujone work? Researchers gradually banged
more nails in the coffin of the thujone and cannabinoid receptors theory, which was conclusively laid to rest by Meschler et
al in 1999, and in 2000 Karin M. Hold and her co-authors at
last established that thujone instead works on the brain's
GABA receptor system. GABA (gamma-aminobutyric acid)
inhibits or moderates the firing of neural synapses, but when

GABA-blockers such as thujone are in operation, the neurones fire too easily, and their signalling goes out of control as they run wild. The inhibiting effect of GABA is essential to the "fine tuning" of the brain, and its loss leads to tremor and convulsions. Benzodiazepine tranquillisers such as Valium have their calming effect by increasing the effectiveness of GABA, and they are the opposite of and antidote to GABA blockers; nicotine, on the other hand, makes the effect of thujone worse, in as much as it lowers the convulsant threshold. As well as finding that thujone blocks GABA receptors in the mammalian brain, Hold and her colleagues established that thujone poisoning is similar to the effects of the prototypical GABA-blocker picrotoxinin, a plant convulsant found in a variety of "loco weed", with similar symptoms and antidotes.

Further, a number of organochlorine insecticides such as dieldrin and DDT work by GABA-blocking, and a strain of fly resistant to dieldrin proved equally resistant to thujone. The symptoms of acute DDT poisoning (excitability, clonic and tonic convulsions sometimes approximating epilepsy, and so on) have a familiar ring to the student of wormwood and thujone. None of these effects are related to alcohol. In fact alcohol, like benzodiazepine tranquillizers, is listed as an antidote to convulsive poisoning by thujone, DDT and dieldrin.

So it seems that absinthe can be said to make you lose your inhibitions in more than one sense. Finally, the pharmacological operation of wormwood ("organically grown" or not) has more in common with DDT – recalling the Mickey Slim cocktail of the 1940s – than it has with cannabis.

———

It sounds grim, but then so do the effects of acute nicotine poisoning: reading them, you would never think that Liszt once said, "A good Cuban cigar closes the door to the vulgarities of the world." The wormwood buzz is agreed to be pleasant in moderation, and the increased firing of neurones must account at least partly for the feelings of mood lift, excitation and inspiration associated with real absinthe. The crucial factor is the correct dose.

It seems probable that nineteenth-century absinthe contained more wormwood than modern absinthe, not least because it was apparently so bitter. I have never had an absinthe that was in need of sugaring. This is borne out by figures, although estimates vary. European Union regulations prohibit absinthe containing more than 10 parts per million, or 10mg per kg, and Hill's contains a token 1.8 ppm (while Sebor and King of Spirits apparently contain the full ten). But the thujone content of absinthe back in the Belle Epoque era has been calculated to have been 60/90 ppm, while one source puts it as high as 260ppm, with a suggestion that with the further thujyl alcohol in wormwood this could go as high as 350 ppm

The strongest commercially manufactured absinthes today are the Swiss 'La Bleue', which seems to have a dubious legal status even its own country and contains 60ppm of thujone, and 'Logan 100', a Czech brand which contains 100ppm and a slightly lower alcohol content than is usual with absinthe, specially designed for the drinker hell-bent on experiencing a thujone jolt. A drinker of La Bleue reports that, "After one glass – I was very present, after two – extremely present, after three – stone-cold sober and very light sensitive, and after four – I was starting to have difficulty with spatial relationships, but was still very mentally focussed. Based on that personal experience, I'd guess that it's quite high in thujone. . ."

Given that alcohol is a depressant and thujone a stimulant, real absinthe fits into the so-called "speedball" family of classic drug combinations consisting of an 'upper' and a 'downer' together. These range from coffee with brandy, through the ugly combination of amphetamines and alcohol, to the 'speedball' proper of cocaine and heroin, and indeed 'Vin Mariani' cocaine wine. This distant relative of Coca-Cola contained 6 mg of cocaine per fluid ounce of wine and enjoyed great popularity during the heyday of absinthe. It was greatly appreciated by Ibsen, Zola, Jules Verne, and Pope Leo XIII, among others; the Pope even awarded Mariani a gold medal for services to mankind.

—

Speedball or not, the jury is still out on whether absinthe is any worse than other alcoholic drinks simply because it contains wormwood. People have argued about this for the last 150 years. Although at least since Dr. Magnan's time it has been clear that wormwood *can* make absinthe worse, whether it does so for most drinkers is still debatable. Certainly it was, and is, possible to get a kick out of thujone, but the real villain of this book must be the alcohol. Medical writers still routinely note that in practice this is the most dangerous and damaging component of absinthe, and it is with alcohol that we should end.

True absinthe involves two paradoxical effects. The alcoholic strength actually protects the drinker from the wormwood, because it is difficult to drink enough to be poisoned by the small amounts present. But on the other hand, it is the water that makes the alcohol so dangerous. While one might regard a neat triple brandy with respect and even distaste, a good absinthe just slips down, cool, clean and refreshing; it is, as it were, the menthol cigarette of lethal alcoholic drinks.

Most of the writers and artists in this book have been alcoholics, from Verlaine and Toulouse Lautrec to Malcolm Lowry and Ernest Hemingway. They have belonged to that large and unhappy band of whom Cyril Connolly once wrote, "I never want to read about another alcoholic; alcoholism is the enemy of art and the curse of Western civilisation. It is neither poetic nor amusing. I am not referring to people getting drunk but to the gradual blotting out of the sensibilities and the destruction of personal relationships involved in the long-drawn social suicide."

Why do writers drink? Not all writers do, of course, but

Tom Dardis has shown in his book on American literary alcoholism that American writers were under cultural pressure to drink in order to live up to an American idea of what being a writer involved. He cites Glenway Westcott – a friend of Hemingway and Fitzgerald – on the difference between American and French literary life. "In France no one expects much of anyone who drinks, but in America the drinker is supposed to drink *and* to produce. Some American writers have done it, but the management of drinking and what is expected of the drinker are very different in France." Absinthe may have inspired some of the figures in this book, but its far more tangible effect on most of their careers, and indeed lives, was to cut them short.

Aside from American cultural pressure, writers in general seem prone to drink. Some may have a grain of bitterness in their characters, either there from the start or brought on by the writing life, and there are distinctive long-term stresses involved, notably not being able to demarcate between life and work. Work always hangs over the writer, who has no real escape from it. Drink, wrote Hemingway, "makes it possible to put up with fools, leave your work alone and not think of it after you knock off. . . and be able to sleep at night."

Frederick Exley similarly reports drinking to switch off, and to think a little less: "Unlike some men, I had never drunk for boldness or charm or wit; I had used alcohol for precisely what it was, a depressant to check the mental exhilaration produced by extended sobriety." That awful 'exhilaration' recalls Baudelaire's brilliantly counter-intuitive note on writing: "Inspiration comes always when man wills it, but it does not always depart when he wishes."

There is a strange beauty to Carolyn Knapp's evocative description of alcoholism in her brilliant autobiographical account, *Drinking*:

> . . . somewhere during that second drink, a switch was
> flipped. . . a melting feeling, a warm light sensation in
> my head, and I felt like safety itself had arrived in

that glass. . . discomfort was diminished, replaced by something that felt like a kind of love.

Like drinking stars. That's how Mary Karr describes it in her memoir, *The Liar's Club*. . . she felt that slow warmth, almost like a light. 'Something like a big sunflower was opening at the very centre of my being', she writes. . . the wine just eased through me, all the way through to my bones. . .

Enough? That's a foreign word to an alcoholic, absolutely unknown. . . . You're always after that insurance, always mindful of it, always so relieved to drink that first drink and feel the warming buzz in the back of your head, always so intent on maintaining the feeling, reinforcing the buzz, adding to it, not losing it. A woman I know named Liz calls alcoholism "the disease of more", a reference to the greediness so many of us tend to feel around liquor, the grabbiness, the sense of impending deprivation and the certainty that we'll never have enough.

There is another spot-hitting description of the drinking life in Patrick McGrath's novel, *The Grotesque*: "Doris is one of those in whom the first drink of the day can arouse a sense of consummate fulfilment unrivalled in the spectrum of human gratification." "I wonder", adds the narrator:

has it ever occurred to you that a certain analogy can be drawn between drinking and suicide? . . . But what the drinker would doubtless spurn is the sudden death, the sudden blessed cessation of experience, and the liberation from the self, that the suicide craves. Sudden death is anathema to the drinker, for the approach to the void must be gradual, it must be attenuated.

Gradual and attenuated? Indeed so. When the French authorities mounted a public health campaign in the 1950s with posters that said "*L'alcool tue lentement*" (alcohol kills you slowly), the abrasive avant-garde group the Lettrists went around writing underneath them "*On n'est pas pressés*" ("We're in no hurry")†.

The leading figure among the Lettrists, and later the Situationists, was Guy Debord. He prided himself – in his impeccably clear Classical prose style, with its icy clarity and paranoid grandiosity – on the fact that "Even though I have read a lot, I have drunk even more. I have written much less than most people who write; but I have drunk much more than most people who drink." Like much of what he wrote, Debord's lapidary description of drinking deserves to be graven on stone. For that matter, it reads as if it already is:

First, like everyone, I appreciated the effect of slight drunkenness; then very soon I grew to like what lies beyond violent drunkenness; when one has passed that stage: a magnificent and terrible peace, the true taste of the passage of time.

† Or more abrasively, "*On s'en fout. On a le temps.*" ("We don't give a fuck. We've got the time.") [Hussey p.56]

Appendix One
Selected Texts

Félicien Rops' engraving *La buveuse d'absinthe*, subject of Joséphin Péladan's poem 'To Félicien Rops'. Copyright Marie-Claude Delahaye.

A LONDON PHANTOM by R. Thurston Hopkins

R.Thurston Hopkins atmospheric "memoir" of Dowson is the source of a famous Dowson quotation, but it may be closer to a short story. Hopkins' veracity has been questioned, not least because he later became a hack writer of mystery stories in the same vein. He was also instrumental in creating the legend of the Mummy's Curse. Still, as Dowson's biographer Jad Adams has written, "it gives the fantastic flavour of evenings spent with Dowson and shows how, even in his wrecked and sometimes deranged state, Dowson could be fascinating company for the right companion."

Towards the end of the eighteen-nineties I was a student at University College, Gower Street, London. That seems to be all that is necessary to say about a fact that is not of the faintest interest to anyone but the writer of this narrative. But what may be of interest to the reader is that it was during this time that there walked into my life (via the Bun House†, a haunt of bohemianism in the Strand) that amazing and erratic poet Ernest Dowson. Thin, small-boned, light brown wavy hair which was always curiously upstanding, blue eyes, a tired voice and nerveless, indeterminate hands, with thin fingers, such as are in the habit of letting things fall and slip from them. That is Dowson as I resurrect him from the mists of the dear dead London of the eighteen-nineties. He wore a disreputable out-of-elbows coat that seemed to be distressingly short above his rump. His collar was, I distinctly remember, tied together with a piece of wide black moire ribbon which

† The Bun Shop, or Bun House, was at 417 the Strand: it is now a wine bar and restaurant, Da Marco's.

acted as a poet's bow and a fastening for his shirt at the same time.

Dowson seldom smiled. His face was lined and grave, and yet it was the round face of a schoolboy and sometimes one might catch a gleam of youth in his blue eyes. At such moments a ghost of a smile would flit over his sombre features and wipe out the fretful expression which generally lurked there.

At that time he carried a small silver-plated revolver in his hip pocket and he seemed ridiculously proud of it. He would produce it, and hand it round for inspection in bars and cafés, without comment, and for no apparent reason at all. I never discovered what risky tortuous paths impinged on Dowson's life, that he should think it necessary to carry a gun; but perhaps he was toying with the idea of suicide. God knows, he must have found life a very distressing affair, for his thirty years existence on earth had been one long catalogue of disillusionments, financial worries and heartbreaks.

I spent many evenings with Dowson in the Bun House. Though the name of this rendezvous has a doughy sound, it never at any time offered buns to its customers. It is just a London tavern, but it was part of the literary and newspaper life of the eighteen-nineties. It was there that I saw Lionel Johnson, the poet, John Evelyn Barlas, poet and anarchist who tried to 'shoot up' the House of Commons, Edgar Wallace, just out of a private soldier's uniform, Arthur Machen in a caped 'Inverness' coat which he told me had been his regular friend for twenty years. "I hope to wear out four of these magnificent cloaks during my lifetime – anyway I can make four last out a hundred years!"

At that time absinthe was a popular spirituous drink amongst the young poets and literary vagabonds, and I can still see Dowson sitting on a high stool, lecturing on the merits of this opalescent anaesthetic. "Whisky and beer for fools; absinthe for poets"; "absinthe has the power of the magicians; it can wipe out or renew the past, annul or foretell the future" were phrases which recurred in his discourse. "Tomorrow one dies" was a saying which was often on his lips, and he would sometimes add, "and nobody will care – it will not stop the traffic passing over London Bridge".

After I had met Dowson a few times at the Bun House we would sometimes rove forlornly about the foggy London streets, initiated bohemians, tasting each other's enthusiasms. Sharing money and confessions, Dowson wielding a cheap Austrian cigar artfully and blowing smoke rings through his nostrils. As we wandered about London at night we often played a sort of game which we called Blind Chivvy. The idea was to find short cuts or round-about-routes from one busy part of London to another by way of slinking alleys and byways which then were not known to the average London man.

One evening we were blind chivvying in a puzzle of by-ways, yards, courts and alleys when we became aware of a dark form following us – a figure wrapped up, intent and carrying a Gladstone bag. We turned and twisted and he turned and twisted. We could not be mistaken – he was following us. Soon our unwanted 'companion' was so close on our heels that we could hear him heavily breathing. At this a foolish feeling of alarm gripped me, but I struggled to save myself from getting panicky.

Nevertheless as soon as we turned into a busy main street I pulled Dowson across to the friendly gas lamps and said to him: "Run like the Devil!"

When we had shaken this unwelcome wayfarer off I asked Dowson if he had had caught sight of the man's face. No, he had not; nor had I. But we both had an idea of a dark wrapped-up scarecrow following us through the empty courts with a debauched looking Gladstone bag in his hand.

A few nights later Dowson and I were in a bar parlour having a couple of frugal 'beers' when I noticed Dowson patting his pockets to locate his cigarette case. Dowson – who wrote that poem 'Cynara' that has since been popularised all over the world by its use as a title and a motif in one of Ronald Colman's famous films – was an absent-minded dreamer who never could return his cigarette case to the same pocket twice running. At that moment somebody slipped through the swing door of the bar. He was tall and thin;

carried a horrible old Gladstone bag; a mummified figure in an overcoat with a crazy old mackintosh over it. His face was almost hidden by a dirty silk scarf which was bound round his jaw as though he had toothache.

Yes! It was the same man who had followed us through the back streets only recently. It is a funny thing to say, but I felt that this figure (or 'personage' shall we say?) was not bound by the limits of youth or age – there was some strange quality about him that was otherworldly. I found it difficult to think of him as a *live* human being.

Meanwhile Dowson fumbled for his cigarette case with ineffective fingers, without result.

Then a voice came from the mummy-like figure: "Try your hip-pocket."

Dowson dived into the hip pocket and found the elusive cigarette case. We looked up and met the eyes of the visitor. Afterwards we tried to recall why we felt that this man – this personage – was so horrible: why he filled us with the essence of terror and repulsion. I do not remember that we could find any sound reason for thinking that he was so ghastly and abnormal. But certainly we did both agree about one thing. That was that our visitor had a *cold* kind of face which as Dowson remarked "reminded him of a bladder of lard." It may be guessed that we did not linger over our beer. The idea of speaking to this personage was intolerable to us and so we emptied our glasses and vamoosed.

Yet once again we were to run into this sinister personage. One evening we had walked towards the house in which Dowson lodged (I think it was 111 Euston Road) and when we were about a hundred yards from the iron railings which stood before the basement we saw once again the man with the dissipated Gladstone bag. We watched (with frightful perplexity) as the man walked up the front steps of Dowson's lodgings. That was enough for us. Somehow the idea of sleeping in the same house with this personage was intolerable to Dowson – for we had guessed that our visitor was looking for a bedroom – and so Dowson arranged to sleep at my home at Crouch End for a night or so.

Before we went to sleep that night we spoke, together and to ourselves, asking each other: Why a derelict hawker with a Gladstone bag could appear to us so evil and dangerous?

Dowson could not be persuaded to return to the Euston Road caravanserai until several days had passed. But when he did enter the house he could not help but observe that his landlady was very agitated about something. She told him that a man who had called and engaged a bedroom for a week had been found dead in his bed the following morning. She said that he had not a penny in his pockets and his Gladstone bag, when opened by the police, contained nothing but garden mould or soft fine earth. No one ever came forward to say who the dead man was, so he was buried in a pauper's grave. He had told Dowson's landlady that his name was Lazarus. As far as I remember, the police could not trace any of his kinsmen or friends.

I asked Dowson what he made of the affair some time afterwards; and the poet shrugged his shoulders and said in his low and hesitating voice: "Let me tell you something, Hopkins. That mould in his bag was graveyard mould. . . And was it not Lazarus 'that had been dead that did come forth from his grave bound in a winding sheet and his face bound about with a napkin'?"

Even after all these years I can still see Dowson's rather pallid face, and the sombre light in his eyes as he said these words.

There are times when I believe that Dowson and I were inclined to exaggerate the strangeness of a not very unusual set of coincidences, but that I must confess is not my final decision about this case. I am more than convinced that this wretched errant soul was dying on his feet – possibly starving and looking for someone who would take pity on him. But his appearance was so forbidding that no one would heed him. Also I believe that, in truth, he may have possessed some abnormal gift of hanging on to his body some days after death had really claimed it.

WORMWOOD: A DRAMA OF PARIS
by Marie Corelli

Marie Corelli (1855–1924) was a best seller in her day, holding the Victorians spellbound with her melodramatic imagination. Even in her own lifetime she was seen as ridiculous, and that is how she is remembered now, although she has some surprising admirers. Erica Jong recalls that when she was getting to know Henry Miller, "he used to rave to me about Marie Corelli".

Weighing in at around 800 pages, *Wormwood* is a 'triple-decker', a popular Victorian format in three volumes – savagely abridged here – during which Corelli maintains a level of unflagging excess. Insanely morbid, it is a book that cries out to have been illustrated by Edward Gorey.

Young, wealthy, and well-bred, Gaston Beauvais has a good position in his father's bank, along with less auspicious literary tendencies. Gaston falls in love with Pauline de Charmilles, whose father is a Count and a friend of Gaston's father, and he asks her father for her hand in marriage. They become engaged.

Unfortunately Pauline falls in love with Silvion Guidel, a handsome and saintly young man who is going to enter the clergy. He is the nephew of Monsieur Vaudron, an old priest much loved and respected by the other characters in the book. Silvion loves Pauline too, and at last she begs Gaston to break off their engagement. Gaston is devastated.

Gaston runs into an acquaintance in park, a wretched artist named André Gessonex. It is a meeting that is going to change his life, because Gessonex introduces Gaston to absinthe:

"Absinthe!" [says Gaston] "Do you like that stuff?"

"Like it? I *love* it! And you?"

"I have never tasted it."

"Never tasted it!" exclaimed Gessonex amazedly. "*Mon Dieu*! You, a born and bred Parisian, have never tasted absinthe?"

I smiled at his excitement.

"Never! I have seen others drinking it often, – but I have not liked the look of it somehow. A repulsive colour to me, – that medicinal green!"

He laughed a trifle nervously, and his hand trembled [. . .]

"I hope you will not compel me to consider you a fool, Beauvais! What an idea that is of yours – 'medicinal green!' Think of melted emeralds instead. There, beside you, you have the most marvellous cordial in all the world, – drink and you will find your sorrows trans-muted – yourself transformed! [. . .] Life without absinthe! – I cannot imagine it!"

He raised his glass glimmering pallidly in the light, – his words, his manner, fascinated me, and a curious thrill ran through my veins. There was something spectral in his expression too, as though the skeleton of the man had become suddenly visible beneath its fleshly covering, – as though Death had for a moment peered through the veil of Life. I fixed my eyes doubtingly on the pale green liquid whose praises he thus sang – had it indeed such a potent charm?"

"Again!" he whispered eagerly, with a strange smile. "Once again! It is like vengeance, – bitter at first, but sweet at last!"

Beauvais finds himself coming to like it, and he begins to be persuaded by Gessonex's speech: "You mean to tell me" I asked incredulously, "that Absinthe, – which I have heard spoken of as the curse of Paris, – is a cure for all human ills?"

Things are going well, and Gessonex is feeling benevolent: "the only good I can possibly do you in return for your many acts of friendship is to introduce you to the 'Fairy with the Green Eyes' – as this exquisite nectar has been poetically termed. It is a charming fairy! – one wave of the opal wand, and sorrow is conveniently guillotined!" Gaston is now under the influence of the new substance:

> "I let him run on uninterruptedly, – I myself was too drowsily comfortable to speak. I watched the smoke of my cigarette curling up to the ceiling in little dusky wreaths, – they seemed to take phosphorescent gleams of colour as they twisted round and round and melted away. A magical period of sudden and complete repose had been granted to me. . .

Gessonex enquires if Beauvais is feeling better: "The 'green fairy' has cured you of your mind's distemper?" Yes, says Beauvais, "whatever was the matter with me, I am now quite myself again." This sets Gessonex laughing like a madman – which indeed he is – and it is the cue for his great speech:

> "Good! I am glad of that! As for me, I am never myself, – I am always somebody else! Droll, is it not? The fact is" – and he lowered his voice to a confidential whisper – "I have had a singular experience in my life, – altogether rare and remarkable. I have killed myself and attended my own funeral! Yes, truly! Candles, priests, black draperies, well-fed long-tailed horses – *toute la baraque*, – no sparing of expense, you understand? My corpse was in an open shell – I have a curious objection to shut-up coffins – open to the night it lay, with the stars staring down upon it – it had a young face then, – and one might easily believe that it also had fine eyes. I chose white violets for the wreath just over the heart, – they are charming flowers, full of delicately suggestive odour, do you not find? – and the long procession to the grave

was followed by the weeping crowds of Paris. 'Dead!', they cried. 'Our Gessonex! The Raphael of France!' Oh, it was a rare sight, *mon ami*! – Never was there such grief in a land before, – I wept myself in sympathy with my lamenting countrymen! I drew aside till all the flowers had been thrown into the open grave, – for I was the sexton, you must remember! – I waited till the cemetery was deserted and in darkness – and then I made haste to bury myself – piling the earth over my dead youth close and fast, levelling it well, and treading it down! The Raphael of France! – There he lay, I thought – and there he might remain, so far as I was concerned – he was only a genius, and as such was no earthly use to anybody.

Gessonex is unmistakably insane, like a stage maniac ("his voice had a strange piteous pathos in it mingled with scorn – and the intense light in his eyes deepened to a sort of fiery fury from which I involuntarily recoiled.") Eventually they part, and as Gessonex disappears around the corner, walking his madman's walk ("his customary half-jaunty, half-tragic style") Beauvais realises what has happened to him. He has become an *absintheur*.

> "I could have shouted aloud in the semi–delirium of feverish intoxication that burnt my brain! . . .my casual meeting with him had been foredoomed! – it had given the Devil time to do good work, – to consume virtue in a breath and conjure up vice from the dead ashes – to turn a feeling heart to stone – and to make of a man a fiend!"

And there endeth the first volume.

Early in Volume Two comes a quotation from Charles Cros† which is pivotal for unfolding the action, and for Gaston's motivation. Gaston's earlier sense of moral good is

† See Chapter Five of this book.

now, he says, not just diminished but "reversed" due to absinthe. "Glorious Absinthe! What is it the poet sings?-

Avec l'absinthe, avec ce feu
On peut se divertir un peu
Jouer son role en quelque drame!

With absinthe one can divert oneself a little, and play a role in a few dramas; this is going to be the rationale of Gaston's mad and callous behaviour. By now, Beauvais talks of himself as a confirmed absintheur, with an addict's craving:

The action of absinthe cannot more be opposed than the action of morphia. Once absorbed into the blood, a clamorous and constant irritation is kept up throughout the system, – an irritation which can only be assuaged and pacified by fresh draughts of the ambrosial poison. . . I made my way down to the Boulevard Montmartre, where I entered one of the best and most brilliant cafés, and at once ordered the elixir that my very soul seemed athirst for! What a sense of tingling expectation quivered in my veins as I prepared the greenish-opal mixture, whose magical influence pushed wide ajar the gates of dreamland! – with what lingering ecstasy I sipped to the uttermost dregs two full glasses of it, – enough, let me tell you, to unsteady a far more slow and stolid brain than mine! The sensations which followed me were both physically and mentally keener than on the previous evening, – and when I at last left the café and walked home at about midnight, my way was encompassed with the strangest enchantments. For example: there was no moon, and clouds were still hanging in the skies heavily enough to obscure all the stars, – yet, as I sauntered leisurely up the Champs Elysées, a bright green planet suddenly swung into dusky space, and showered its lustre full upon my path. Its dazzling beams completely surrounded me, and made the wet leaves of the trees overhead shine like jewels; and I tranquilly watched the burning halo spreading about me in the fashion of a wide watery rim, knowing all the time that it was but an image of my fancy. Elixir vitae! – the secret so ardently sought for by philosophers and alchemists! – I had found it, even I! – I was as a god in the power I had obtained to create and enjoy the creations of my own fertile brain. . .

. . . we of Paris care nothing as to whether our thoughts run in wholesome or morbid channels so long as self-indulgence is satiated. My thoughts, for instance, were poisoned, – but I was satisfied with their poisonous tendency!

Gaston's hallucinations continue as he reaches his front door:

I found the door draped with solemn black, as if for a funeral, and saw written across it in pale yet lustrous emerald scintillations –

LA MORT HABITE ICI

Gaston develops a new callousness in his dealings with Pauline: "I had the ruling of the game, I and my 'green eyed fairy', whose magical advice I now followed unhesitatingly." He has changed, so that good seems unnatural and absurd, and his former habits and ideas are completely reversed due to absinthe, as he explains

Give me the fairest youth that ever gladdened his mother's heart, – let him be hero, saint, poet, whatever you will, – let me make of him an *absintheur*!- and from hero he shall change to coward, from saint to libertine, from poet to brute! You doubt me? Come then to Paris, – study our present absinthe-drinking generation, absintheurs, – and then, – why then give glory to the English Darwin! For he was a wise man in his time, though in his ability to look back, he perhaps lost the power to foresee. He traced, or thought he could trace, man's ascent from the monkey, – but he could not calculate man's descent to the monkey again. He did not study the Parisians closely enough for that!

Darwinism is one of several contemporary strands Corelli introduces into the book: there are also strong links with Zolaesque 'Naturalism', and with ideas of pathological 'Degeneration', as expounded by Max Nordau in his book of the same name.

Silvion has meanwhile joined the priesthood, so he is unable to marry Pauline, and Gaston offers to marry her after all. "I know why you do it", says Pauline, "– for my father's sake – and for the sake of good M. Vaudron, – to save honour and prevent scandal". Little does she know that Gaston is simply playing his role in a drama, Charles Cros-style. The night before their wedding he drinks his "favourite nectar, – glass after glass" until he starts to hallucinate. The walls of his room seem to him like "transparent glass shot throughout with emerald flame. Surrounded on all sides by phantoms – beautiful, hideous, angelic, devilish – I reeled to my couch in a sort of waking swoon, conscious of strange sounds everywhere."

He feels himself divided into "two persons, who opposed each other in deadly combat", and the next morning:

I was seized with a remarkable sensation, as though some great force were, so to speak, being hurled through me, compelling me to do strange deeds without clearly recognising their nature. . . I though of that white half-naked witch who had been my chief companion in the flying phantasmagoria of the past wild night. How swiftly she had led me into the forgotten abodes of the dead. . . Oh, she was a blithe brave phantom, that Absinthe-witch of mine!

At the altar he suddenly refuses to marry Pauline, publicly accusing her of being Silvion's cast-off mistress. Pauline collapses, but Gaston feels it all merely as a little drama: "a curious scene, – quite stagey in fact, like a set from a romantic opera – I could have laughed aloud".

When Gaston meets his father in the street, Beauvais senior is disgusted by what Gaston has done to Pauline. A madman, he says, or "a delirious absintheur. .a beast" might be capable of such useless ferocity, but not a rational human being. Gaston doesn't let on his secret, but later he relishes his situation: instead of marrying Pauline, "in my heart of hearts a wondrous wedlock was consummated, – an indissoluble union with the fair wild Absinthe-witch of my dreams! – she and she alone should be part of my flesh and blood from henceforth, I swore!"

Pauline has now gone missing, and her cousin Héloïse St.Cyr begs Gaston to help find her. Like Baudelaire's address to his *'hypocrite lecteur'*, Gaston then addresses his readers directly, believing they are secretly as selfish as he is:

> Let us then metaphorically shake hands upon our declared brotherhood, – for though you may be, and no doubt are, highly respectable, while I am altogether disreputable, – though you may be everything that society approves while I am an absinthe-drinking out-cast from polite life, a skulking pariah of the slums and back streets of Paris, we are both at one – yes, my dear friend, I assure you, – entirely at one! – in the worship of Self!

Pauline's father, the Count, summons Gaston. A servant shows Gaston to the Count's study, where the Count is sitting rigidly upright in an armchair. On the table is an open case of pistols, and Gaston realises – while simultaneously sneering at the idea of honour – that the Count intends to fight a duel with him. But what of the Count, sitting there and saying nothing? The Count seems to be looking at Gaston with "old world dignity" and "speechless but majestic scorn", when suddenly his jaw drops; he is already dead. Gaston's actions have effectively killed him, but, "My career was stainless, save for the green trail of the Absinthe-slime which no one saw."

He blames Pauline: "I took a sort of grim and awful pleasure in regarding her as a *parricide!*"

"From his period", says Gaston, "I may begin to date my rapid downward career": a career which has nonetheless "brought to me, personally, the wildest and most unpurchasable varieties of pleasure." Gaston checks into an obscure hotel under a false name, in order to live out his new life to the full. And when he goes walking around Paris he keeps carefully to the back streets, not only to avoid a chance meeting with old acquaintances but because that is where he is most likely to find Pauline, now that she is disgraced.

On one of his walks by the Seine, Gaston sees a priest standing by the river, and he recognises him. "You! – you!" he whispers, choked with rage, "Silvion Guidel!" Silvion is unaware of the terrible story; he thinks that Gaston and Pauline have married. Gaston fills him in: Pauline is on the streets, and her father is dead. Silvion reminds Gaston that Pauline never loved him, and Gaston falls on his throat, strangling him after a fierce struggle and throwing his dead body into the river.

A week or so later, in a miserable back street, Gaston catches a glimpse of Pauline, but he loses her again. In the same district he suddenly hears a loud laugh; it is Gessonex, the laughing madman, who lives in this slum: "with the oddest gestures of fantastic courtesy he invited me to follow him!"

Gessonex's domestic arrangements are not very pretty. He lives with a half-feral child who catches rats and eats them (Gessonex, in contrast, has reached a stage where he considers food "a vulgar superfluity"). The child, says Gessonex, is "a production of absinthe. . . of Absinthe and Mania together". As in Zola's *Rougon-Macquart* novels, tracing the effects of poverty and alcohol on a family over several generations, the child is a study in heredity and environment, the offspring of a line degenerated by absinthe. His grandfather was a renowned scientist, but his father drank absinthe and became an actor. He took up with a dancer named Fatima, but the "emerald elixir" drove him mad, until he became convinced that Fatima was "a scaly serpent whose basilisk eyes attracted him in spite of his will, and whose sinuous embraces suffocated him."

He ended in a lunatic asylum, where he succeeded in strangling himself, and the child is the offspring of "the absintheur and his 'serpent', – begotten of mania and born of apathy." Gessonex takes a scientific interest in him: "I think I know now how we can physiologically resolve ourselves back to the primary Brute period, if we choose, – by living entirely on Absinthe!" This is exactly what Gessonex would like to see: "Civilisation is a curse, – Morality an enormous hindrance to freedom."

Gessonex shows Gaston his masterpiece – a painting of a priest breaking open a beautiful woman's coffin in despair – before suggesting that they should do something "amusing"; they should visit the Paris morgue (which was a popular sight in those days; Dickens always visited the Morgue when he was in Paris).

> "Because it is dusk, mon ami, – and because the charm of the electric light will give grace to the dead! If you have never been there at this hour, it will be a new experience for you, – really it is a most interesting study to any one of an artistic temperament! I prefer it to the theatre!"

As they are leaving, Gaston gives the child a couple of francs, causing it to emit "an eldritch screech of rapture" that makes the ceiling ring, before kissing the money. "He is a droll little creature!" says Gessonex.

As they walk towards the Morgue, Gessonex raises his battered hat to drab and broken down women with fantastic courtesy. In the Morgue they find the hideously rotted and disfigured corpse of Silvion Guidel, testing Gaston's self-control. The morgue keeper thinks the priest is a suicide, but Gessonex, with his knowledge of anatomy, believes the priest to have been murdered. Gaston is understandably keen to change the subject, and when Gessonex makes a sketch of the dead priest, Gaston tears it into little pieces: "I thought it was a bit of waste paper! Forgive me! – I often get frightfully abstracted every now and then, – *ever since I took to drinking absinthe!*"

In the street, both men are getting nervous: Gessonex sees the apparition of a creditor behind him, and soon afterwards Gaston thinks he sees Silvion in the street. After brief digressions on Zola, on atheism, and on the moral state of Paris, Gaston is glad to duck into a café. "In what resort of fiends and apes could I hide myself. . .?" he wonders.

Gaston is further down the slippery slope in Volume Three. Walking near the Avenue de l'Opéra, he sees a ship being built and launched upon a green sea, only to break up and give way to a skeleton. "All the work of my Absinthe-witch! – her magic lantern of strange pictures was never exhausted!" People walking around under her influence are not uncommon in Paris: "There are plenty of people in the *furia* of Absinthe. . . men who would ensnare the merest child in woman's shape, and not only outrage her, but murder and mutilate her afterwards."

Gaston meets his father in the street again, and this time he tells him the truth: he is an *absintheur*. Beauvais senior is appalled:

> "You tell me you have become an absintheur, – do you know what that means?"
> "I believe I do," I replied indifferently. "It means, in the end, – death."
> "Oh, if it meant only death!" he exclaimed passionately. . . . "But it means more than this – it means crime of the most revolting character – it means brutality, cruelty, apathy, sensuality, and mania! Have you realised the doom you create for yourself, or have you never thought thus far?"
> I gave a gesture of weariness.
> "*Mon Père*, you excite yourself quite unnecessarily! [. . .] and even suppose I do become a maniac as you so amiably suggest I have heard that maniacs are really very

enviable sort of people. They imagine themselves to be kings, emperors, popes, and what not, – it is just as agreeable an existence as any other, I should imagine!"

"Enough!" and my father fixed his eyes upon me. . . "I want to hear no more special pleadings for the most degrading and loathsome vice of this our city and age".

With that he removes Gaston from the bank, but Gaston is beyond caring.

" I hate all things honest! It is part of my new profession to do so" – and I laughed wildly – "Honesty is a mortal affront to an *absintheur*! – did you not know that? However, though the offence is great, I will not fight you for it – we will part friends! Adieu!"

Gaston reports two other encounters in his wanderings: first, he sees an English woman in the Champs Elysées, "the breathing incarnation of sweet and stainless womanhood" which makes Gaston, who knows himself to be a low and filthy *absintheur*, "slink back as she passed, – slink and crouch in hiding". His next encounter is more congenial. He is meditatively stirring the "emerald potion" in a café when who should come up, as jaunty as ever, but Gessonex. Lifting his hat with a flourish, he glances appreciatively at Gaston's drink:

"The old cordial!" he said with a laugh. "What a blessed remedy for all the ills of life it is, to be sure! Almost as excellent as death, – only not quite so certain in its effects."

Gessonex sits down with a drink, and buys himself a copy of *Journal Pour Rire*, which brings out a surprisingly moral side in Gaston: a particular cartoon in it is "so gratuitously indecent that, though I was accustomed to see Parisians enjoy both pictorial and literary garbage with the zest of vultures tearing carrion, I was somewhat surprised at their tolerating so marked an instance of absolute grossness". Hardly has

Gessonex bought his *Journal* when a shot rings out: perhaps despairing of the uncommercial nature of his own work, Gessonex has shot himself in the head. Alive he starved, but no sooner is he dead than he is acclaimed a great genius.

Gaston meets Héloïse St.Cyr, who is appalled at his reduced condition. Too late she tells him that she was once in love with him, but that she feels nothing for him any longer. They talk of Pauline − *still missing* − her father − *dead* − and Silvion − *missing too.* "What has become of him, do you think?" says Gaston suddenly − "Perhaps he is dead?" "Perhaps" − he adds, beginning to laugh like a madman "he is murdered! Have you ever thought of that?" Their eyes meet, and Héloïse cries out in horror before she turns and runs for her life.

Gaston is still obsessed with finding Pauline; "this was the only object apart from Absinthe which interested me in the least." And one day he does, singing in the gutter with her hand outstretched for coins from passers-by. She tells him again of her pure love for Silvion Guidel, which goads Gaston to tell her what has become of him: "He is dead, I say! − stone dead! − who should know it better than I, seeing that I − *murdered* him!"

"What fools women are!" says Gaston to himself.

A mere word! − . . . '*Murder*,' for example − a word of six letters, it has a ludicrously appalling effect on human nerves! On the silly Pauline it fell like a thunderbolt. . .

Pauline collapses and lies unconscious. As she lies there, Gaston is moved to kiss her. She recovers consciousness and starts screaming "Murderer! Murderer! . . . *au secours! Au secours!*" (Help! Help!) Grabbing her, Gaston reiterates that he killed Silvion, forcing her to listen to the full story while she shudders and moans. Even as Gaston speaks, he is haunted by the pale phosphorescent apparition of Silvion creeping and skulking about: "There he is!" he says to Pauline. Suddenly Pauline breaks into a run, pursued by Gaston, until she reaches Pont Neuf. She dives off the parapet into the dark and swirling waters of the Seine.

"Pauline! Pauline!" Gaston cries to the waters – "I loved you! You broke my heart! You ruined my life! You made me what I am! Pauline! Pauline! I loved you!" He sinks into unconsciousness. Next day he wakes, still lying on Pont Neuf, and thinks back on the events of the night. "How strange it seemed! As the critics would say – how *melodramatic*!"

Gaston's thoughts are interrupted by the terrifying spectacle of a green-eyed leopard on the bridge, until he sees an early morning workman walk through it. Gaston gets up and walks, knowing that the phantom leopard is still behind him. Gessonex used to peer anxiously behind him, Gaston remembers, "And I idly wondered what sort of creature the Absinthe-fairy had sent to him so persistently that he should have seen no other way out of it but suicide."

Gaston has almost reached rock bottom. "And here I am, an *absintheur* in the City Of Absinthe, and glory is neither for me, nor for thee Paris, thou frivolous, godless, lascivious dominion of Sin!" Gaston haunts the Morgue, desperate to see Pauline again, and after two days her unidentified body is brought in. His first thought is that she must have a proper burial, but then he takes a perverse pleasure in the idea of her being thrown into the general pauper's ditch.

> The brain of a confirmed absintheur accepts the most fiendish idea as both beautiful and just. If you doubt what I say, make inquiries at any of the large lunatic asylums in France, – ask to be told of some of the aberrations of absinthe-maniacs, who form the largest percentage of brains gone incurably wrong, – and you will hear enough to form material for a hundred worse histories than mine!

The mortuary keeper can see that Gaston is interested in this particular body, but Gaston denies knowing her: "a *fille de joie*, no doubt!" Suddenly he sees "a pair of steadfast, sorrowful, lustrous eyes" flash "wondering reproach" at him. It is Héloïse, come to claim her cousin. Gaston has been cheated of his vengeance.

"What was there to do now? Nothing – but to drink Absinthe! With the death of Pauline every other definite object in living had ended. I cared for nobody; – while as far as my former place in society was concerned I had apparently left no blank." Now, in Père Lachaise cemetery, he watches Pauline's funeral from a distance: "I – I only had wrought all the misery on this once proud and now broken-down, bereaved family! – I, and Absinthe! If I had remained the same Gaston Beauvais that I once had been, – if on the night Pauline had made her wild confession of shame to me, I had listened to the voice of mercy in my heart – if I had never met André Gessonex. . . imagine! – so much hangs on an 'if'!"

Night falls and Gaston is still hiding.

The guardians of Père-la-Chaise, patrolled the place as usual and locked the gates – but I was left a prisoner within, which was precisely what I desired. Once alone – all alone in the darkness of the night, I flung up my arms in delirious ecstasy – this City of the Dead was mine for the time! – mine, all these moulding corpses in the clay! I was sole ruler of this wide domain of graves! I rushed to the shut-up marble prison of Pauline – I threw myself on the ground before it, – I wept and raved and swore, and called her by every endearing name I could think of! – the awful silence maddened me! I beat at the iron grating with my fists till they bled; "Pauline!" I cried – "Pauline!"

By now Gaston can see, "Fiery wheels in the air, – great, glittering birds of prey swooping down with talons out-stretched to clutch at me, – whirlpools of green in the ground into which it seemed I must fall headlong as I walked." Gaston feels the need to confess to a priest, and confesses to Père Vaudron. Vaudron is driven half-mad by the revelation that Gaston has murdered his beloved nephew. Vaudron can offer him no forgiveness, but Gaston reminds him that he has to keep the secret of the confessional.

After another binge on absinthe, Gaston becomes so ill that

a doctor is called. He tells him that his sufferings are due to absinthe:

"You must give it up," he said decisively, "at once, – and for ever. It is a detestable habit, – a horrible craze of the Parisians. Who are positively deteriorating in blood and brain by reason of the their passion for this poison. What the next generation will be, I dread to think!"[. . .] "I must inform you that if you persist drinking absinthe you will become a hopeless maniac."

Gaston has one last hope. He remembers Héloïse St.Cyr. He will go to her, and ask her pity, and try to give up absinthe for her sake; only Héloïse can free him from the curse of absinthe. He goes to the St.Cyr mansion, but its aspect has changed. The doors are open and it is draped in black. Someone has died. It must be the old Comtesse, thinks Gaston, as he presses further in among the incense and white lilies. But the figure lying in the *chapelle ardente* is Héloïse. "Dead!" cries Gaston, "Dead! Grovelling on the ground in wild agony, I clutched handfuls of the flowers with which her funeral couch was strewn – I groaned – I sobbed – I raved! – I could have killed myself then in the furious frenzy of my horror and despair."

Gaston has lost everything. In a sudden flash he realises that there is a god, the God who made wormwood. Finally, he kills his last vestiges of conscience and becomes wholly an absintheur:

Absintheur, pur et simple! – voila tout! I am a thing more abject than the lowest beggar that crawls through Paris whining for a sou! – I am a slinking, shuffling beast, half monkey, half man, whose aspect is so vile, whose body is so shaken with delirium, whose eyes are so murderous, that if you met me by chance in the day-time, you would probably shriek for sheer alarm! But you will not see me thus – daylight and I are not friends. I have become like a bat or an owl in my hatred of the sun! – . . . At night I live; – at night I creep out with the other obscene things of Paris, and by my very presence, add fresh pollution to the moral poisons in the air! I gain pence by the meanest errands, – I help others to vice, – and whenever I have the opportunity, I draw down weak youths. Mothers' darlings, to the brink of ruin, and topple them over – if I can! [. . .]For twenty francs, I will murder or steal, – all true absintheurs are purchasable! For they are the degradation of Paris, – the canker of the city – the slaves of mean insatiable madness which nothing but death can cure.

Finally another absinthe addict, a derelict chemist, gives Gaston a phial of lethal poison in exchange for absinthe – "a mere friendly exchange of poisons" – which Gaston intends to swallow as soon as he has the courage.

——

Corelli was not well liked by the Wilde-Smithers-Dowson set. Wilde told William Rothenstein that a prison warder had asked him about Marie Corelli's morals, to which he had replied that there was nothing wrong with her morals, but as for her writing, "she ought to be here." Ernest Dowson reports in a letter to his friend Arthur Moore that, "My people, meaning well doubtless, brought me a book of Marie Corelli's to read." It would be interesting to know which one it was. Whichever, it is not likely to have cheered him up very much.

FRENCH POETRY

The subject of absinthe drinking spawned a great deal of French poetry, much of which can be found in Marie-Claude Delahaye's book, *Absinthe Muse Des Poètes*. The following is a very small sample.

Raoul Ponchon (1848–1937) was a prolific versifier, publishing a staggering 150,000 poems over forty-odd years – he started late – of which around 7,000 are devoted to drinking. This one, from 1886, shows the persistent association between absinthe and death.

Absinthe

Absinthe, je t'adore, certes!
Il me semble, quand je te bois,
Humer l'âme des jeunes bois,
Pendant la belle saison verte!

Ton frais parfum me deconcerte,
Et dans ton opale je vois
Des cieux habites autrefois,
Comme par une porte ouverte.

Qu'importe, o recours des maudits!
Que tu sois un vain paradis,
Si tu contentes mon envie;

Et si, devant que j'entre au port,
Tu me fais supporter la vie,
En m'habituant à la mort.

Absinthe, I adore you, truly!
It seems, when I drink you,
I inhale the young forest's soul,
During the beautiful green season.

Your perfume disconcerts me
And in your opalescence
I see the full heavens of yore,
As through an open door.

What matter, O refuge of the damned!
That you a vain paradise be,
If you appease my need;

And if, before I enter the door,
You make me put up with life,
By accustoming me to death.

Raoul Ponchon

Gustave Kahn (1859–1936) was associated with the Symbolist movement, and later wrote a history of it. Mallarmé praised him for writing something which was neither prose nor poetry, like the following paean to absinthe as an all-embracing female object:

Absinthe, mère des bonheurs, o
liqueur infinie, tu miroites en mon verre
comme les yeux verts et pales de la
maîtresse que jadis j'aimais. Absinthe,
mère des bonheurs, comme Elle, tu
laisses dans le corps un souvenir de lointaines douleurs;
absinthe, mère
des rages folles et des ivresses titubantes,
ou l'on peut, sans se croire
un fou, se dire aime de sa maîtresse.
Absinthe, ton parfum me berce. . .

Absinthe, mother of all happiness, O
infinite liquor, you glint in my glass
green and pale like the eyes of the
mistress I once loved. Absinthe, mother
of happiness, like Her, you leave in the
body a memory of distant pain; absinthe,
the mother of insane rages and of staggering drunkenness,
where one can say, without thinking oneself
a madman, that one is loved by one's mistress.
Absinthe, your fragrance soothes me. . .

Gustave Kahn

Joséphin Péladan (1850–1918) was a key figure in the nineteenth–century French occult revival, and founded his own mystical order, the *Salon de la Rose-Croix*. A man with a taste for exoticism and ritual, he was known for hosting "aesthetic" evenings. The subject of the following poem is Félicien Rops' picture, *La Buveuse d'Absinthe*, of which J-K. Huysmans wrote "the girl bitten by the green poison leans her exhausted spine on a column of the Bal Mabille and it seems that the duplicate of Syphilitic Death is going to cut the ravaged thread of her life."

To Félicien Rops

Ô Rops, je suis troublé. Le doute m'a tordu
L'âme! – Si tu reviens de l'enfer effroyable,
Quel démon t'a fait lire en son crâne fendu
Les éternels secrets de ce suppôt du Diable.
La Femme? Tu l'as peint, le Sphinx impénétrable;
Mais l'Énigme survit devant moi confondu.
Parle, dis, qu'as-tu vu dans l'abîme insondable
De ses yeux transparents comme ceux d'un pendu.

Quels éclairs ont nimbé tes fillettes polies?

Quel stupre assez pervers, quel amour devaste
Mets des reflets d'absinthe en leurs mélancolies!

À quelle basse horreur sonne ta Vérité?
Rops, fais parler Satan, prêcheur d'impiété,
Qu'il écrase mon front sous des monts de folie!

O Rops, I am troubled. Doubt has twisted my soul
If you come back from the frightful hell,
What demon made you read in his split open head
The eternal secrets of that tool of the Devil,
Woman? You have painted her, the impenetrable Sphinx
But the enigma lives on before me, confusing me.
Speak, tell what you have seen in the plumbless abyss
Of her eyes, clear like those of a hanged man.

What lightning flashes have haloed your nice young ladies?
What perverted defilements, what devastated love
Put the glitter of absinthe into their melancholy

From what deep horror rings your truth?
Rops, make Satan speak, that preacher of godlessness,
So he can shatter my brow under mountains of madness.

Joséphin Péladan

Antonin Artaud (1896–1948) moved from an early involvement with surrealism to develop his own more idiosyncratic
ideas about the so-called "Theatre of Cruelty", bringing a
primitive and ritualistic element into drama. Meanwhile his
life increasingly fell apart in mental illness and drug addiction.
This weirdly schizoid early poem invokes an era which was
already distant by the time it was written.

Verlaine Boit

Il y aura toujours des grues au coin des rues,
Coquillages perdus sue les grèves stellaires
Du soir bleu qui n'est pas d'ici ni de la terre,
Où roulent des cabs aux élytres éperdues.

Et roulent moins que dans ma tête confondue
La pierre verte de l'absinthe au fond du verre,

Où je bois la perdition et les tonnerres
A venir du Seigneur pour calciner mon âme nue.

Ah! Qu'ils tournent les fuseaux mêlés des rues
Et filent l'entrelacs des hommes et des femmes
Ainsi qu'une araignée qui tisserait sa trame
Avec les filaments des âmes reconnues.

'*Verlaine Drinks*' – Antonin Artaud

There will always be whores on street corners,
Lost shells stranded on the stellar shores
Of a blue dusk which belongs neither here nor on earth
Where taxis roll by like bewildered beetles.

But they roll less than in my whirling head
The green gem of absinthe deep in the glass
Where I drink perdition and the thunder
Of the Lord's judgement to roast my naked soul.

Ah! How the tangled spindles of the streets
Turn and spin the fabric of men and women,
As if a spider were weaving her web
With the filaments of uncovered souls.

RAYMOND QUENEAU – THE FLIGHT OF ICARUS

The following little drama is part of Raymond Queneau's obscurely comic novel in the form of a play, *The Flight of Icarus*, and it looks back on the all–important ritual of preparing an absinthe properly.

At the Globe and Two Worlds Tavern in the rue Blanche there was only one free table, which seemed to be waiting for Icarus. It was in fact waiting for him. Icarus sat down, a slow but sure waiter came in and asked him what he wished to partake of. Icarus didn't know. He looked at the nearby tables; their occupants were drinking absinthe. He pointed to that milky liquid, believing it to be harmless. In the glass he was brought, the beverage appeared to be green; Icarus might well have thought this was an optical illusion had he known what an optical illusion was; he also brought a strangely shaped spoon, a lump of sugar and a carafe of water.

Icarus pours the water on the absinthe, which assumes the colour of milt. Exclamations from the neighbouring tables.

FIRST DRINKER: Disgraceful! It's a massacre!

SECOND DRINKER: The fellow's never drunk absinthe in his life!

FIRST DRINKER: Vandalism! Pure vandalism!

SECOND DRINKER: Let's be indulgent; let's simply call it ignorance.

FIRST DRINKER: (*to Icarus*) My young friend, have you never drunk absinthe before?

ICARUS: Never, Monsieur. I didn't even know that it was called absinthe.

SECOND DRINKER: Where've you come from, then?

ICARUS: Er. . .

FIRST DRINKER: What does it matter! My young friend, I'm going to teach you to prepare a glass of absinthe.

ICARUS: Thank you, Monsieur.

FIRST DRINKER: In the first place, do you know what absinthe is?

ICARUS: No, Monsieur.

FIRST DRINKER: She is our comforter, alas, our consolation, she is our only hope, she is our aim, our goal, and like an elixir – which she is, of course – the source of our elation, it is she who lends us strength to reach the end of the road.

SECOND DRINKER: What's more, she is an angel whose magnetic fingers hold the gifts of blessed sleep, of ecstatic dreams untold.

FIRST DRINKER: Kindly don't interrupt me, Monsieur. That is precisely what I was about to say and, I may add, with the poet: she is the glory of the Gods, the mystic crock of gold.

ICARUS: I'd never dare drink that.

FIRST DRINKER: Not that, no! You've ruined it by slopping all that tap-water over it in such barbaric fashion! Never! (*to the waiter*) Bring Monsieur another absinthe.

The waiter brings another absinthe. Icarus stretches his hand out towards his glass.

FIRST DRINKER: Stop, idiot! (*Icarus rapidly withdraws his hand.*) You don't drink it like that! I'll show you. You place the spoon on the glass in which the absinthe already reposes, and then you put a lump of sugar on the aforementioned spoon, whose singular shape will not have escaped your notice.

Then, very slowly, you pour the water over the sugar lump, which will start to dissolve and drop by drop a fecundating and sacchariferous rain will fall into the elixir and cause it to become cloudy.

Once again you pour on a little water which beads, and beads, and so on, until the sugar has dissolved, but the elixir has not acquired too aqueous a consistency. Observe it, my young friend, watch the operation taking effect. . . an inconceivable alchemy. . .

ICARUS: Isn't it pretty?

He stretches his hand out towards his glass.

THIRD DRINKER: And now pour the contents out on the floor.

THE TWO OTHERS: Blasphemy!

CHORUS OF WAITERS: Blasphemy!

THE PROPRIETOR: Hell and damnation!

ICARUS: (*bewildered*) What am I to do?

This continues until the door opens and a young woman ["LN"] comes in.

FIRST HALF OF THE CHORUS: You shall be the judge!

SECOND HALF: You shall be the arbiter!

FIRST HALF: You shall be our Solomon!

[. . .]

LN: What's going on?

THIRD DRINKER: I don't see why this whore. . .

LN: That's what I am, and I'm proud of it. Whore I am and whore I remain. But why a judge, an arbiter, a Solomon?

FIRST DRINKER: Come over here. Look at this young man.

LN: Isn't he handsome!

SECOND DRINKER: Should he drink his absinthe?

THIRD DRINKER: Or shouldn't he? But I don't see why this whore. . .

ICARUS: Mademoiselle. . .

LN: Monsieur.

ICARUS: I shall do what you tell me to do, Mademoiselle.

THIRD DRINKER: So young, and already a lost soul. . . Absinthism and grisette. . .

He disappears abruptly.

LN: [*indicating Icarus*] Who is he?

FIRST DRINKER: I don't know him, and you can see he's not an habitué. Just a beginner. He didn't even know how to prepare his absinthe. . .

CHORUS OF DRINKERS: Well! Shall he drink it or shan't he?

LN: (*to Icarus*) Drink it, young man!

ICARUS: (wets his lips and makes a grimace).

[. . .]

ICARUS: (*putting down his glass*) I shall only try it again if Mademoiselle tells me to.

LN: Mademoiselle does tell you to. Have another sip. *Icarus drinks a mouthful. He smiles politely, and then imbibes another mouthful.*

SECOND DRINKER: Well, what do you think of it?

ICARUS: (*after a third, a fourth, a fifth mouthful, positively*). How far away my nurse's milk seems. . . how the heavenly bodies are increasing and multiplying. . . how the night fades into the pale nebulae. It is already blue, the opalescent sea is hushed. . . how far away I seem from all that. . . in the vicinity of the star called Absinthe. . .

[. . .]

FIRST DRINKER: Ha ha! Well, I'll stand another round.

SECOND DRINKER: Me too.

LN: Be reasonable. You'll make the young man ill.

ICARUS: But I'm quite all right; my head feels hot and my liver feels cold, which at the moment isn't at all unpleasant.

FIRST DRINKER: You see! Waiter, another round!

ICARUS: I don't know how to thank you.

LN: You can thank him later.

SECOND DRINKER: He must be able to appreciate the third round.

LN: (*to Icarus*) Will you be able to hold out until then?

ICARUS: I'm floating a little.

The third round is brought.

FIRST DRINKER: (*observing Icarus preparing his absinthe*). Not too bad. He's improving.

SECOND DRINKER: He still pours the water rather too
  quickly.
LN: You're always criticising! (*to Icarus*). A very good
  beginning, pet.
Later in the book we find Icarus in the Globe and Two
  Worlds bar again. He is no longer a beginner, and he
  is appropriately 'high flown':
ICARUS: (*sitting in front of his fifth absinthe*). I might
  compare absinthe to a Montgolfier. It elevates the
  spirit as the balloon elevates the nacelle. It transports
  the soul as the balloon transports the traveller. It
  multiplies the mirages of the imagination as the
  balloon multiplies one's points of view over the
  terrestrial sphere. It is the flux which carries dreams as
  the balloon allows itself to be guided by the wind. Let
  us drink, then, let us swim in the milky, greenish wave
  of disseminated oneiric images, in the company of
  my surrounding habitués: their faces are sinister but
  their absinthed hearts absinthe themselves along
  abstruse and maybe abyssine abscissae.

*In due course Icarus has his fall. LN reappears later, and announces
that she has given up prostitution to become a dressmaker, making
solely bloomers for lady bicyclists. The bicycle, she says, "will give the
Frenchwoman the liberty her Anglo-Saxon sisters have already
discovered."*

ALL THE DRINKERS Bravo! Hurrah for the Bike!. . .
  They drink their absinthes.

ABSINTHE IN SPAIN

It is one of life's mysteries why the absinthe revival didn't come from Barcelona, where the absinthe is better, rather than Eastern Europe.

The Bar Marsella ("Marseilles") in the notorious Barrio Chino district, described here by British travel writer Robert Elms, was also frequented by Guy Debord during his exile in Spain. Debord liked the louche atmosphere of the Barrio Chino, and his biographer Andrew Hussey writes "Debord's endless thirst was often slaked in the Bar Marsella on Carrer nou de la Rambla, a dim-lit bar which specialised in a form of absinthe which had long been illegal in France: it is still there. . ." As for Elms:

> Over on the other side, the wild side, of the Ramblas, the barrio Chino is a mysteriously Chineseless China town, a dripping tenderloin where things go on. Secreted behind the huge undercover food market, the Chino is just as maze-like as the Gothic quarter, though it lacks the beauty and the charm of that ancient district. It is a messy and undeniably dark district occasionally punctuated by quiet and quite beautiful little squares – except they tend to be made a little less attractive by the used needles lying on the floor. Still you can't help liking it, or at least I couldn't; despite being the true home of the lowest life this city has to offer, the barrio Chino, certainly during the day, has never felt like a particularly dangerous place to be – providing of course you watch your step. For in among its sometimes filthy streets there are some great treasures.

. . .

I stumbled upon the bar Marseilles on my first ignorant excursion into the barrio Chino on that first weekend in Barcelona. People have been stumbling out of there for years. A black and white television plays noiselessly in the corner of this large, scruffy, barely furnished bar. But then few people bar the huge barmaid are looking. Some are playing an animated game of cards or dominoes in the corner, but most sit alone and stare hard at their drinks. For Marseilles is an absinthe bar.

Absinthe is drunk with dreamy ceremony, a fork placed over the top of a glass with a sugar cube resting on its prongs, water is dripped slowly onto the sugar and the sweet solution runs into the dark green liquid. Despite all the romantic associations with Paris at its peak, the stuff is so toxic and absinthism is so virulent an addiction that the drink has been banned in most parts of the world, but not in the barrio Chino. Here even bad dreams are allowed.

When I finally allowed myself to try absinthe I ended up losing a day which survives now only as shards, but which definitely included sitting with the working women of the barrio who I believe showed me a certain kindness. Later on, in a time not obscured by the green liquid, I discovered in the Chino, on a square lined with lumpy prostitutes, that there is a small plaque celebrating Alexander Fleming, such is the affection of this diseased place for the man who discovered penicillin.

ABSINTHE L.A. STYLE

D.J.Levien's 1998 absinthe pulp fiction, *Wormwood*, is a product of the current revival. It features Nathan Pitch, an embittered cog in the Hollywood star machine, who becomes increasingly involved with absinthe after encountering it in an underground club.

> Underground clubs were a staple of the city's nightlife. They ran by word of mouth among a secret, selective network. I had never been a member, while Ronnie, it appeared, was. Usually the clubs, housed in strangely sterile banquet rooms or small, dark, hot holes, offered something that regular bars did not. Nudity, or certain sexual proclivities involving leather or foot worship, was often on the block, on other occasions, designer drugs. Most just stayed open far later than was legal. The clubs issued invitations or employed cryptic password systems governing admittance, and given these parameters, and their shrouded locations, I had never been to one.
>
> Now, entering the ancient hotel's lobby, my heart was quick with excitement. I walked through the vaultlike entrance and up a cavernous marble staircase that led into the ballroom housing the club for tonight, or this week, or however long it would be there. The pale stone gave the underlit space a cool, museum-like feel. A threadbare tapestry ran the length of the floor, and I followed it past heavy oak and fabric chairs, to a doorway blocked by several young, vibrant people in high-style clothes who crowded the door, eager to enter. Heavy bass computer-generated music pulsated from beyond them. Conversations were muffled, possibly

because of the size of the place, but it sounded as if the walls were hung with wet blankets. A few tried to talk their way through the bulky doormen who wanted none of it, but my name had been left on a list by Ronnie, and I flowed through the bottleneck. My hand was stamped with an ink that made it glow, and I stepped into the main room.

The club room was reminiscent of a marble cathedral, but the lightless air reaching towards the ceiling was filled with smoke. This room was not muffled and cool like the foyer, and the people inside were not pious worshippers. Rather, it was alive and hot, and bodies pressed together on a dance floor. They moved to two different kinds of music – the techno I had heard and also classic disco – coming from separate sound systems on opposite sides of the hall which crashed together and showered down in a cacophony. The fusion, the activity and the humidity were causing condensation along lighting scaffolds which hung from the ceiling, and water drops were falling like noncommital rain. I stared at several seductive dancers gyrating on top of towering speakers, and then I realised they weren't dancing, but were unclothed and being painted, as they writhed, in neon colours by would-be artists kneeling at their feet.

The room smelled like perfume-sweat and cloves and camphor, and made me want to find Ronnie and dance with abandon. I looked for the bar, where I was to meet her, and where I would have to have a drink, or several, to reach the place these people inhabited. Spotting the bar across the room, I threaded my way through the revellers and chairs as I advanced towards it. I ordered a drink, and just as the bartender delivered, I felt a pair of soft, cool hands cover my eyes. I made a pretence of feeling her rings before yelling above the din, "Veronica Sylvan?" She spun around and kissed me, spun me around again and led me after her.

"Leave that," she said, gesturing to my drink.

The way she guided me across the floor made me feel

like I was at the end of a stunted conga line, and my shouts of, "How are you?" and, "Where are we going?" went unheard or unheeded by her. We finally arrived at a passageway that looked like it led to the kitchen, but was blocked by a short velvet rope between two brass posts, and a large man wearing an earpiece and microphone. He raised a handheld ultraviolet light at us, but seeing Ronnie, he lowered it, unclipped the rope, and moved it aside. I mumbled thanks and Ronnie dragged me, not into a kitchen, but rather a small sitting room populated by a number of thin, impossibly attractive women and a few heavy, but very tan, men. One of the men, moustachioed and dressed like an Edwardian, I recognised as a producer of sexual thrillers that were constantly surrounded by rumours of his on-set perversion. Everyone in the room was sprawled lethargically on plumply stuffed couches, and though seeing was difficult due to the stygian atmosphere, I made out several bottles of greenish liquid, and several more bellshaped glasses, littering the small tables in front of us.

"Care for an absinthe, dear?" Ronnie asked. My eyes adjusted to the dark, and I looked at her. She was stunning and a little outrageous in a crushed velvet cloche and a man's cut suit of dark silk that draped open, showing her black lace bra.

"Absinthe," I repeated. After witnessing it at several functions, I had done some research and knew it had disappeared early in the century through a combination of laws and intolerance. "I thought the stuff makes you insane?" I asked, communicating a fact I had learned.

"Only when it contains too much wormwood, friend," a refined but obese man spoke from across the room. "Wormwood is the root that gives absinthe potency. Without wormwood you are drinking mere pastis."

Ronnie placed a glass in my hand and directed me to a sofa. "Sit," she said.

"So is there wormwood in this variety? How do you know if it contains too much?" I asked.

"Don't be silly, darling, the wormwood is what makes it what it is. But this batch has the right amount," she said, pouring a small splash of the green liquid into each of our glasses. She then laid a silver strainer-type spoon shaped like the Eiffel Tower across each, rested a few sugar cubes on top of them, and began trickling water over the apparatus and into the glasses. Witnessing the process, I remembered the people with the teacups and flask at Asylum the night we had met.

"All these people?" I asked, gesturing out toward the main room of the club.

"Some. Some are on cocaine or other drugs. Some are just drunk. Some are sober. What's the difference?" she said, removing the strainers and stirring the sodden sugar cubes into the mixture, which was now turning a cloudy whitish-green.

"No difference." I shrugged, accepting the glass she offered.

She raised hers and we touched rims. I paused for a moment, breathing deeply, but knew that I was going ahead and saw no sense in waiting. I drank a healthy slug, draining half the glass. It was faintly licorice tasting and refreshing, not minty, though, as I expected due to the colour. It was cold too, from the water, I supposed.

"Do you like?" Ronnie asked, curling into me.

"I think so," I said, swallowing the rest, feeling its tendrils reach out into my blood.

As if from a great distance I heard the mustachioed man say to somebody, "Yes. *Chernobyl*. That's the word for wormwood in the Russian tongue. The coincidence is quite devastating, no?" I realised he was talking to me when he clapped me warmly on the shoulder.

"This stuff could bring back the days of ennui," I mused lazily, now knowing why all in the room were laid out like so on the couches.

"No, my good man, ennui is passé", said the

mustachioed man on his way out of the room. "These are the days of fear. Strictly fear." I shuddered and drank again.

As the night wore on, and the absinthe flowed, I began to feel a sensation of forgetfulness take hold of me. I briefly fought to recall something that Oscar Wilde had said about absinthe. *The first stage is like ordinary drinking, the second when you begin to see monstrous and cruel things, but if you persevere, you will enter upon the third stage, where you see things that you want to see, wonderful curious things. . .* But his words melted away, as did the sucking gravity-like feeling that had once trapped my feet and held them to the earth.

The usual exhaustion and incoherence that accompany heavy drinking was far off as Ronnie continued to pour. She moved closer to me too with each glass, and soon it was as if we were communicating deeply with one another although neither of us spoke. Others in the room began to drift away. I did not witness them walk out, but suddenly they were no longer present. All at once Ronnie and I were suddenly alone in the room, except for the cozy velvet furniture, and then we were all over one another. Our hungry mouths found fabric, then flesh as we grappled blindly. My equilibrium left me as I entered her. I felt I was mounting boundless horizons, tumbling through an ocean of green effluvium, then went into blackness.

Returning to sentience much later, I was disappointed to find her gone. I rubbed my eyes and peered around the room, discovering I was completely alone. I had a brief moment when I felt the same accordion-like feeling in my chest that I had earlier, but I tucked my shirt in, drew myself back together, and gave myself a sprinkle in the face from one of the leftover water decanters. I checked my watch and found it was past four o'clock, but amazingly the music still pumped relentlessly outside. Walking back into the slightly less populated club, I began to look for her.

244

A quarter of an hour elapsed, and after wading through the crowd of dwindling revellers, I was still empty-handed. My spirits began to sink along with my hopes of finding her as the absinthe faded, and I realised I was utterly alone. I located a pay phone and dialled Ronnie's number, only to reach her answering machine. I swore the filthy machine was against me. With no sign of her, or any of the others from the private room, and still a little lit from the strange head the absinthe brought, I went to my car. Upon finding it intact, I headed for home.

Along the way, fighting to stay focused, I finally recalled what Oscar Wilde had said of absinthe. I had gotten it slightly wrong the first time, I supposed, because I was already well past the fourth glass when I had thought of it, but now his words reverberated in me. *After the first glass you see things as you wish they were. After the second, you see things as they are not. Finally you see things as they really are, and that is the most horrible thing in the world. . .*

THE UNREPENTANT
CRONSHAW

Somerset Maugham has a memorable picture of the unrepentant absinthe drinker, Cronshaw, who also seems to be in possession of the secret of life. He figures in Maugham's 1915 novel, *Of Human Bondage*. Cronshaw has returned from Paris and is now living at "43 Hyde Street", Soho. It is in a shabby restaurant in Dean Street that Philip, the idealistic young doctor, meets Cronshaw again.

Cronshaw had before him a glass of absinthe. It was nearly three years since they had met, and Philip was shocked by the change in his appearance. He had been rather corpulent, but now he had a dried-up, yellow look: the skin of his neck was loose and wrinkled: his clothes hung about him as though they had been bought for someone else; and his collar, three or four sizes too large, added to the slatternliness of his appearance. His hands trembled continually. Philip remembered the handwriting which scrawled over the page with shapeless, haphazard letters. Cronshaw was evidently very ill.

'I eat little these days,' he said. 'I'm very sick in the mornings. I'm just having some soup for my dinner, and then I shall have a bit of cheese.'

Philip's glance unconsciously went to the absinthe, and Cronshaw, seeing it, gave him the quizzical look with which he reproved the admonitions of common sense.

'You have diagnosed my case, and you think it's very wrong of me to drink absinthe.'

'You've evidently got cirrhosis of the liver,' said Philip.

'Evidently.'

He looked at Philip in the way which had formerly had the power of making him feel incredibly narrow. It seemed to point out that what he was thinking was distressingly obvious; and when you have agreed with the obvious what more is there to say? Philip changed the topic.

'When are you going back to Paris?'

'I'm not going back to Paris. I'm going to die.'

The very naturalness with which he said this startled Philip. He thought of half a dozen things to say, but they seemed futile. He knew that Cronshaw was a dying man.

'Are you going to settle in London then?' he asked lamely.

'What is London to me? I am a fish out of water. I walk through the crowded streets, men jostle me, and I seem to walk in a dead city. I felt that I couldn't die in Paris. I wanted to die among my own people. I don't know what hidden instinct drew me back at the last.'

[. . .]

'I don't know why you talk of dying,' [Philip] said.

'I had pneumonia a couple of winters ago, and they told me then it was a miracle that I came through. It appears I'm extremely liable to it, and another bout will kill me.'

'Oh, what nonsense! You're not so bad as all that. You've only got to take precautions. Why don't you give up drinking?'

'Because I don't choose. It doesn't matter what a man does if he's ready to take the consequences. Well, I'm ready to take the consequences. You talk glibly of giving up drinking, but it's the only thing I've got left now. What do you think life would be to me without it? Can you understand the happiness I get out of my absinthe? I yearn for it; and when I drink it I savour every drop, and afterwards I feel my soul swimming in ineffable happiness. It disgusts you. You are a puritan and in your heart you despise sensual pleasures. Sensual pleasures are the most violent and the most exquisite. I am a man blessed with vivid senses, and I have indulged them with all my soul. I have to pay the penalty now, and I am ready to pay.'

Philip looked at him for a while steadily.

'Aren't you afraid?'

For a moment Cronshaw did not answer. He seemed to consider his reply.

'Sometimes, when I'm alone.' He looked at Philip. 'You think that's a condemnation? You're wrong. I'm not afraid of my fear. It's folly, the Christian argument that you should live always in view of your death. The only way to live is to forget that you're going to die. Death is unimportant. The fear of it should never influence a single action of the wise man. I know that I shall die struggling for breath, and I know that I shall be horribly afraid. I know that I shall not be able to keep myself from regretting bitterly the life that has brought me to such a pass; but I disown that regret. I now, weak, old, diseased, poor, dying, hold still my soul in my hands, and I regret nothing.'

'D'you remember that Persian carpet you gave me?' asked Philip.

Cronshaw smiled his old, slow smile of past days.

'I told you that it would give you an answer to your question when you asked me what was the meaning of life. Well, have you discovered the answer?'

'No,' smiled Philip. 'Won't you tell it me?'

'No, no, I can't do that. The answer is meaningless unless you discover it for yourself.'

Appendix Two
Some Available Brands

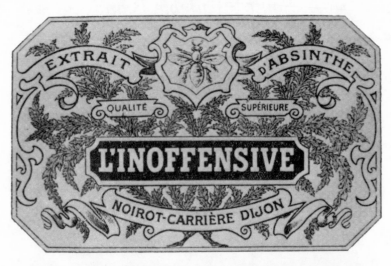

The charm of old labels. Anti-Semite Brand, launched in the wake of the Dreyfus Affair. Pernod, the great absinthe firm, was partly Jewish-owned. The Inoffensive Brand, on the other hand, was inoffensive because it contained no thujone. Copyright Marie-Claude Delahaye.

Since *Hill's* absinthe came in from the cold in 1998, a tidal wave of absinthe and would-be-absinthe drinks has hit the market. Several of these are not absinthe at all. Someone has to say it. But broadly speaking, there are two styles of absinthe: there is the true French (or Spanish) style, which is very much like Pernod, except stronger, and often greenish rather than yellow. This should "louche" or go cloudy when water is added. Then there is the East European "Bohemian" style, which is often bluish, doesn't louche, and is frequently compared to things like window-cleaning fluid. I say "style" because some of the worst East European-style absinthes are now made in France. Conversely, a couple of East European brands are good.

All comments are given 'without prejudice', as they say in legal circles. So in a darkened room, after invoking the departed spirit of George Saintsbury, off we go.

PÈRE KERMANN'S ABSINTHE (60% alcohol) French, but East European-style

By far the best thing about this is the label, which features a nice old monk sitting in his cell like a giant hamster and writing "Mon Absinthe Sera Tonique et Digestif" in an olde booke. The advice underneath is worth a second glance too: "Avec une morale saine et une hygiene rationelle l'homme ne meurt que de vieillesse." With healthy morality and sensible living, a man need only die of old age. Which is no doubt true, but what is it doing on a bottle? What are they trying to tell us here?

The entertainment comes to an abrupt end when you actually taste the drink, which is pretty horrible. The taste is very synthetic, with a hint of vanilla flavouring and perhaps a faint suggestion of something like Curaçao; the artificial-looking colour already primes you to think of Curaçao. It is not aniseedy, and the thin, burning, mouthwash-type taste is basically watered raw alcohol with some artificial flavourings. It is also lighter and slightly bluer in colour than absinthe ideally should be, and it fails to louche; it just dilutes.

Looking at the label on the back in more detail, we find this only purports to be "a reminiscence of the French notorious banned drink" and that it contains "wormwood Artemisia Vulgaris". This is not the true wormwood (Artemisia Absinthium), but the appropriately named mugwort. For aftershave drinkers only.

Dowson rating: zero

TRENET (60% alcohol) French, but East European-style

This is very much like *Père Kermann's*; almost suspiciously so. If anything, it tasted slightly staler and more medicinal, like a long forgotten cough syrup. But that makes it sound more pleasant than it is.

Again, it only promises to "remind you of the notorious banned drink". The best thing about this, compared to *Kermann's*, is that it has the good manners to come in small bottles, so it only costs three pounds to find out that you don't like it. However, it has been sighted more recently in large bottles shaped like the Eiffel Tower.

I am told both *Père Kermann's* and *Trenet* are manufactured in Le Havre on the Channel Coast, conveniently close to the know-nothing British.

Dowson rating: zero

HAPSBURG (72.5% alcohol) Bulgarian

Very green and very strong. Some aniseed flavour competes with sheer alcohol and somewhat murkier and staler artificial-type flavourings. Again, not especially pleasant.

Dowson rating: one

PRAGUE (60% alcohol) Czech

At last, after the previous trio, we're getting into the realms of something less poisonous, although it's still nothing to get wildly excited about. A reasonably aniseedy taste is combined with a touch of mintiness.

The label advises that it is "best served with sugar or honey, and may be diluted with tonic or spring water to taste". Given that most East European absinthes are agreed to taste like anti-dandruff shampoo, this might seem like an incongruously elegant nod towards gracious living. But to be fair, it's not so bad.

Dowson rating: three

HILL'S (70% alcohol) Czech

This is the granddaddy of the Czech absinthes, the brand that started it all. It's an open secret that this translucent bluish drink is not very pleasant, although it certainly gets you drunk. As we have seen earlier in this book, the flavour has attracted various insulting comparisons. But to taste this is to realise what brands like *Trenet* and *Père Kermann* are imitating. In comparison to them, this is richer, fuller, almost spicier. It is not very aniseedy and it doesn't louche, but mixing it with water gives off a faint bouquet of something like cinnamon.

Dowson rating: three

SEBOR (55% alcohol) Czech

The slightly tacky and exploitational UK advertising mentions Van Gogh's ear, and promises a much stronger hallucinogenic effect than its major UK competitor, which is presumably a now outdated reference to *Hill's*. *Sebor* contains 10ppm thujone, while Hill's apparently contains a nominal 1.8ppm or less. I didn't see lizards on the wall, mutilate myself, or get the urge to beat my loved ones to a bloody pulp, but this is a very good brand nevertheless.

Very green, slightly darker than most, *Sebor* is smooth with a little aniseed flavour combined with a strong liquorice. Above all it has a rich, herbal, 'medicinal' taste which is very aromatic and slightly peppery. This strong dry herbal quality reminds me a little of *Underberg*, and of *King of Spirits*. It also has a pleasantly dry aroma, like old dark wedding cake.

I find that – initially at least – this seems to produce a stimulating, 'bracing' quality of intoxication. This was comfortably well ahead of the other East European absinthes (in fact it's a different animal) until *King of Spirits* arrived. It louches slightly with ice and cold water.

Dowson rating: four

KING OF SPIRITS (70%) Czech

Who is this ferrety-looking little maniac on the label, somehow shiftier than your full-blown schizophrenic but clearly not an entirely well man? According to the caption it is supposed to be Vincent Van Gogh, although you'd hardly know it. So I've grown to think of this as Maniac Brand.

King of Spirits is distinctive in colour; it's much more organic-looking. After the chemical blue-greens of some other brands, this one has the colour of green olive oil. But it doesn't move like olive oil; it positively jumps and leaps while you examine the label, like the thin, volatile, highly alcoholic liquid it is. And in the bottom of the bottle, like a little compost heap, lies a pile of leaves, stalk, seeds and what have you.

It is agreeably bitter – some people find it too bitter – and for me at least it produces a distinct mood lift and a perhaps paradoxical sense of 'sharpening', along with a tendency to laugh. *This is the stuff*, I thought, when I first tried it, and then the word "*herbedaceous*" erupted into my head, bringing memories of a circa 1970 children's TV programme called *The Herbs* ("I'm Bayleaf, I'm the gardener. . ."). I recommended Maniac to a friend, who similarly reported that "it puts a smile on your face", and quickly. Someone rang him after he'd been drinking it, and he found he couldn't stop giggling on the phone. Nonetheless he stopped drinking it after suffering from stomach pains.

This and *Sebor* are distinctly akin, although this is stronger and more bitter. For my part I'm very fond of this, in moderation, and I feel the world would be a sadder place if they stopped making it.

Dowson rating: four

MARI MAYANS (70% alcohol) Spanish

Manufactured in Ibiza and coming (at least sometimes) in serial-numbered 'collector's bottles', this has apparently been going strong since 1880. Absinthe was never banned in Spain. *Mari Mayans* is pleasantly smooth and full with a very strong, fresh, fairly uncomplicated aniseed flavour like *Pernod*, with liquorice around the edges. The almost confectionary cleanness and purity of flavour masks the great alcoholic strength; bear in mind that *Pernod*, for example, is only 40% alcohol, and even that is still stronger than whisky. This is the most aniseedy brand tested.

It is a somewhat electronic pale green and louches with an opalescent vengeance; you half expect the resulting radioactive-looking substance to glow in the dark. Very good indeed, and another personal favourite.

Dowson rating: five

LA FÉE (68% alcohol) French

This is the hot new contender from France, where it is now manufactured for export only. It is apparently based on an authentic nineteenth-century recipe and it comes with the enthusiastic franchise-style endorsement of Mrs. Absinthe herself, Marie-Claude Delahaye, who runs the Absinthe Museum and is probably the world authority on the subject; her signature is blazoned across the back label. It owes its existence to her complaints about *Hill's* and belongs to the same importers, Green Bohemia, the outfit with *The Idler* connection.

This is less 'clean' than *Mari Mayans*, less sweet, and less overwhelmingly aniseedy, with a greater herbal complexity. There is a medicinal note of sweetish linctus at the front, and plenty of aniseed, followed by hints of woodland pond and even an undertaste reminiscent of the brown spirits such as whisky and rum; possibly due to the presence of caramel. Its woody notes give it not just the flavour of aniseed but a taste of aniseed *seed*, like getting to the centre of an aniseed ball and finding the bitter, roasty little black bit in the middle. This seedy quality slightly recalled drinks such as kummel.

Adding water makes it pleasantly opalescent, and it also cleans the flavour up to some extent, removing the sweet linctus and allowing aniseed and herbal bitters to predominate. Like *Mari Mayans*, the addition of a fair quantity of iced water – the label recommends diluting it as much as six to eight times – makes a very refreshing drink, if one can ever use such an innocuous word about something so lethally alcoholic. This is again very good indeed, and likely to eclipse *Hill's*. It ended joint favourite with *Mari Mayans*, the two of them retaining their distinct and separate identities.

Dowson rating: five

—

It would be ephemeral to include prices, but at the turn of the century (twenty-first) *Hill's*, *Mari Mayan*, *King of Spirits* and *Sebor* were all in the region of forty to fifty pounds.

This modest selection is nothing like all the absinthes there are, but it includes the major brands. I have also heard good reports of the Spanish brand *Deva*. There are now forty or fifty absinthes worldwide, including curiosities like *Absenta Serpis* (which is red) and rare beasts like *La Bleue*, a Swiss brand with informal, semi-underground distribution, which contains a solid 60ppm of thujone, and *Logan 100*, a phenomenally expensive Czech brand, which contains 100 ppm.

A New Orleans chemist and biologist named Ted Breaux has spent several years studying absinthe and has recreated the recipe for Belle Epoque Pernod, aided in his research by a couple of very scarce century-old bottles of the real thing. Breaux is reportedly soon to launch his own brand commercially, for distribution outside of the USA. This is eagerly awaited in some quarters.

NOTES

PROLOGUE

This miserable tale can be found in Zolotow (1971), and subsequent books.

CHAPTER ONE: WHAT DOES ABSINTHE MEAN?

". . . do you know what that means?" Marie Corelli, *Wormwood: A Drama of Paris* Vol.III p.36.

". . . putting straitjackets on . . ." Georges Ohnet, cited in Barnaby Conrad, *Absinthe: History in a Bottle* p.6

". . . cocaine of the nineteenth century" R.Nadelson 'Sweet Taste of Decadence' *Metropolitan Home* Nov.1982 cited in Doris Lanier, *Absinthe: The Cocaine of the Nineteenth Century* (Jefferson, McFarland and Co., 1995) p.1. A comparison between absinthe and cocaine had already been made by Robert Hughes in a 1979 Toulouse-Lautrec review in *Time*, reprinted in *Nothing If Not Critical: Selected Essays on Art and Artists* (Harvill, 1990) p.127

". . . deliberate denial of normal life . . ." Conrad p.x

". . . eroticism and decadent sensuality" Lanier p.1

". . . eat through solid rock." Don Conklin 'Absinthe is making a comeback' *College Hill Independent*

. . . transgression and death." Richard Klein *Cigarettes are Sublime* p.x

". . . not good, not beautiful, but sublime." ibid. p.2

". . . not entirely a fake" Somerset Maugham *The Magician, together with A Fragment of Autobiography* p.viii.

". . . Garcon! Un Pernod!" Aleister Crowley, *The Confessions of Aleister Crowley* p.574

". . . graces and virtues that adorn no other liquor." Crowley, 'The Green Goddess'

". . . without bodily disturbances" ibid.

". . . exalts my soul in ecstasy" 'La Légende de l'Absinthe'

"deliciously colonial" Crowley, *Confessions* p.499

". . . not really a wholesome drink . . ." ibid.

"Social mission" see C.Baldick *The Social Mission of English Criticism* (O.U.P. 1983)

". . . such a skunk as that." George Orwell, *The Road to Wigan Pier* (Gollancz, 1937) p.167

". . . neither had done". Cited in John Gross, *The Rise and Fall of the Man of Letters* (Weidenfeld and Nicolson, 1969) p.142

". . . more than one absinthe a day." George Saintsbury, *Notes on a Cellar-Book* pp.141–5

"ideal drink . . ." *Roland Barthes by Roland Barthes* p.96

". . . PARTY LIKE IT'S 1899!" advert, *The Idler* No.25, 1999

CHAPTER TWO: THE NINETIES

". . . the words 'vieux jeu' and 'rococo' were faintly audible." Max Beerbohm, 'Enoch Soames' in *The Bodley Head Max Beerbohm* p.58

". . . trusting and encouraging" ibid. p.62

". . . fantastic attenuations of weariness . . ." Holbrook Jackson *The Eighteen Nineties* (Jonathan Cape, 1927), new preface

". . . strange litany of fluted lust and hopelessness." Peter Ackroyd, introduction, *A Catalogue of Rare Books Offered for Sale from the collection of Giles Gordon: Oscar Wilde, Aubrey Beardsley and the 1890s* (London, Gekoski, 1994)

". . . so very 1890 . . ." Richard Le Gallienne *The Romantic '90s* p.192

"I hope you drink absinthe, Le Gallienne . . ." ibid.

". . . diabolism and nameless iniquity." ibid.

"Did not Paul Verlaine drink it . . ." ibid.

"So it was with a pleasant shudder . . ." ibid.

"too fierce a potion" ibid. p.193

". . . effect on the intellectual and imaginative faculties." ibid. p.194

Johnson is generally reported to have died after falling from a bar stool, but Le Gallienne attributes his end to being hit by a hansom cab.

"... the Café So-and-So" Lionel Johnson 'The Cultured Faun', in *The Anti-Jacobin* 1891, cited in R.K.R.Thornton, *Poetry of the Nineties* pp.20–21

"... globes of some unnatural fruit" Arthur Symons, 'London' *Arthur Symons: Selected Writings* p.60

"... Rocked on this dreamy and indifferent tide" 'The Absinthe Drinker' ibid. p.34

"... and drown deliciously" 'The Opium Smoker' ibid. p.29

"... powers, effects and variations." ibid. p.90

"... the last trumpet should have sounded ..." cited R.Ellmann *Oscar Wilde* p.301

"... through which he got his visions and desires." ibid. p.346

"... has no message for me" ibid. p.562

"... suits my style so well" ibid.

"... glass of absinthe and a sunset?" ibid.

"... why it drives men mad" ibid. 469

"... when I might be drinking my absinthe?" *Arthur Machen: A Bibliography* by Henry Danielson, with Notes by Arthur Machen, pp.31–2

"... – tulip – heads – brushing against my shins." J. Fothergill *My Three Inns* p.139

"The Morgue yawns for me ..." Ellmann *Wilde* p.580

"One or the other of us has to go." ibid. p.581

"... life and soul of the party." ibid.

"... produces all the effects of drunkenness" ibid. p.562

"If you're French in your taste ..." William Schwenk Gilbert, *Lost Bab Ballads* p.100

"... These are some of the words you hear" *The Complete Poetical Works of Robert Williams Buchanan* p.399

"... a very bad man." Gross p.145

"... the sickly gnome." Buchanan p.390

"... Born by broods in paper covers!" ibid. p.393

"... the louder to confess." F.Harald Williams *Confessions of a Poet* p.461

secret Bovril drinking: Robert Hichens, *The Green Carnation* pp.13ff.

". . . blended so well with the colour of absinthe." ibid. p.18

". . . The mind has its West End and its Whitechapel." ibid. p.9

". . . like absinthe – original, n'est-ce pas?" *The Savoy: Nineties Experiment* ed. Stanley Weintraub p.xviii

". . . model of my penis about his person." Peter Raby, *Aubrey Beardsley and the Nineties* p.85

". . . diabolical monocle." James G.Nelson *Publisher to the Decadents: Leonard Smithers in the Careers of Beardsley, Wilde, Dowson* p.65

". . . and one for the Police." Wilde *Letters* p.1063

". . . erotomaniac in Europe" ibid. p.924

". . . very nice." ibid. p.1101

". . . have gone back to absinthe." Smithers to Wilde, ibid. 1012 n.

"Dowson sends his love . . ." ibid.

". . . extreme horror" Ranger Gull, cited in Jad Adams *Madder Music, Stronger Wine: The Life of Ernest Dowson, Poet and Decadent* p.173

. . . Russian novel – R.A.Walker cited in Nelson p.283

CHAPTER THREE: THE LIFE AND DEATH OF ERNEST DOWSON

I have been indebted throughout this chapter to Jad Adams's superb biography of Dowson, *Madder Music, Stronger Wine* (I.B.Tauris, 2000)

". . . that curious love of the sordid . . ."Arthur Symons, 'A Literary Causerie: On a Book of Verses' *The Savoy* No.4 (August, 1896) p.93

"gone with the wind" from Dowson's poem 'Cynara'; "Since Death is coming to me . . . . Let me meet it, a stranger in a strange land" from Dowson's *Savoy* short story, 'The Dying of Francis Donne' (*Savoy* No.4, August 1896); "days of wine and roses", from Dowson's poem 'Vitae Summa Brevis'.

"Why was this book ever written?" Nelson p.235

". . . gets on one's nerves and is cruel." Raby, p.36

"... over my holy places." Dowson *Letters* p.213

"To Dorothy ..." Adams p.55

"a bankrupt concern" ibid. p.15

"... the drear oblivion of lost things." 'Dregs' cited Adams pp.156–7

"... whether subtly or defiantly." William Thomas, cited Adams p.12

"... like a protoplasm in the embryo of a troglodyte.." Dowson, *Letters* p.77

"... absinthe has the power of the magicians ..." Cited in Thurston Hopkins 'A London Phantom'

"... How wonderful it is!" Dowson, *Letters* p.175

"... as many things seem nowadays." ibid. p.174

"... madman when he got drink or drugs." Adams p.92

"... some act of absurd violence." ibid. p.102

"... and vomiting insults." ibid. p.101

"... clean or dirty", W.B.Yeats 'The Tragic Generation' in *Autobiographies* p.311

"... like Browning and Mrs Browning!" ibid. p.327

"... my head is full of noises." Dowson *Letters* p.307

"Whisky v Absinthe" ibid. p.35

"Good Old Café Royal" ibid. p.94

"... that may restore me." ibid. p.96

"... be it never so deleterious." ibid. p.107

"... putting money to the wrong account." Vincent O'Sullivan, *Aspects of Wilde* (1936) cited Adams pp.125–26

"... The picture on *Hunger* grows more like Ernest daily" Wilde *Letters* 1151; 1153

"... and Ernest Dowson, who is here, never." ibid. p.898

"... under the apple trees." ibid. p.900

"... *les saouls ne soient pas toujours poètes*" Ellmann p.542

"... it will entirely restore my character." Adams p.145

"I decided this morning to take a Pernod ..." Wilde, *Letters* p.901

"... and we want you." ibid. p.907

". . . we dare not even look at them." Dowson *Letters* p.317

". . . message from Satan . . ." ibid. p.325

". . . an absinthe and afterwards a breakfast." ibid. p.326

dipping his crucifix into his absinthe – Ranger Gull, cited Adams p.155

". . . through the whole crowded congregation." Dowson *Letters* p.327

". . . out of the ordinary." Adams p.146

". . . a most extraordinary series of hallucinations . . ." Conder cited Adams p.158

". . . come down off its shelf and strangle me." Adams p.159

". . . His conversation is undiluted vitriol." Adams p.159

"in the future" Adams p.166

". . . God bless you." Adams p.168

". . . for he knew what love is." Wilde, *Letters* p.1173

Eighteen Nineties Society and The Lost Club: personal communication from Ray Russell

". . . if they did I have forgotten." W.B.Yeats *The Oxford Book of Modern Verse 1892–1935* p.xi

CHAPTER FOUR: MEANWHILE IN FRANCE

"Dr. Martin told me . . ." *Pages from the Goncourt Journals* ed. Robert Baldick p.392

"Mad dog" and "absinthes himself"; anecdotes in Conrad p.viii

Edmond Bougeois poem cited Delahaye *L'Absinthe: Art et Histoire* p.74

". . . the mark of a neurasthenic idler." Baudelaire, *Intimate Journals* p.50

Jules Bertaut, *Le Boulevard*, cited in Marie-Claude Delahaye *L'Absinthe: Art et Histoire* p.86

"always with this hard gem-like flame . . .", Pater *The Renaissance* p.236

". . . gorgeous iridescence of decay:" Eugene Lee-Hamilton, in R.K.R.Thornton, *Poetry of the Nineties* p.41

"... meant that he took sugar with his absinthe" cited Conrad p.ix

"a hideous mug ..." Antoine Adam, cited Lanier p.50

"like an orang-utan escaped ..." Lepelletier, cited Lanier p.50

"... great trouble in dragging him away." Joanna Richardson *Verlaine* p.26

"... absinthe day and night." *A Poet's Confession* cited Conrad p.25

"... laden with perfumes of dreadful delight." Richardson p.288

"... One absinthe, if you please, mademoiselle." ibid. p.95

"... incapable of getting back to the school without assistance." Lanier p.63

"... Excuse all horrors" cited Conrad p.33

"... absinthe-corollas" Edmund Gosse, 'A First Sight of Verlaine' *The Savoy* No.2 (April, 1896) p.113

"Chinese, if you like ..." ibid. p.116

"... installed in front of a splendid verte." cited Richardson p.247

"... all his happiness, all his life." Bergen Applegate, cited Lanier p.47

"degeneracy ... melancholy magic" Max Nordau *Degeneration* pp.119–127

"... long been considered an absolute monster ..." Richardson p.292

"... I have my reasons." 'A François Coppée', in *Dédicaces* p.10

"... Absinthe!" *Paul Verlaine: Confessions of a Poet* trans. J.Richardson pp.105–7

"... *liberals.*" Enid Starkie, *Arthur Rimbaud* p.155

"... the dark dream by which he is surrounded." Baudelaire, cited Enid Starkie *Rimbaud* p.117

"I is an other" [*Je est un autre*] 1871 letter to Georges Izambard, *Rimbaud: Complete Works, Selected Letters* ed. Wallace Fowlie p.305

"... derangement of all the senses" ibid. p.307

"... poisons taken by the Sybil!" Starkie p.132

"... lie down in the shit!" *Rimbaud: Complete Works* p.315

"... Near some floating bits of wood." ibid. p.132

"... pensive drowned figure sometimes sinks." ibid. pp.115–17

"... I liked stupid paintings, door panels, stage sets ..." ibid. pp.193–5

"columns of amethyst, angels in marble and wood ..." Starkie p.369

"... life, and elsewhere." 'First Surrealist Manifesto' (1924), cited in Breton, 'Surrealism, Yesterday, To-day and Tomorrow' in *This Quarter* Vol.V No.1, Surrealist Number (September 1932)

CHAPTER FIVE: GENIUS UNREWARDED

Hebrew and Sanskrit: Richardson, *Verlaine* p.18.

Telegraph, photography and communication with planets – ibid.

"... engine run on empty" André Breton *Anthology of Black Humour* p.120

artificial rubies – ibid.

"... strangest book that he had ever read" *The Picture of Dorian Gray* p.125. There are other sources suggested for this Yellow Book.

"... icily comic observations" J.K.Huysmans, *Against Nature* p.194

"... suffering, poverty, and neglect" *Wormwood* Vol.1 p.105

'Lendemain' and "making some dramas" *Wormwood* Vol.2 p.7

"I wonder if we shouldn't go out and be bohemian ..." cited Michael Meyer *Strindberg: A Biography* p.451

"Concerning absinthe ..." ibid. p.372

"... London Bridge, where the throng bears a truly occult appearance" ibid. p.373

"air electricity ... silkworms" ibid.331

"... and the imp crouching on the floor" ibid. 330

"For instance, Rontgen rays ..." ibid.

"... and a murderous homosexual." Goncourts p.399

"... descended from the Templars by way of the Funambules" ibid. pp.100–101

"... to a padded cell" Richardson *Verlaine* p.245

"sacred book" cited in Edmund Wilson, *Axel's Castle* p.258

"... Orient which you carry within yourself" cited *Axel's Castle* p.263

"JARRY in absinthe" 'First Surrealist Manifesto', cited *This Quarter* Surrealist Number (Sept.1932) p.18

". . . his own revolver, which sobered him up instantly." Keith Beaumont *Alfred Jarry* pp.125–6

". . . makes it muddy." Roger Shattuck, *The Banquet Years* p.157

"most horrible of faces" Beaumont *Jarry* p.157

". . . like a very nice renter" Wilde *Letters* p.1075

". . . frightful attacks of *delirium tremens*" Shattuck p.164

". . . no human characteristic" ibid.

". . . and the Green Fairy would claim them both." David Sweetman, *Toulouse-Lautrec and the Fin-de-Siecle* p.433

". . . and just downright crude" ibid. p.425

". . . the Fascist and the Stalinist" Breton *Black Humour* p.213

"After us, the Savage God" Yeats *Autobiographies* p.349

". . . annihilated as a principle" cited Shattuck p.168

". . . to fly a black flag over the roof." Breton, *Anthology of Black Humour* p.212

"direct his dream", Shattuck p.157

". . . of super-reality" Breton, 1924 Manifesto, cited Beaumont *Alfred Jarry* p.161

"precocious imbecility" Shattuck p.154

". . . life is continuous" Jarry *Days and Nights* p.103

the Leao people and their 'flying heads' – see Beaumont *Alfred Jarry* pp.162–3

". . . probable obedience of the world at large." Jarry, *Days and Nights* p.102

". . . was flounder" Shattuck p.166

". . . on an empty stomach does more good" Beaumont *Alfred Jarry* p.270

". . . and that was my only illness" ibid.269

". . . not having always had enough to eat." Shattuck 170

Alphone Allais 'Absinthe' in *The World of Alphonse Allais* ed. Miles Kington pp.106–8

CHAPTER SIX: FROM ANTIQUITY TO THE GREEN HOUR

Ebers . . . Paracelsus: all widely repeated in previous works on absinthe, e.g. Lanier Ch.1

Culpeper, "Wormwood is an herb of Mars . . ." cited Lanier p.6

"Take the Iuce of wormewode . . ." cited in O.E.D.

Tusser's *Husbandrie* "It is a comfort for the hart and braine . . ." cited Lanier p.4

". . . produce a dream of the person he loves." Lady Wilkinson, *Weeds and Wild Flowers* (1858) p.353 cited in O.E.D.

"grew up in the winding track of the serpent . . ." cited Lanier 3

"and the name of the star is called Wormwood . . ." King James Bible, Revelations 8:10

further Jacobean references: O.E.D.

The Dr.Ordinaire story is widely repeated in previous works, e.g. Zolotow (1971) and Conrad Ch.7.

16 – 400 – 20,000 litres: Conrad 90–91.

125,000 litres a day: ibid. p.93.

"like a drunkard' s breath" ibid. p.94

Ricard's camel: Ricard obituary, *Telegraph* 15th November 1997

"Before those wars . . ." cited Richardson *Verlaine* p.245

"He takes his first drink at one café . . . Absinthe gets its work done more speedily." ibid. p.245

"As the night closes in you watch with fascination . . ." Ian Littlewood, *Paris: a Literary Companion* p.194

". . . asylum, charity ward, or morgue." Marie-Claude Delahaye, *L'Absinthe: muse des poètes* p.42

"It strikes me as the death of Bohemia . . ." Goncourts p.57

"Being a dramatist isn't an art . . ." ibid. p.44

". . . destruction of the French army." Flaubert *Dictionary of Received Ideas* p.1

genius of . . . death of any real genius: axiom of Dr. G.J.Witkowski, c.1878, cited Delahaye *muse des poètes* p.11

"I've drunk four absinthes . . ." cartoon, ibid. p.87

Niagara Falls: cartoon, ibid. p.181

'The Decadent' cartoon, ibid. p.149

. . . after the eighth that genius arrives: cartoon, ibid. p.286

CHAPTER SEVEN: BEFORE THE BAN

"talking about Chien Vert . . ." Goncourts pp.253–4

". . . that dreadful absinthe tinted with sulphate of zinc" ibid. p.362

". . . as a corpse possessed by a dream" ibid. p.42

". . . absinthe for women" Conrad p.52

Lanier cites an advertisement: Lanier p.28

"Woman has a particular taste for absinthe . . ." Conrad p.79

"Absinthe has always accentuated certain traits . . ." ibid. p.131

"What doctors fear the most . . ." Lanier p.28

". . . the beastliness of men." Zola, *Nana* p.254

"An absinthe drinker! . . ." cited in *Manet and his Critics* George Heard Hamilton. Proust recalled it slightly differently: "My friend, there is only one drinker of absinthe round here, and it's the painter who produced this insanity." See Anne Coffin Hanson, *Manet and the Modern Tradition* p.157

". . . the best tits in Europe." Daniel Farson, *Soho in the Fifties* (Michael Joseph, 1987) p.54

". . . sat and aestheticized till two o'clock in the morning." Littlewood, *Paris: A Literary Companion* p.195

"The perfection of ugliness . . ." cited in Ronald Pickvance, 'L'Absinthe in England' *Apollo* May 15th 1963, p.396. All further details of this picture's reception from Pickvance.

". . . didn't he slaughter me!" cited in Conrad p.53

". . . he was an absinthe drinker." Zola, *L'Assomoir* p.411

"I am an old Parisian . . ." cited Delahaye *Art et Histoire* p.104

"Our fathers still knew the time.." ibid. p.105

". . . more time and money to waste in drink." Lanier p.44

". . . absinthe kills you but it makes you live." Cartoon in Delahaye *muse des poètes* p.264

"... It's my absinthe." Goncourts p.132

"... feeling her blood freeze." Zola, *Nana* p.343

"... the man of the people, the workman" Conrad 22

"... something different ... from chronic alcoholism." *The Lancet* March 6th 1869 p.334

"... from 39 centigrade to 42" *The Lancet* Sept.7th 1872 p.341

"... 246 times more likely to become insane ..." Lanier p.35

"... truly 'madness in a bottle'" ibid.

"... nine out of ten are due to absinthe poisoning" ibid. p.38

Lawrence Alloway conjures up the "Bohemian monster" in his 'Discussion' printed after W.R.Bett, 'Vincent Van Gogh (1853–90) Artist and Addict' *The British Journal of Addiction* Vol.51, Nos. 1 and 2, 1954, p.13

"... entirely painted in absinthe" Sweetman p.421

"... like the temptation of the devil." Julia Frey, *Toulouse-Lautrec: A Life* p.145

"... you will be sorry to hear was taken to a lunatic asylum yesterday" Dowson *Letters* p.406

"Old fool" Sweetman p.500

Matisses's painting drives you mad: Delahaye, *Muse des Peintres* p.141

"I was sitting said Alfie at a cafe ..." cited Brooks Adams, 'Picasso's Absinthe Glasses: Six Drinks to the End of an Era' *Artforum* April 1980

"... end of an era." ibid.

"... *memento mori*" ibid.

"recalls the Satanic lull ..." ibid.

three orders of representation: see Werner Spies, *Picasso Sculpture: With a Complete Catalogue* p.50

CHAPTER EIGHT: AFTER THE BAN

"The spirit of the boulevard is dead ..." Conrad p.135

"green fairy's fang" James Joyce, *Ulysses* p.53

"froggreen wormwood" ibid. p.52

"Nos omnes biberimus viridum toxicum . . ." ibid. p.559

"greeneyed monster" ibid. p.690

". . . absintheminded . . ." *Finnegans Wake* 464.17

". . . python enfolding and crushing its victim." Lanier p.154

". . . You imbibe your absinthe frappé" Lanier p123

"almost as fatal as cocaine . . ." ibid.

". . . collapsed and was put to bed" Tom Dardis, *The Thirsty Muse: Alcohol and the American Writer* p.215

". . . FOR BEING DEAD" ibid. p.253

". . . for all our parties" ibid. p.42

". . . consumed in quantities" Lanier p.139

". . . not as benign as it might appear" Dardis p.164

". . . drinking before virtually all of them." ibid.

woodworms and wormwood – Conrad p.137

". . . distorted my reflexes" Hemingway, cited Conrad 131

". . . one cup of it took the place of the evening papers . . ." Ernest Hemingway, *For Whom The Bell Tolls* p.51

". . . a few drops at a time." ibid.

". . . There is nothing like absinthe" ibid.197

"delicate anaesthesia" ibid. 51

". . . become very cultured and improve ourselves." Victor Arwas, *Alastair: Illustrator of Decadence* p.17

". . . perfume, pagan, phantom . . ." Cited in Geoffrey Wolff *Black Sun* p.138

". . . like a pearl in a cup of dead green absinthe" ibid. p.140

"preposterous, *outré*, umotivated gloom" ibid. p.139

". . . Flowers of Dissolution, Fleurs du Mal" ibid p.139

"shadows hot from hell" Arwas, *Alastair* p.18

". . . and two bottles of absinthe" Conrad p.141

". . . into which I decanted the absinthe . . ." ibid.

". . . a Verlaine jag with absinthe . . ." Wolff p.163

". . . die with one's beloved." Conrad p.143

". . . vote of confidence . . ." ibid.

". . . hand fluttered, lifted, and fell back." Anne Rice, *Interview with the Vampire* p.150

". . . drugs their forefathers made famous" cited in *The Times* 24 August 1994 p.10

"Victo-grunge" ibid.

"To the treasures and pleasures of the grave . . ." Poppy Z.Brite *His Mouth Will Taste of Wormwood* p.1

". . . 'with or without?' – i.e. with or without absinthe." C.W.J.Brasher, 'Absinthe and Absinthe Drinking in England' *The Lancet* April 26 1930, p.944

". . . . But I daresay I should like it now." Alec Waugh, *In Praise of Wine* p.180

". . . curious property of doubling the effect of every drink that is taken after it . . ." H Warner Allen, cited in Zolotow p.172

"gazing into the opalescent depths . . ." Evelyn Waugh, *Decline and Fall* p.133

". . . his glass of crimson syrup." Evelyn Waugh, *Scoop* p.129

". . . and ordered some more absinthe." ibid.

"delowryum tremens" and other Lowry material from Gordon Bowker, *Pursued by Furies*, (Harper Collins, 1993) cited in P.Baker 'Delowryum Tremens' *Times Literary Supplement* Dec.31st 1993

". . . a florid demon brandished a pitchfork at him" Malcolm Lowry, *Under The Volcano* p.10

". . . hidden in drawers at Consulates . . ." ibid. p.307

"Money came from the blue eyes of home . . ." Samuel Beckett *A Dream of Fair to Middling Women* p.37

". . . the stout that helped to bloat the sadness of sad evenings." ibid. p.143

". . . the old Bohemian hardened by many years of drinking absinthe and cafés of Montmartre" Harriet Vyner *Groovy Bob* p.13

CHAPTER NINE: THE ABSINTHE REVIVAL

"One winter, as I stood in a Prague bar . . ." John Moore, 'The Return of Absinthe' *The Idler* Winter 1997 p.39

". . . to a not completely dissimilar end" ibid.

"... surreal and obscene" ibid.

"... if you are interested in importing it." ibid. p.41

"... horror of alcohol awareness campaigners" Stuart Miller 'Green Fairy Fires Spirits After Long Absinthe' *Guardian* Dec.1st 1998

"... that kind of publicity." Tom Hodgkinson ;'Absinthe – that's the spirit' *Telegraph* 3 Dec 1988

"... decadent fin-de-siècle drink." Joanna Simon 'Absinthe Minded' *Sunday Times* 17 Jan 1999

"horrible ..." ibid

"aquavit on steroids ..." Ben Macintyre 'One green bottle makes fools of us all' *Times* 5 Dec 98

"... Vosene shampoo ..." Richard Neill, 'Absinthe makes the head pound harder' *Telegraph* 8 Feb 1997

"... a long lasting drink" ibid.

"It works!" cited T.Hodgkinson, 'Wild Green Fairy Liquid' *Loaded* Feb 1999

"... disgusting, alien rubbish" cited Tony Allen-Mills 'French start bar brawl for 'real' absinthe' *Sun Times* 18 April 1999

"... turning in their graves" ibid.

"... *farniente, de douceur de vivre*" Delahaye, *Histoire de la Fée Verte* p.94

"... stronger and not yellow" Dick Bradsell in *Class: the magazine of bar culture* reproduced at eabsinthe.com

Damien Hirst reported to be considering absinthe-inspired works 'Peterborough' *Telegraph* 8 Dec 1998

"... poison ... illegal ... doolally" cited Adam Helliker 'Lethal Tipple' *Sun.Telegraph* 2 May 1999

"... clearly has mind altering properties" cited in 'Baron's son fights drinking ban after 'poison' absinthe' *Evening Standard* 16 June 1999

"... any other substance that can be misused." Cited in *The Publican* 'Sales of absinthe are set to rise ...' 11 Feb 1999 reproduced on eabsinthe.com

"We shall be keeping a very close eye ..." cited Tom Baldwin, 'Labour poised to ban absinthe' *Sunday Telegraph* 27 Dec 1998

"... he will ban it" Michael Bywater 'Why Government is bad for you' *Telegraph* 25 Feb 1999

CHAPTER TEN: THE RITUALS OF ABSINTHE

The first three quotations on the enduring appeal of the ritual are from the Net: the first from a marketing site, the second from 'Princess Xanax' at Erowid, and the third from Kallisti at Sepulchritude.

". . . similar to using intravenous drugs" John Moore, 'The Return of Absinthe' p.39

". . . ceremonial and etiquette . . ." Saintsbury p.144

The late 19thc cartoon with the old French colonial and the boy in the tree is by Testevuide, reproduced in Delahaye *Art et Histoire* p.49

". . . a purée parfaite!" cited in Delahaye *Muse des Poètes* p.20

". . . a single drop more might have instantly degraded the sacred potion." Marcel Pagnol, *The Time of Secrets* pp.85–6

"30ml" in Strang J, Arnold WN, Peters T. 'Absinthe: what's your poison?' *British Medical Journal* [online version] 18th Dec.1999; 319; pp.1590–92

". . . Satie or Ravel, to get in the mood" Barnaby Conrad in *USA Today* 18 August 1997

"The professors of absinthe were already at their station . . ." Conrad *Absinthe* p.22

"It is a solemn trial for the amateur . . . ." Lanier p.16

"What a moment for the beginner! . . ." Lanier p.17

"In every circle of young men one finds a veteran . . ." Marie-Claude Delahaye, *L'Absinthe: Histoire de la Fée Verte* pp.89–90

Both the *vidangeur* and *minuit* are attributed to Toulouse-Lautrec. The various names and variations are from the 'Dictionnaire' of Delahaye's *L'Absinthe: Art et Histoire* pp. 36–43.

". . . Purple Haze . . ." Stuart Mangrum, "Absinthe, the Potent Green Fairy' in *Proust Said That* issue no.7

". . . the whole lot out of the window." Valentin, variant comic strips reproduced in Delahaye *Muse des Poètes* p.22 and Delahaye *Muse des Peintres* p.21

"new views . . . and unique feelings" W.N.Arnold 'Absinthe' *Scientific American* June 1989 p.86

"euphoria without drunkenness" Lanier p.23

". . . you stare beyond the walls" Kallisti at sepulchritude.com

". . . a clarity that you don't have with those two." Lilith, cited in 'Absinthe Devotees: The Green Fog' wired.com August 2000

"It brings one to a more clear concise focal point . . ." 'Princess Xanax' at erowid.com

"Users noted the 'double whammy' . . ." 'Absinthe' *Clinical Toxicology Review* Vol.18 No.4 Jan 1996

". . . I want to die!" T.Hodgkinson 'Wild Green Fairy Liquid' *Loaded* Feb 1999

". . . a lower class of rubbish to be spouted." ibid.

". . . a generalised feeling of being insulted and persecuted." Lancereaux cited Meyer *Strindberg* p.356

". . . on account of the essential oils it contains" Lancereaux cited in Brasher 1930 p.945

"Many of these perfume drinkers are women . . ." ibid.

"great injury to the nervous system" cited Arnold, 'Absinthe', *Scientific American* June 1989 p.90

". . . like a devil's furnace, of pale sulphur."cited Lanier p.85

"the satyric figure of a dwarf . . ." W.R.Bett 'Vincent Van Gogh: Artist and Addict' *British Journal of Addiction* Vol.51 Nos.1–2 p.7

". . . occipital lobe, which controls vision." D.Wilkins and B.Schultz, *Art Past, Art Present* (New York, Abrams, 1990) cited Lanier p.86

". . . without a care in the world." cited Lanier 88

"affinity" W.N.Arnold 'Vincent Van Gogh and the thujone connection' *Journal of the American Medical Association* Vol.260 no.20 Nov.25 1988 p.3042

"I fight this insomnia with a very, very strong dose of camphor . . ." ibid. p.3043

". . . any more than when we are dead we can take the train." cited Lanier p.89

". . . as though they held him in a strong embrace." U.F.Vandenbroucke, cited in Arnold 'Vincent Van Gogh and the thujone connection' p.3044

". . . three days of drowsiness or sleep." Adam Gottlieb *Legal Highs* p.53

". . . mainly consisting of thujone." ibid. p.52

"I'll keep y'all informed (if I can remember!)" 'Kurt' 'Absinthe: My Dance with the Green Fairy' at entheogen.com

"agitated, incoherent, and disoriented state" etc. S.D. Weisbord, J.B. Soule, P.L. Kimmel 'Poison on Line: Acute Renal Failure Caused by Oil of Wormwood Purchased Through the Internet' *New England Journal of Medicine* Vol.337 no.12 p.825

". . . I am sorry for any pain this has caused you." letter published on gumbopages.com

". . . but getting to that point is quite dangerous." Lilith, in Frauenfelder 'Absinthe Devotees' wired.com

"liquid joint" Frauenfelder op.cit

". . . ever invented by the mind of man" Zolotow 'Absinthe' p.174

". . . a morbid craving." Eric Newby *A Short Walk in the Hindu Kush* p.163

". . . continued to gorge themselves." ibid. p.174

Meschler et al. – Meschler J, Marsh C, Land B, Howlett 'Failure of the active component of absinthe to bind the cannabinoid receptor' International Cannabinoid Research Society paper (1997), cited in Matthew Baggot *Absinthe FAQ* [net]

260/350ppm: Strang et al. 'Absinthe: What's Your Poison?'

". . . based on that personal experience, I'd guess it's quite high in thujone." Anon. at Sepulchritude.com 'Absinthe Guide'

". . . alcoholism is the enemy of art and the curse of Western civilisation . . ." Cyril Connolly cited Dardis p.9

"In France no one expects very much from anyone who drinks . . ." Glenway Westcott cited Dardis p.11

". . . put up with fools, leave your work alone and not think of it after you knock off . . ." Hemingway, cited Dardis p.202

". . . a depressant to check the mental exhilaration produced by extended sobriety" F. Exley, *A Fan's Notes* (Penguin, 1990) p.31

". . . but does not always depart when he wishes." Baudelaire, *Intimate Journals* p.13

"somewhere during that second drink, a switch was flipped . . . . never have enough." Caroline Knapp, *Drinking* p.53

". . . the approach to the void must be gradual, it must be attenuated." Patrick McGrath, *The Grotesque* (Penguin, 1990) p.133

"*On n'est pas pressés*" Ralph Rumney *Le Consul* (Paris, Editions Allia, 1999) p.27

". . . *On a le temps.*" Cited A.Hussey *The Game of War: The Life and Death of Guy Debord* p.56

". . . drunk much more than most people who drink." Guy Debord *Panegyric* trans. James Brook (Verso, 1991) p.34

". . . the true taste of the passage of time." ibid. p.35

BIBLIOGRAPHY

Ackroyd, Peter (introduction) *A Catalogue of Rare Books Offered for Sale from the collection of Giles Gordon: Oscar Wilde, Aubrey Beardsley and the 1890s* (Gekoski, 1994)

Adams, Brooks 'Six Drinks to the End of an Era' *Artforum* (April, 1980)

Adams, Jad *Madder Music, Stronger Wine: The Life of Ernest Dowson, Poet and Decadent* (I.B.Tauris, 2000)

Allais, Alphonse 'Absinthe' in *The World of Alphonse Allais* ed. Miles Kington (Chatto and Windus, 1976)

Allen-Mills, Tony 'French start bar brawl for 'real' absinthe' *Sunday Times* 18 April 1999

Alloway, Lawrence [reply to W.R.Bett; see Bett]

Applegate, Bergen *Verlaine: his absinthe-tinted song* (Chicago, Alderbrink Press, 1916)

Arnold, Wilfred Niels 'Absinthe', *Scientific American* 260 (June, 1989)

Arnold, Wilfred Niels 'Vincent Van Gogh and the Thujone Connnection' *Journal of the American Medical Association* 260:20 (Nov. 25th 1988)

Arnold, WN, Loftus LS 'Vincent Van Gogh's Illness: Acute Intermittent Porphyria?' *British Medical Journal* 1991; 303; 1589–91

Arwas, Victor *Alastair: Illustrator of Decadence* (Thames and Hudson, 1979)

Asbury, Herbert *The French Quarter* (New York, Knopf, 1936)

Baldwin, Tom 'Labour poised to ban absinthe' *Sunday Telegraph* 27 Dec 1998

Balesta, Henri *Absinthe et Absintheurs* (Paris, Marpon, 1860)

Barthes, Roland *Roland Barthes by Roland Barthes* (NY, Hill and Wang, 1977)

Baudelaire, Charles *Intimate Journals*, with a preface by Christopher Isherwood (Black Spring Press, 1989)

Baudelaire, Charles *Baudelaire: The Complete Verse* ed. Francis Scarfe (Anvil Press, 1986)

Baudelaire, Charles *Petites Poèmes en Prose: Le Spleen de Paris* ed. Henri Lemaitre (Paris, Garnier, 1974)

Beaumont, Keith *Alfred Jarry: a critical and biographical study* (Leicester University Press, 1984)

Beckett, Samuel *A Dream of Fair to Middling Women* (Dublin, Black Cat, 1992)

Beerbohm, Max 'Enoch Soames' in *The Bodley Head Max Beerbohm* (Bodley Head, 1970)

Bett, W.R. 'Vincent Van Gogh (1853–90): Artist and Addict' *British Journal of Addiction* 51, Nos.1 and 2, April 1954

Brasher, C.W.J. 'Absinthe and absinthe drinking in England' *The Lancet* April 26, 1930

Breton, André *Anthology of Black Humor* (San Francisco, City Lights, 1997)

Breton, André 'Surrealism, Yesterday, To-day and Tomorrow', *This Quarter* Vol.V No.1, Surrealist Number (Paris, September 1932)

Brite, Poppy Z. *His Mouth Will Taste of Wormwood* (Penguin, 1995)

Buchanan, Robert Williams *The Complete Poetical Works of Robert Williams Buchanan* (Chatto and Windus, 1901)

Bywater, Michael, 'Why Government is bad for you' *Telegraph* 25 Feb 1999

Castillo, J del, et al. 'Marijuana, absinthe and the central nervous system' *Nature* Vol.253 (January 31, 1975)

Conklin, Don 'Absinthe is making a comeback' *College Hill Independent* 17th April 1997

Conrad, Barnaby *Absinthe: History in a Bottle* (San Francisco, Chronicle Books, 1988)

Corelli, Marie *Wormwood: A Drama of Paris* in 3 volumes (Richard Bentley and Son, 1890)

Crosby, Harry *Shadows of the Sun – The Diaries of Harry Crosby* ed. Edward Germain (Santa Barbara, Black Sparrow, 1977)

Crowley, Aleister *The Confessions of Aleister Crowley* (Jonathan Cape, 1969)

Crowley, Aleister (as 'Jeanne la Goulue)'La Légende de l'Absinthe' *The International* (New York, October 1917)

Crowley, Aleister 'The Green Goddess' *The International* (New York, February 1918)

Dardis, Tom *The Thirsty Muse: Alcohol and the American Writer* (Abacus, 1990)

Debord, Guy *Panegyric* trans. James Brook (Verso, 1991)

Delahaye, Marie-Claude *L'Absinthe, histoire de la fée verte* (Paris, Berger-Levrault, 1987)

Delahaye, Marie-Claude *L'Absinthe: Art et Histoire* (Paris, Editions Trame Way, 1990)

Delahaye, Marie-Claude, and Noel, Benoit *L'Absinthe: muse des peintres* (Paris, Editions de l'Amateur, 1999)

Delahaye, Marie-Claude *L'Absinthe: muse des poètes* (Auvers-sur-Oise, Musée de l'Absinthe, 2000)

Dobson, Roger 'A Palimpsest of Three Impostors' *Faunus* No 7 Spring 2001

Dowson, Ernest *The Letters of Ernest Dowson*, ed. Desmond Flower and Henry Maas (Cassell, 1967)

Dubois, Claude *Apaches, Voyous et Gonzes Poilus* (Paris, editions Parigramme, 1996)

Ellman, Richard *Oscar Wilde* (New York, Knopf, 1988)

Elms, Robert *Spain: A Portrait the General* (Heinemann, 1992)

Fitzgerald, F.Scott *The Beautiful and the Damned* (Collins, 1922)

Flaubert, Gustave, *The Dictionary of Received Ideas* (Penguin, 1994)

Fothergill, John, *My Three Inns* (Chatto and Windus, 1949)

Frauenfelder, Mark, 'Absinthe Devotees: The Green Fog', August 2000 [wired.com]

Frey, Julia, *Toulouse-Lautrec: A Life* (Weidenfeld and Nicolson, 1994)

Gide, André *The Counterfeiters* (NY, Knopf, 1927)

Gilbert, W.S., *Lost Bab Ballads* ed.Townley Searle (Putnams, 1932)

Goncourt, Edmond and Jules de *Pages From The Goncourt Journals* ed.Robert Baldick (O.U.P., 1962)

Gosse, Edmund 'A First Sight of Verlaine' *Savoy* No.2 (April, 1896)

Gottlieb, Adam *Legal Highs* (Manhattan Beach Calif., 20th Century Alchemist, 1992 [1973])

Gross, John, *The Rise and Fall of the Man of Letters* (Weidenfeld and Nicolson, 1969)

Guyot, Yves. *L'absinthe et le délire persecuteur* (Paris, 1907)

Hamilton, George Heard, *Manet and his Critics* (Yale, 1986)

Hanson, Anne Coffin, *Manet and the Modern Tradition* (Yale, 1977)

Helliker, Adam, 'Lethal Tipple' *Sunday Telegraph* 2 May 1999

Hemingway, Ernest *For Whom the Bell Tolls* (Jonathan Cape, 1941)

Hemingway, Ernest *Death in the Afternoon* (Jonathan Cape, 1932)

[Hichens, Robert] Anon. *The Green Carnation* (William Heinemann, 1894)

Hodgkinson, Tom, 'Absinthe – that's the spirit' *Telegraph* 3 Dec 1998

Hodgkinson, Tom 'Wild Green Fairy Liquid' *Loaded* February 1999

Hold KM, Sirisoma NS, Ikeda T, Narahashi T, Casida JE 'Alpha-thujone (the active component of absinthe): gamma-aminobutyric acid type A receptor modulation and metabolic detoxification' *Proceedings of the National Academy of Sciences* 97:8 (April 11, 2000)

Hopkins, R.Thurston, 'A London Phantom' printed as Appendix D of Ernest Dowson *Letters*

Hughes, Robert, *Nothing If Not Critical: Selected Essays on Art and Artists* (Harvill, 1990)

Hussey, Andrew *The Game of War: The Life and Death of Guy Debord* (Jonathan Cape, 2001)

Huysmans, J.K. *Against Nature* (Penguin, 1976)

Jackson, Holbrook, *The Eighteen Nineties* (Jonathan Cape, 1927)

Jarry, Alfred *Days and Nights* (Atlas, 1989)

Jones, Thomas *The Art of Distilling Simple and Compound Waters on the Most Modern and Improved Principles* (London, n.d. c.1840)

Joyce, James, *Ulysses* (Bodley Head, 1960)

Joyce, James, *Finnegans Wake* (Faber, 1939)

Kernahan, Coulson 'Two Absinthe-Minded Beggars' *Chamber's Journal* (June 1930)

Kington, Miles, *The World of Alphonse Allais* (Chatto)

Klein, Richard, *Cigarettes Are Sublime* (Picador, 1995)

Knapp, Caroline *Drinking* (Quartet, 1997)

'Kurt' 'Absinthe: My Dance with the Green Fairy' [entheogen.com]

Lancet, The March 6th 1869 'Absinthe and Alcohol'

Lancet, The Sept 7th 1872 'New researches on the properties of absinthe'

Lancet, The [see also Brasher]

Lanier, Doris, *Absinthe: The Cocaine of the Nineteenth Century* (Jefferson, McFarland and Co., 1995)

Le Gallienne, Richard *The Romantic '90s* (Putnams, 1925)

Levien. D.J. *Wormwood* (Allison and Busby, 1998)

Littlewood, Ian *Paris: A Literary Companion* (John Murray, 1987)

Lowry, Malcolm *Under the Volcano* (Jonathan Cape, 1947)

Machen, Arthur, *Arthur Machen: A Bibliography* by Henry Danielson, with Notes by Arthur Machen (Henry Danielson, 1923)

Macintyre, Ben 'One green bottle makes fools of us all' *Times* 5 Dec 98

Mangrum, Stuart 'Absinthe, the Potent Green Fairy' in *Proust Said That* issue no.7 [proust.com]

Maugham, W.Somerset *Of Human Bondage* (Heinemann, 1915)

Maugham, W.Somerset *The Magician, together with A Fragment of Autobiography* (Heinemann, 1956)

Mew, J. and Ashton, J. *Drinks of the World* (Leadenhall Press, 1892)

Meyer, Michael *Strindberg: A Biography* (Secker and Warburg, 1985)

Miller, Stuart, 'Green Fairy Fires Spirits After Long Absinthe' *Guardian* Dec.1st 1998

[Monson case] 'Baron's son fights drinking ban after 'poison' absinthe' *Evening Standard* 16 June 1999

Moore, John, 'The Return of Absinthe' *The Idler* (Winter, 1997)

Morrow, William Chambers 'Over an Absinthe Bottle' in *The Ape, the Idiot, and other People* (Philadelphia, Lippincott, 1897)

Nadelson, Regina 'The Sweet Taste of Decadence' *Metropolitan Home* Nov 1982

Neill, Richard, 'Absinthe makes the head pound harder' *Telegraph* 8 Feb 1997

Nelson, James G. *Publisher to the Decadents: Leonard Smithers in the Careers of Beardsley, Wilde, Dowson* (Pennsylvania, Pennsylvania State University Press, 2000)

Newby, Eric *A Short Walk in the Hindu Kush* (Picador, 1981)

Nordau, Max *Degeneration* (Heinemann, 1895)

Olsen, Richard W. 'Absinthe and gamma-aminobutyric acid receptors' *Proceedings of the National Academy of Sciences* 97:9 April 25, 2000

O'Sullivan, Vincent *Aspects of Wilde* (New York, Henry Holt, 1936)

Pagnol, Marcel *The Time of Secrets* trans. Rita Barisse (Hamish Hamilton, 1962)

Pater, Walter *The Renaissance* (Macmillan, 1910 [1873])

Pickvance, Ronald 'L'Absinthe in England' *Apollo* 77 (May 15th, 1963)

Pinto-Scognamilio, W. 'Effetti del tuyone sull'attività spontanea e sul comportamento condizionato del ratto' *Bolletino Chimico Farmaceutico* no.107, 1968

Queneau, Raymond *The Flight of Icarus* trans. Barbara Wright (Calder and Boyars, 1973)

Raby, Peter *Aubrey Beardsley and the Nineties* (Collins and Brown, 1998)

Ricard, Paul, obituary in *Daily Telegraph* 15th November 1997

Rice, Anne *Interview with the Vampire* (Raven, 1976)

Richardson, Joanna, *Verlaine* (Weidenfeld and Nicolson, 1971)

Rimbaud, Arthur *Rimbaud: Complete Works, Selected Letters* ed. Wallace Fowlie (University of Chicago Press, 1966)

Saintsbury, George, *Notes on a Cellar-Book* (Macmillan, 1921)

Seigel, Jerrold *Bohemian Paris: Culture, Politics and the Boundaries of Bourgeois Life, 1830–1930* (Viking, 1986)

Shattuck, Roger *The Banquet Years* (Faber, 1959)

Simon, Joanna, 'Absinthe Minded' *Sunday Times* 17 Jan 1999

Spies, Werner, *Picasso Sculpture: With a Complete Catalogue* (Thames and Hudson, 1972)

Starkie, Enid *Arthur Rimbaud* (Faber, 1938)

Strang J, Arnold WN, Peters T 'Absinthe: what's your poison?' *British Medical Journal* 18th Dec.1999 [online version] vol.319; pp.1590–92

Sweetman, David *Toulouse-Lautrec and the Fin-de-Siècle* (Hodder and Stoughton, 1999)

Symons, Arthur, 'A Literary Causerie: On a Book of Verses' *The Savoy* No.4 (August, 1896)

Symons, Arthur, *Arthur Symons: Selected Writings*, ed. Roger Holdsworth (Carcanet, 1974)

Symons, Arthur *Arthur Symons: Selected Letters, 1880–1935* ed. Karl Beckson and John M.Munro (Macmillan, 1989)

Tarling, W.J. *The Café Royal Cocktail Book* compiled by W.J.Tarling, illus. Frederick Carter (Publications from Pall Mall, 1937)

Thornton, R.K.R (ed.) *Poetry of the Nineties* (Penguin, 1970)

Verlaine, Paul *Confessions of a Poet* trans. Joanna Richardson (Thames and Hudson, 1950)

Verlaine, Paul, 'À François Coppée', in *Dédicaces* (Paris, Leon Vanier, 1894)

Vogt, Donald D 'Absinthium; A 19thc drug of abuse' *Journal of Ethnopharmacology* Vol.4, 1981

Vyner, Harriet, *Groovy Bob: The Life and Times of Robert Fraser* (Faber, 1999)

Waugh, Alec, *In Praise of Wine* (Cassell, 1959)

Waugh, Evelyn *Decline and Fall* (Penguin, 1973)

Waugh, Evelyn *Scoop* (Penguin, 1973)

Weber, Eugen *France: Fin-de-Siècle* (Harvard University Press, 1986)

Weintraub, Stanley, *The Savoy: Nineties Experiment* (Pennsylvania University Press, 1996)

Weisbord SD, Soule JB, and Kimmel PL 'Poison on line: acute renal failure caused by oil of wormwood purchased through the internet *New England Journal of Medicine* 337 no.12: p.825 (1997)

Wilde, Oscar, *The Picture of Dorian Gray* (O.U.P. 1974)

Wilde, Oscar *The Complete Letters of Oscar Wilde* ed. Merlin Holland and Rupert Hart-Davis (Fourth Estate, 2000)

Williams, F.Harald, *Confessions of a Poet* (Hutchinson, 1894)

Wilson, Edmund, *Axel's Castle* (Penguin, 1993)

Wolff, Geoffrey *Black Sun* (New York, Random House, 1976)

Woolf, Alan D 'Absinthe' *Clinical Toxicology Review* (Massachusets, Massachusets Poison Control System) vol.18 no.4 January 1996

Wu, C. 'Toxin in absinthe makes neurons run wild' *Science News*, April 1, 2000

Yeats, W.B. *Autobiographies* (Macmillan, 1955)

Yeats, W.B. [intro] *The Oxford Book of Modern Verse 1892–1935* (Oxford, 1936)

Zola, Emile, *L'Assomoir* trans. Leonard Tancock (Penguin, 1970)

Zola, Emile, *Nana* trans. George Holden (Penguin, 1972)

Zolotow, Maurice 'Absinthe' *Playboy* (June 1971)

INTERNET

"Absinthe" currently (as of midsummer 2001) brings up 54,400 or so hits on the Internet, using the search engine Google. Much of this is ephemeral or low grade material, like the piece suggesting "Perhaps these artists of the 19th century stumbled upon a key that may, in the future, allow us to genetically alter our children to be artistic prodigies." However, several absinthe sites stand out, particularly 'Le Fée Verte' at the American Gothic site Sepulchritude (Sepulchritude.com), and Matthew Baggott's excellent 'Absinthe FAQ' or "frequently asked questions", which is currently disseminated on various sites. There are other absinthe sites which are high quality but primarily promotional, commercial, marketing sites of one kind or another. The engaging New Orleans website 'The Gumbo Pages' (gumbopages.com) contains only a little about absinthe, but is of interest because it contains the other side of the "internet wormwood overdose" story.

THE ABSINTHE MUSEUM

Marie-Claude Delahaye's excellent absinthe museum, Le Musée de l'Absinthe, can be found at 44 rue Callé, 95430 Auvers-sur-Oise.

ACKNOWLEDGEMENTS

Any modern writer on absinthe is indebted to the work of Marie-Claude Delahaye, who has largely rescued French absinthe drinking from cultural oblivion. Her books on the subject are an indispensable resource. I have also very much enjoyed Barnaby Conrad's impressively researched and superbly illustrated book on the subject, and learned things too from Doris Lanier's.

Various individuals gave me their time and effort, and responded with great kindness to my requests for help or information, including Liz Brooks, Kathy Brunner, Nishi Chaturvedi, Geoffrey Elborn, Ben Fernee, Dr Edward Fetherstone, Richard Hutton, John Moore, Ian Pindar, Ray Russell, Max Rutherston, and Gavin Semple.

In Appendix One, the extract from *The Flight of Icarus* by Raymond Queneau is reprinted by permission of Calder Publications (London). The extract from *Wormwood* by D.J.Levien is reprinted by permission of Allison and Busby (London). The extract from *Of Human Bondage* by W.Somerset Maugham, published by William Heinemann, is reprinted by permission of the Random House Group Ltd. Antonin Artaud's poem *'Verlaine Boit'* is copyright Editions Gallimard, 1976 and is reprinted by permission of the publisher. The author and publishers have tried to trace the copyright holders of R.Thurston Hopkins without success, and would be glad to hear from them.

'L'Absinthe' by Benasset appears by permission of the Musée Carnavalet. The William Rothenstein portrait of Ernest Dowson appears by permission of Lucy Dynevor, and the photograph is copyright of the National Portrait Gallery. The picture of Verlaine in the Café Procope appears by permission of the Bibliothèque Nationale. William Orpen's 'The Absinthe Drinker' appears by permission of Kit Orpen. The photograph of Toulouse-Lautrec's absinthe cane appears by permission of the Musée Toulouse-Lautrec at Albi. 'L'Absinthe' by Apoux, and the poisoned guinea-pig, appear by permission of Roger-Viollet, Paris. The photograph of Victor Berlemont in Soho's French Pub appears by permission of Hulton-Getty. Félicien Rops' picture 'La Buveuse de l'Absinthe', the cartoon of a man throwing an absinthe out of the window, and the two labels before Appendix Two all appear by permission of Marie-Claude Delahaye.

INDEX